New CLAiT

for Office 2003

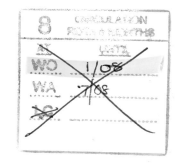

ALAN CLARKE

Hodder Arnold

A MEMBER OF THE HODDER HEADLINE GROUP

Orders: please contact Bookpoint Ltd, 130 Milton Park, Abingdon, Oxon OX14 4SB. Telephone: (44) 01235 827720, Fax: (44) 01235 400454. Lines are open from 9.00 – 5.00, Monday to Saturday, with a 24 hour message answering service. Email address: orders@bookpoint.co.uk

British Library Cataloguing in Publication Data

A catalogue record for this title is available from The British Library

ISBN 978 0 340 94202 4

First published 2007

Impression number   10 9 8 7 6 5 4 3 2 1
Year   2011 2010 2009 2008 2007
Copyright © 2007 Alan Clarke

Figure 1.6 reproduced with permission of Photodisc. Figure 1.8 © Jose Luis Pelnez, Inc./CORBIS. Figure 1.10 © Simon Belcher/Alamy
Typeset by Fakenham Photosetting Limited, Fakenham, Norfolk
Printed in Italy for Hodder Arnold, an imprint of Hodder Education and a member of the Hodder Headline Group, an Hachette Livre UK company, 338 Euston Road, London NW1 3BH.

Contents

Acknowledgements

To my wife and sons for their help and support during the writing of the book and particularly to Christine for improving my grammar and spelling and Peter for checking the technical content of the book.

The author and publisher wish to acknowledge the following for use of on-screen images: CorelDRAW®, Atomz.com, NIACE, The National Archive, Google™ and the Microsoft® Corporation.

Screen shots reprinted by permission from Microsoft® Corporation.

Screen shots are copyright Corel Corporation and Corel Corporation Limited, reprinted by permission.

Microsoft and Corel Trademarks are acknowledged.

OCR does not endorse the use of one software package over another, and all CLAiT qualifications are written in generic form. This book is written using the Microsoft® Office suite as examples, simply to provide clear support to the majority of candidates who will be using that package. The use of any other form of software is equally appropriate and acceptable to OCR.

Introduction

New CLAiT is an initial information and communication technology course and does not assume that you have any prior experience of using computers, applications (e.g. word-processing) or the Internet. It is suitable for people new to computing and is a qualification offered by OCR, who are a major qualification-awarding body. The qualification conforms to the National Qualifications Framework.

In August 2005 New CLAiT was revised to produce a straightforward structure of eight units. You can achieve a Certificate by completing three units or a Diploma by completing five units. All eight units are covered within this book. For both the certificate and diploma you must complete the core unit (Unit 1) amongst your chosen units.

The book is based on Microsoft® Office 2003, Internet Explorer 7 and the Windows® XP operating system. However, the exercises have been selected so that they are in many cases suitable for other versions of Microsoft® Office. Only the e-Image Creation unit employs an application not based on Microsoft® Office. This is the drawing package CorelDRAW® 10.

The assessment of each unit is based on a practical test which places an emphasis on undertaking a task by accurately following instructions. For most units there is a choice of assessment methods such as local or computer-based. Your tutor will be able to provide you with detailed guidance about the nature of the assessment.

Chapter 1

Unit 1

File Management and e-Document Production

This chapter will help you to use a computer, manage your data and produce documents. You will be able to:

- identify and use a personal computer, monitor, keyboard and mouse
- identify and use operating system software
- use an operating system to create and manage files and folders
- identify and use a word processor to enter text, numbers and symbols
- format basic paragraphs and document properties .

The chapter covers the contents of the New CLAiT mandatory unit. It contains information and helps you practise the skills which are essential to the successful completion of the unit.

Assessment

This unit does not assume any previous experience of using a computer. You will be assessed through a practical realistic assignment which is designed to allow you to demonstrate your knowledge and skills against each objective. Your tutor can provide you with more guidance.

What is a computer?

A computer consists of two main components: hardware and software. The hardware is the physical element of the equipment that you can see when you look at a computer. Figure 1.1 illustrates a desktop computer, Figure 1.2 shows a tower computer and Figure 1.7 a laptop computer. These are some of the variations of personal computers. In the first two examples you will see a monitor which resembles a television, a box that contains the electronic heart of the computer (Central Processing Unit), a keyboard (Figure 1.6) and a mouse (Figure 1.8). The laptop computer integrates these features into a single structure. The views of the computer may seem complicated and you may wonder what the purposes of all the parts and connections are. For OCR New CLAiT you do not need to know but if you are interested you will find an explanation in the summary section at the end of the chapter.

All computers are different so when you look at your own computer it will be similar but not identical. The on-switch is often positioned on the front of the computer but in many models

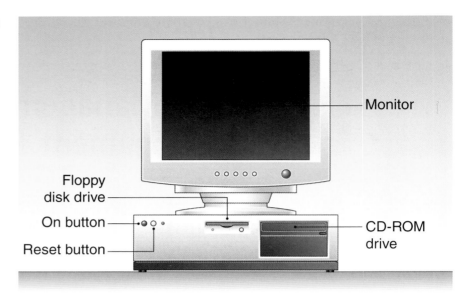

there is a second switch on the back of the computer. The second switch is usually the power supply control so it needs to be on in order for the front switch to operate. When the computer is switched on a small light near to the on-switch is sometimes illuminated.

Figure 1.1 Desktop computer

Software is the set of instructions that controls the hardware. It controls the operations of the hardware such as saving information, electronic communications, word-processing and many other applications. Software is divided into two main types.

The operating system – this is the program that controls and connects the application software and hardware. It provides all the standard features of the computer (e.g. saving information, printing and display of information on the monitor screen). This book is based on the Microsoft

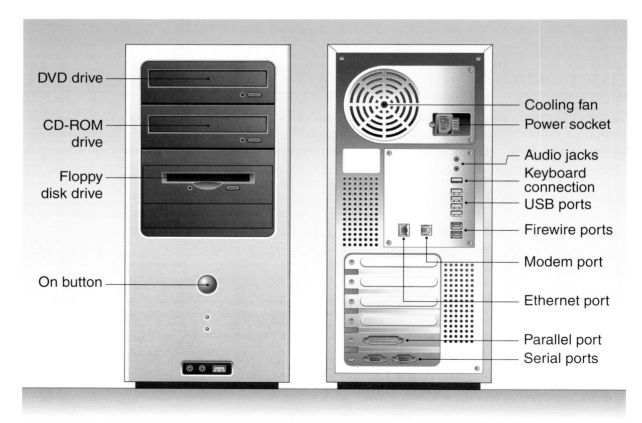

Figure 1.2 Tower computer

Windows® XP operating system. However, there are other versions of this product and also other completely different systems (e.g. Linux®).

Applications – these are programs that help you carry out specialist tasks (e.g. word-processing, drawing pictures, communicating and designing presentations). The later chapters consider applications in considerable detail.

Exercise 1

Investigate the hardware

1 Before you switch on your computer, and with all the hardware disconnected from the power supply, carry out a visual inspection of the equipment. Observe the different connections and pieces of hardware.

2 Identify whether the computer is a desktop, tower or laptop, then locate the printer, keyboard (Figure 1.6) and mouse (Figure 1.8). These are the main components of a computer system's hardware. If you are considering a laptop then identify how these features are incorporated into the structure.

3 Inspect the back of the computer and you will observe a number of connections and cables. These link the different parts together and allow information to pass between the different elements (e.g. the computer sends information to the printer so it can produce a document).

4 Locate the on-switch or switches.

Switching on

When you switch on a computer you are instructing the operating system, which is software stored in the computer's hard disk, to start the computer following a set procedure. If the computer is connected to the power supply then you will hear the hard disk making noises while searching for instructions. The monitor will display some of the instructions but these are probably meaningless to all but those users at an expert level.

You may notice that the light on the floppy disk drive or other parts of the computer are illuminated. The standard start-up (or 'boot-up') procedure involves checking the floppy drive for a disk. If you have left one in the drive then the start-up sequence will be interrupted. This seems unusual but is actually a safety feature – if you have a hard disk failure it allows you to investigate the problem.

After a few moments the Microsoft Windows® logo will appear on the screen. The system will continue to make noises until eventually the logo disappears and is replaced by what is known as a dialog box in the middle of the screen. This will ask you for your User name and Password . You can change both once you have access to the computer. Once you have entered the correct name and password you click on to the OK button using the mouse pointer. This will present you with the Microsoft Windows® desktop (Figure 1.3). This illustration has been kept simple but on many desktops there will be many more small pictures (known as icons) representing different software applications.

Figure 1.3 shows some icons on the main desktop area. Three important ones are:

- My Computer – this links you to the areas of the computer where information is stored (known as drives). Drives include the hard disk which stores the bulk of the information as well as CD-ROM and floppy disk drives which allow information to be placed in portable form. My Computer also links you to resources connected to the computer, such as printers

- Recycle Bin – this is a place where deleted files are kept so that if you make a mistake you can reclaim them

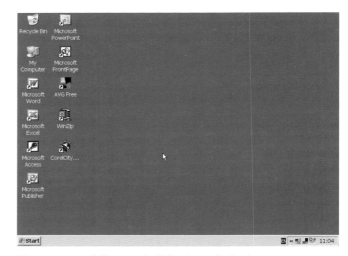

Figure 1.3 Microsoft Windows® desktop

- Application icons – these allow you to load the application (e.g. Microsoft® Word, Microsoft PowerPoint®, Winzip® and AVG virus protection).

At the bottom of the desktop there is a grey bar – the taskbar. At the right end of the taskbar is an area called the notification area in which a range of small icons is shown. These represent programs that are currently working. Other icons on the toolbar allow you to access the applications they represent while at the left end is the button called Start . Clicking on this provides access to a range of applications and other services and is also the way to switch off the computer.

Exercise 2

Switching on (booting up) your computer

1 With the computer, monitor and other hardware connected to the power supply, press the on-switch on the front of the computer and on the monitor. In both cases a small light will be illuminated and you will hear the whirring and clicking sounds of the computer starting.

2 If nothing happens then check that the power switch at the rear of the computer is in the on position.

3 Observe what happens – the time to start (boot) the computer can vary considerably depending on what is connected to the machine and how it is configured, so do not be concerned if it takes a few minutes.

4 Eventually you will see the dialog box requesting your User name and Password . Once these have been entered you will see something similar to Figure 1.3 appear.

Opening applications

There are several ways of loading an application such as word-processing (Microsoft® Word) and spreadsheets (Microsoft Excel®). The two most used are:

- The Start button
- The application icon displayed on the Windows® desktop.

In the bottom left-hand corner of the Windows desktop (Figure 1.3) is a button called Start. This allows you to access many applications and standard features of the operating system. If you single-click on Start, a menu will pop up, which is shown in Figure 1.4. If you place the mouse pointer over the All Programs item it will become highlighted (i.e. the background will change colour) and a new menu will appear alongside. This is shown in Figure 1.5.

The programs menu will vary in length and number of items depending on what applications you have installed on your computer. In this case all the Microsoft® Office 2003 applications are available to you. You should notice that All Programs and other items sometimes have a small black triangle next to them. This indicates that if you highlight this item by placing your pointer over it then another menu will open.

To load Microsoft® Word, single-click on the Word option on the All Programs menu (Figure 1.5). The Microsoft® Word application will open. An alternative way of loading the application is to double-click on the Word icon on the Windows® desktop.

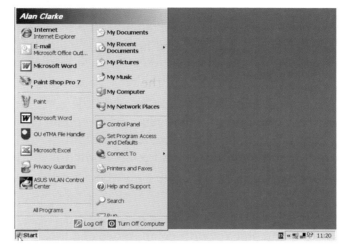

Figure 1.4 Start menu

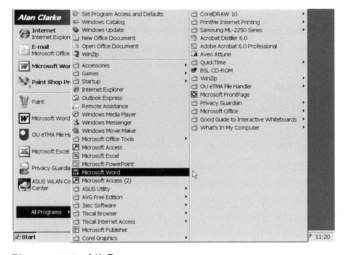

Figure 1.5 All Programs menu

File Management and e-Document Production

5

Switch off

Switching off a computer must be done in the correct way or you run the risk of damaging your system. To switch off a computer using the Microsoft Windows® XP operating system requires you to click on the Start button. A menu (list of options) will appear (Figure 1.4) and if you select the Turn Off Computer option then a small box entitled Turn off computer will appear.

The Turn off computer box provides several options and in most cases you will want to select Turn Off . You select an option by clicking on its icon. If you click on the Cancel button you will return to the desktop. If you position your pointer over an option then a short statement will appear explaining its purpose.

The process of shutting down involves the computer making noises and the screen showing a variety of images. The time required to complete the process varies but does not take very long. When the shut-down is complete, the light on the computer will be switched off. However, the light on the monitor will still remain on until you press its switch.

Input

Users communicate with computers using input devices such as:

■ a keyboard (Figure 1.6)
■ a mouse (Figure 1.8).

There is a variety of input devices depending on how you need to interact with the computer system. When you input information into the computer it usually responds by displaying the information on the monitor screen.

A keyboard is similar to a typewriter and is designed to allow you to enter text into the computer. A keyboard and a typewriter have alphabetical keys and are laid out identically. There are also other keys which are common to them both, e.g.

Figure 1.6 Keyboard

■ space bar
■ capital lock
■ shift
■ punctuation keys.

The major difference, however, is that the keyboard has a number of additional keys. These are:

■ a row of number keys towards the top of the keyboard and a separate number pad on the right
■ enter keys which are used to confirm that you want to enter information into the computer
■ a top row of keys labelled F1 to F12 which carry out particular functions

■ a number of other special-purpose keys whose role will gradually emerge as you work through the book.

Exercise 3

Exploring the keyboard

1 Work your way across the keyboard. You will notice that it is divided into four main areas:
   - function keys across the top of the keyboard
   - number pad on the right of the keyboard
   - main alphabetical keys – notice the QWERTY layout (this is the sequence of alphabetical keys along the top left of the keyboard)
   - various other keys sandwiched between the QWERTY and number pad areas (e.g. Enter).

2 Identify the following keys: Ctrl, Alt, Home, Pg Up and Num Lock. These are special-purpose keys, and eventually you will learn their purposes. For the moment you simply need to know where they are. This will help you once you start to use applications.

3 To enter upper-case letters requires that the shift and character keys are pressed together. This is also the way symbols on the top half of some of the keys are entered.

4 Some keyboards have a small Microsoft Windows® symbol on a key. This is a shortcut equivalent to pressing the Start button on the Microsoft Windows® desktop. This might not seem useful at the moment but its importance will become apparent later.

There are other types of keyboard and various specialist ones have been devised for particular tasks.

Figure 1.7 illustrates a laptop computer keyboard. This is smaller and so is suitable for a laptop computer which is designed to be portable. The main difference from a desktop keyboard is the lack of a number pad.

A mouse is a small palm-sized device which is usually connected to your computer by a cable, although wireless mice are now becoming very popular. Most new computers are now supplied with a wireless mouse. The mouse is linked to an on-screen pointer which normally appears as an arrow and mirrors the movements made by the mouse.

Figure 1.7 Laptop computer

Figure 1.8 shows a two-button mouse which is the type most widely used, but single- and three-button mice are also available. This book will only discuss a two-button mouse.

If you move the mouse, the on-screen pointer moves in the same way. If you move right, the pointer goes right, if you move left then the pointer goes left and so on. The buttons on the mouse allow you to communicate with the computer. The mouse normally sits on a small mat which is called, not surprisingly, a mouse mat. This helps the mouse move smoothly across the surface.

Figure 1.8 Mouse

Other input devices exist which will also control the screen pointer. A trackball works by your manipulating a ball and clicking buttons to control the pointer and make selections. Laptop computers have a variety of devices using touch buttons, pads and thumb balls to control on-screen pointers.

Exercise 4

Using a mouse – right-handed users

1 Place your right hand with your index finger on the left-hand button and your middle finger on the right button.

2 Move the mouse and watch how the pointer responds on the screen.

3 Practise using the mouse until you are comfortable – move the pointer up, down, left, right and diagonally until you can accurately control the pointer. Notice where you move the mouse to achieve the desired result.

Alternative Exercise 4

Using a mouse – left-handed users

1 You can adjust the mouse to make it suitable for left-handed people. This involves clicking on the Start button and Control Panel to reveal the Control Panel window. Double-click on the Mouse icon. This will reveal the Mouse Properties window and you can select the left-handed option by clicking on the radio button labelled Switch primary and secondary buttons and then the OK button.

2 Place your left hand with your index finger on the right-hand button and your middle finger on the left button.

3 Move the mouse and watch how the pointer responds on the screen.

4 Practise using the mouse until you are comfortable – move the pointer up, down, left, right and diagonally until you can accurately control the pointer. Notice where you move the mouse to achieve the desired result.

Note – remember that if you select the left-hand mouse options then you will need to take this into account when reading the instructions in this book.

It is very important that you learn to use a mouse accurately and effectively. This will take practice. The main skills are:

- accurately moving the on-screen pointer until it touches objects on the screen. Often they will be animated or a text box will appear to explain their purpose.
- single-clicking the left mouse button as this communicates a command to the computer to start a process
- single-clicking the right mouse button to communicate a command to the computer to show some extra features such as revealing an extra menu of choices

- double-clicking the left mouse button which communicates a command to the computer to start a process
- clicking and dragging (if you press the left-hand mouse button but do not release it while the pointer is resting on an object on the screen and then you move the mouse, the object will be dragged across the screen until you release the button).

Exercise 5

Practising your mouse skills

1 You can practise your mouse skills in many ways but it can be fun to play a game which is supplied as part of the Windows® operating system. This is a card game called Solitaire played using the mouse pointer to move the cards.

2 To load the games program requires using the mouse and can be quite a challenge if this is the first time you have used a mouse – but do keep trying.

3 The first step is to single-click with the left mouse button on the Start button. A list of options will appear above the button. This is called a menu and is a standard way of presenting an option in Microsoft Windows® and in applications.

Step 1: Slide the mouse up the menu until you highlight the All Programs option (the background changes to a new colour).

Step 2: At the end of the word Programs you will see a small pointer (triangle) which tells you that there are more options available. If you leave the mouse pointer over All Programs a new menu will appear to the right.

Step 3: Slide your mouse pointer in a straight line to the right until you highlight an option in the new menu, then move the pointer up the menu until you reach the option Games.

Step 4: If you leave your pointer over Games another menu to the right will appear. Again, in a straight line slide your pointer to the right until a new option is highlighted. Move the pointer until it is now over the option Solitaire.

Step 5: With the option highlighted, single-click on the left mouse button and you will see the Solitaire game appear. It will provide you with an opportunity to practise moving and controlling the precise direction of the mouse pointer.

4 Figure 1.9 illustrates the Solitaire game after a few cards have been played. The game has the same rules as the card game. You turn cards over by single-clicking on the pile. Move cards by clicking the left mouse button on the one of your choice and holding the button down and dragging the card to its new location.

5 Try to play a game. If you find that every time you drag a card to a new location it returns to its original position, it is because you are making an illegal move.

6 Keep playing until you are confident about dragging and dropping and clicking with the left button. These are key elements in using a mouse but there are two further important actions. These are double-clicking and single-clicking with the right mouse button and there will be opportunities to improve these skills in other parts of the book.

continued

However, double-clicking (which is clicking the left mouse button twice rapidly) needs practice. People often find it difficult initially to click twice quickly enough. If you find that after double-clicking no action results, it is probably because you are leaving too long an interval between the clicks. Keep trying to click twice as quickly as you can. You will eventually get it right.

7 To close the Solitaire window you need to single-click with the left mouse button on the button marked with an X in the top right-hand corner of the Solitaire window. Figure 1.9 shows the three buttons that allow the window to be minimized to a button on the Desktop taskbar, maximized to fill the entire display, or closed (i.e. buttons left to right). Experiment with expanding the window to fill the whole display and minimizing it to a button. When the window is maximized you can reduce it in size by using the same buttons.

8 These controls appear on all windows. It is a standard part of the operating system.

Applications can be displayed as a window (a rectangular area), the whole display or a single button on the taskbar.

9 When you have finished playing Solitaire, close the window.

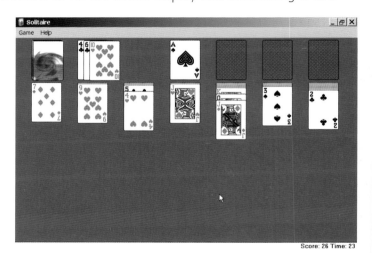

Figure 1.9 Solitaire

Graphic User Interface

Microsoft Windows® and the vast majority of modern software uses a Graphic User Interface (GUI). A GUI is a highly visual interface combining the use of a pointing device (e.g. a mouse) with visual links to applications, commands and options. The visual links take the form of small pictures called icons, buttons (small rectangles) or menus (i.e. lists of options). GUIs are easy to learn and to use since you do not need to remember a large number of commands, but only to recognize them when they appear on the screen. Most GUIs are consistent meaning that you can work out what to do even when you are using a new part of the system.

A key feature of a GUI, Microsoft Windows® and Microsoft® Office is the window. This is a rectangular enclosed area in which applications, files and messages are displayed. Windows can be moved and resized (i.e. a window can fill a whole screen or be reduced to a small picture on the edge of the display). Windows can be stacked on top of each other so that at first you can sometimes lose a window because it is hidden under another one.

While you are still learning about Windows®, using a mouse and GUIs, you probably feel confused and uncertain but this will change with practice. GUIs have made learning about using information and communication technology far easier than earlier computers based on command interfaces.

Storing and locating information

Computers have a permanent store for information, programs (applications) and data. This is called the hard disk or hard drive and it can hold an enormous amount of information. It is often designated by the letter C with a colon, so drive C: is the hard drive. The hard disk is normally a permanent part of the computer, although there are computers that allow you to remove a hard drive, but these are relatively rare. Information can be stored in smaller amounts on a floppy disk which is a portable storage device that you can carry from one computer to another. The floppy drive is often designated as the A: drive.

Figure 1.10 illustrates a floppy disk. The disk is inserted into the drive with the label on the top, the metal slider entering first. The disk is firmly pushed into the drive until it clicks. It is not possible to insert a disk the wrong way round so if it does not go in, you are holding it the wrong way up.

There are other portable storage devices that can hold far more data than a floppy disk. The memory stick is a small device which you can plug into a computer's USB port. It then becomes a new drive on which you can store information. Memory sticks are sometimes called flash or pen drives and even dongles. Some computers have CD-RW (i.e. compact disk read-write) or DVD-RW (i.e. DVD read-write) drives which enable you to save information on to disks.

Figure 1.10 Floppy disk

Exercise 6

Inserting a floppy disk

1 Try to insert a floppy disk into the drive (Figures 1.1 and 1.2). Remember to push the disk firmly into the drive, but if it will not enter then check you are inserting it the right way (i.e. label on top and metal slider first).

2 The floppy will make a noise when it is in place and it will be inside the computer so that you cannot reach it. To remove the disk you need to press the button which is located near to the drive. This button will pop out as the floppy disk is pushed in.

3 Press the button and see the disk emerge.

4 Repeat the action of inserting and removing the disk until you are confident.

The Windows® operating system provides you with the means to search the hard disk and floppy disks when they are inserted into the drive. Windows Explorer lets you view the contents of the computer drives. Figure 1.11 illustrates Windows Explorer showing the contents of the C: drive (hard drive).

Windows Explorer is a file management application provided within Microsoft Windows®. The Explorer's application window is divided into a number of areas. These are:

■ Title bar (e.g. Windows (C:))

■ Menu bar

■ Toolbar

■ Address (i.e. shows the location or path of the highlighted folder)

■ Folders (left-hand side of the display) – showing the structure of folders stored on the hard disk, floppy disks, CD-ROMs or other storage media. The plus sign indicates that the folder has more folders stored within it. If you click on the plus sign, the structure will be opened up to show these folders. The revealed folders may also be shown with a plus sign, indicating further folders stored within the revealed one.

■ Contents of the folder (right-hand side of the display). This shows the files and folders stored within the highlighted folder.

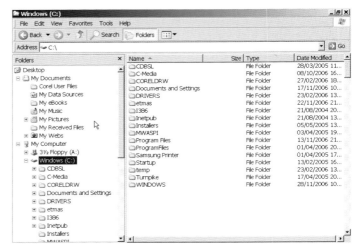

Figure 1.11   Windows Explorer

Information is stored in a computer in what are known as files. All files have a unique name and they are normally grouped with related files and stored within folders. This is rather similar to the storage of paper records in cardboard files and it is

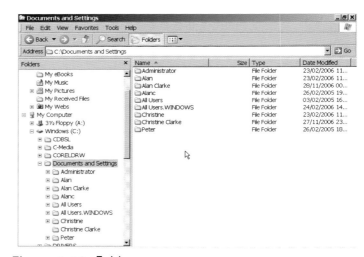

Figure 1.12   Folders

intended to help you locate them again when you have a large number of files. In the computer it is also possible to store folders within other folders. In Figure 1.11 you will notice many small plus signs in the left-hand area of the display. This indicates that these folders contain other folders. Clicking on the plus sign will open up the folder to reveal what it contains. These are shown in the right-hand window. Figure 1.12 shows a group of folders within the Documents and Settings folder, each with a unique name.

Figure 1.13 shows the folders stored within the Alanc folder. If the My Documents folder is highlighted then the files stored in it are shown. The different types of files take on different forms or formats depending on the information they contain. Here we see examples of

Microsoft® Word, Rich Text Format, WinZip®, Text Document, HTML file, Corel, R.A.V.E.® and Microsoft® Access.

Windows Explorer provides functions in the File menu to delete or rename your files. You highlight the file you need to work on by single-clicking on it, then select the File menu and the options Delete or Rename. In the Edit menu you are also provided with options to copy (Copy and Paste) or move (Cut and Paste) the file to another

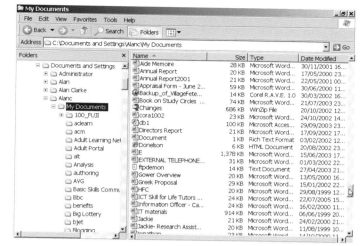

Figure 1.13 Files

folder. To locate a file you need to click on the folder to reveal what other folders or files are stored within.

It is not always easy when you first start to use a computer to distinguish between different types of files. Applications (e.g. word processors) are stored as files, documents produced by the applications are also stored as files and so on. In a way everything is a file. You distinguish between them by considering the small picture (icon) in front of the filename and the extension at the end of the name (i.e. the letters following the full stop – .bmp, .gif, .doc and .txt). There are many different types of files.

You can change the appearance of folders and files in Windows Explorer and in other Microsoft® applications. They can appear as:

- Icons
- Tiles
- List (i.e. similar to Details but without the information about size, type and date of modification)
- Details (e.g. Figures 1.11, 1.12 and 1.13)
- Thumbnails (i.e. useful if you are viewing pictures since each appears as a small image making it easy for you to select the one you want).

In order to change the appearance within Windows Explorer select the View menu and choose the appropriate option (i.e. icons, tiles, list, details and thumbnails). Alternatively choose the View icon on the toolbar and the options will be displayed, allowing you to select one. The selected option is shown by a black spot placed alongside the item.

Exercise 7

Windows Explorer

1 Open Windows Explorer by clicking on the Start button, then highlighting All Programs and Accessories to reveal a menu of options. Click on the Windows Explorer item. This will open Explorer (Figure 1.11).

2 Explore the application by clicking on the plus signs to open up the folder structure. Keep clicking on new plus signs that are revealed and observe what changes.

3 Highlight a folder in the left-hand list and observe the changes in the right-hand area of the window. This area shows what a highlighted folder contains. You can also click on folders in the right-hand area to open them. Again notice any changes this causes.

4 When you click on a folder in the left-hand list you will notice the picture of the folder itself changes to look like an open folder.

5 Use Explorer to investigate what is stored on the computer's hard disk. However, do not select Delete or Rename or any option within the menus since you may cause changes that harm your computer.

6 When you have investigated the structure, close Explorer by clicking on the close button in the top right-hand corner of the window or select the File menu and the Close option.

The Windows® operating system provides you with a way of finding files and folders if you cannot remember a particular file location.

If you click on the Start button, a menu will pop up containing an option called Search (in other versions of Windows® this is sometimes called Find). If you click on Search, the Search Results window appears (Figure 1.14).

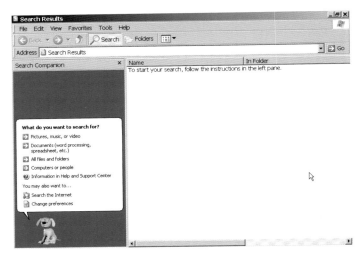

Figure 1.14 Search Results

Exercise 8

Finding a file

1 Load the Search Results window (Figure 1.14). On the left-hand side of the window are a series of options to help you search for different types of files and folders (e.g. Documents). Select the `Documents` option by clicking on it and observe what happens (Figure 1.15). The display changes to ask you to specify the nature of the file you are seeking (e.g. name or part of the name of the file and the last time you changed it). Enter the name of a file (e.g. clait) and select the `Don't remember` option and click on the `Search` button. If you make a mistake you can go back a step by selecting the `Back` button.

2 Observe what happens and you should see the search results on the right-hand side of the display fill with a list of files and folders. These all have your search term in their titles.

3 When the search is completed you will need to review the list to identify the particular file you are searching for. If you want to open the file, double-click on the chosen item. The file will open inside the application which created it (e.g. text files in a word processor).

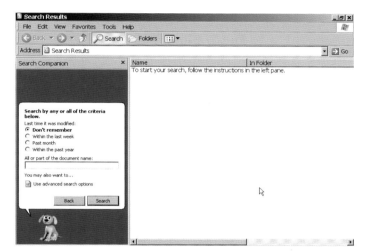

Figure 1.15 **What do you want to search for?**

4 Explore the search function by entering new names, selecting different modification dates and try the advanced search functions (i.e. click on `Use advanced search options`). Try the different options and see what happens.

5 The Advanced Options lets you search specific drives and offers two additional features:

a. What size is it? (i.e. lets you specify the size of the file you are seeking)

b. More advanced options.

The more advanced options include allowing you to specify case sensitivity (i.e. match filename with lower-case or capital letters).

6 Continue until you are confident in locating files. Try locating files on a floppy disk (A:) as well as on the hard disk (C:).

7 Close the function by using the `Close` button in the right-hand corner of the window.

Create and manage files and folders

In addition to being able to find files and folders it is important that you are able to manage them. Microsoft Windows® operating system provides a range of functions to allow you to:

- Create and name folders (directories)
- Open, close and save files
- Delete files and folders
- Rename files and folders
- Print the file structure
- Cut, copy and paste
- Move files and folders
- Copy files and folders.

Windows Explorer is designed to manage your files and folders. It allows you to create, delete and rename files and folders. The `File` menu (Figure 1.16) offers you functions to create, name, open, close and rename files and folders. The `Edit` menu has the options to cut, copy, paste, move and copy files and folders.

Figure 1.16 shows the following functions:

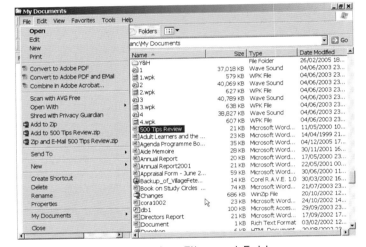

Figure 1.16 Manipulating Files and Folders

- `New` – creates a new folder in the folder currently being viewed in Windows Explorer
- `Delete` – deletes the file or folder highlighted
- `Rename` – allows you to change the name of the file or folder highlighted.

Other options are available within the `Edit` menu:

- `Move To Folder` – moves the highlighted file or folder to a new folder (this is the same process as Cut and Paste)
- `Copy To Folder` – copies the highlighted file or folder to a new folder (this is the same process as Copy and Paste)
- `Undo` – this lets you change your mind since it undoes the last action you have undertaken
- `Cut` – enables you to cut out a file or folder with the intention of moving it to a new location using the Paste option
- `Copy` – allows you to copy a file or folder to a new location using the Paste option but leaving the original file or folder unaffected
- `Paste` – lets you place a copied or cut file or folder in a new location.

Manipulating Folders

1 Insert a floppy disk into the drive.

2 Open Windows Explorer by clicking on the Start button, highlighting All Programs and Accessories and selecting Windows Explorer . The application will appear (Figure 1.11) either in a window or filling the whole screen.

3 Click on the 3½ Floppy (A:) option (Figure 1.17). If the floppy disk drive is empty then no files or folders will be shown on the right-hand side of the display. If you cannot see the Floppy option, scroll up and down the window or click on the My Computer folder to display the drives. Floppy is at the top of the list.

4 You are going to create a new folder, so select the File menu, highlight New and click on the Folder option. A new folder will appear on the right-hand side of the display with the name New Folder. The cursor (a cursor is a small flashing bar that shows you where your text will appear when you enter it from the keyboard) will be flashing in the name box and you should enter a name for the folder from the keyboard. In this case call it Master.

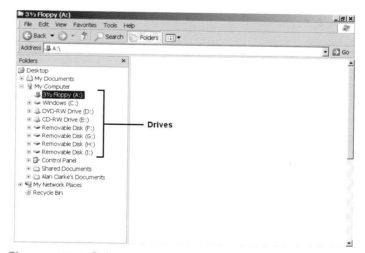

Figure 1.17 Drives

5 The Master folder is stored on the floppy disk because this was the drive selected when the folder was created.

6 Double-click on Master and you will see the right-hand side is clear because this folder is empty. However, on the left-hand side the Master folder will appear (Figure 1.18) and because it has been selected the folder icon is shown open.

7 Create a new folder and name it Master1. Open Master1 and create another new folder called Master2. You now have three folders stored one within another. Figure 1.19 shows the structure.

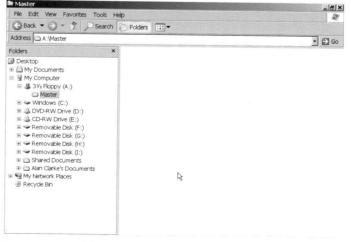

Figure 1.18 Master folder open

8   Highlight Master1 folder by clicking on it, then select File menu and the Rename option. You can change the name to New Master. Repeat the process for Master2 and rename it Modern Master.

9   Highlight Modern Master (single-click) and then select the Copy option from the Edit menu. Highlight the Master folder and select the Paste option from the Edit menu. You will see the Modern Master folder copied into the Master Folder. The original Modern Master folder is still in place. Figure 1.20 shows the new structure.

10 The process of using the function has now been illustrated. You must highlight the folder you wish to operate on and then select the function. Now practise using the other ones. Undo lets you remove your last action so none of your changes need be permanent:

a) Delete a folder

b) Cut and paste a folder

c) Copy To Folder

d) Move To Folder.

11 When you select either Copy To Folder or

    Move To Folder a new window appears called Move Items or Copy Items (Figure 1.21). This allows you to find

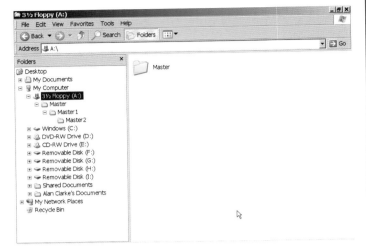

Figure 1.19 Structure

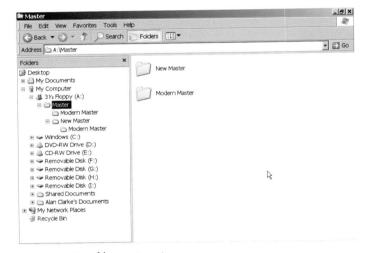

Figure 1.20 New structure

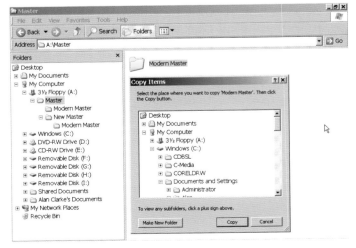

Figure 1.21 Copy Items window

continued

the folder you want to copy or move the file or folder to. Notice that in the Copy Items or Move Items window you can create a new folder using the Make New Folder button in the bottom left-hand corner of the window.

12 Continue trying the different functions until you are confident.

13 Close Windows Explorer by clicking on the File Menu and the Close option.

Creating and printing documents

The Windows® operating system includes other applications in addition to Windows Explorer. These include:

- Paint – a straightforward drawing application
- WordPad – a basic word processor
- Notepad – a text editor which is a limited word processor
- Calculator – an on-screen calculator
- Address Book – this allows you to keep details of people's names, e-mail addresses and telephone numbers.

These can be accessed in a similar way to Solitaire by clicking the Start button, highlighting the All Programs and Accessories options in the menu and then single-clicking on the application of your choice. In addition to these applications you can install other ones.

Word processors are one of the most widely used computer applications. In the next exercises, you are going to use Microsoft® Word (Figure 1.22) to create a short document, save it to floppy disk and print it. Microsoft® Word is a powerful word processor though there are many other word processors available and other applications such as text editors. The difference between a word processor and a text editor is mainly the degree of sophistication. Text editors are used principally for producing simple messages while a word processor provides the tools for writing a wide range of documents (e.g. from a letter to a book). Word processors provide tools for presenting and formatting information and are often WYSIWYG, which stands for What You See Is What You Get. This means that the way the words are presented on the screen is how they will be printed. They help you write by providing a wide range of features and functions such as spelling and grammar checkers and offer you considerable

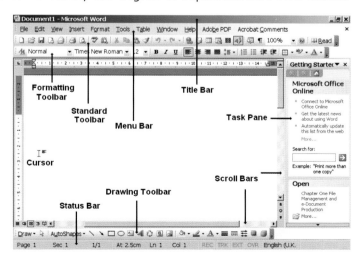

Figure 1.22 Microsoft® Word

freedom to change the words, presentation, layout and appearance of your documents.

If you have never used a keyboard to enter text it may feel strange at first, but you will rapidly realize how useful a word processor is. Windows® includes a text editor called Notepad which is shown in Figure 1.23.

The Microsoft® Word display consists of four main areas:

Figure 1.23 Notepad

- menus and toolbars which provide you with access to the word processor controls (e.g. Standard, Formatting and Drawing toolbars)
- task pane (e.g. Getting Started)
- the working area where you enter your words to create documents
- the status bar (reading from left to right) shows:
  - Page 1 – the page you are on (e.g. the first page)
  - Sec 1 – the section of the document you are on
  - 1/1 – shows you that you are looking at the first page of your document which is one page long
  - At 2.5 cm – tells you that you are entering text that will be 2.5 cm below the top of the page when it is printed
  - Ln 1 – you are entering text into the first line of your document
  - Col 1 – you are entering text in the first character position of the document.

Exercise 10

Creating a document

1 Open Microsoft® Word by clicking on the Start button, highlighting the All Programs option to open a menu of options and single-clicking on Microsoft Word . The application will open (Figure 1.23). Maximize the window using the control buttons in the top right-hand corner of the window.

2 On the first line of the work area you will see a flashing upright line. This is called the cursor and indicates where any text or numbers that you enter will appear on the screen. Press any letter or number on the keyboard. You will see your selected character appear and the cursor move one space to the right, indicating where the next one will be entered. To remove your character press the Backspace key.This is marked with a left-pointing arrow and will delete any character to the left of the cursor. There is also the Delete key which removes characters to the right of the cursor. This is located in the bottom right of the keyboard below the number pad.

3 Move the mouse pointer around the display and you will see that it changes shape. It is no longer shaped liked an arrow when it moves across the work area but is like the letter I.

4 Using the keyboard enter:

My name is .... I live in .... and I am .... years old.

Fill in the blanks with your own details – name, town/city and age.

To enter a capital letter (upper-case character) you need to hold down the Shift key and then press the letter of your choice. If you want to enter everything in upper case press the Capitals Lock (i.e. Caps Lock) key once. To return to lower case, press Caps Lock again. For the current exercises you only need to enter single upper-case letters.

5 If you make a mistake then you can remove it using the Backspace key.

6 When you have entered the text then move your mouse pointer until it is immediately in front of – I live in ... and then single-click. You will see the cursor move to this new position. This is how you move the cursor using the mouse, although there are other ways such as by using the arrow keys on the keyboard.

7 If you press the Enter key then the text will be broken into two parts as shown below.

My name is ....

I live in .... and I am .... years old.

The Enter key inserts a new line but if you continue typing text, the words will automatically go to the next line when you reach the end of the previous one. This is called text-wrapping. If you hold down any key you will see the character appear many times and wrap around when it reaches the end of a line.

8 If you single-click on the menu item File (Figure 1.24) a menu will drop down. This provides a number of standard features which, if you click on them, give you access to useful functions such as:

■ New – creates a new document

■ Open – opens an existing document so that you can amend it

■ Save – allows you to save your document to the computer's store on the hard disk or on a floppy disk

■ Save As – allows you to save an existing file under a different name

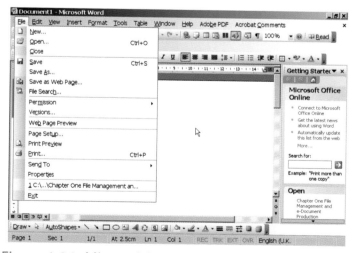

Figure 1.24 Microsoft® Word File Menu

continued

- <u>P</u>rint – allows you to print your document on a connected printer
- E<u>x</u>it – an alternative to using the Close button.

You will notice that the menu covers part of the text you have entered but will disappear if you click your mouse anywhere outside of the menu area. Above the E<u>x</u>it option is a list of files (e.g. C:\..\Chapter One File Management an …). These are the most recent documents that have been opened by Word. You can access them by clicking on them.

9 Close Word by selecting the File menu and the E<u>x</u>it option unless you want to progress immediately to Exercise 11.

Printing

Printers provide you with the means to output your computer work to produce letters, reports and other paper documents. There are several different types and three widely available types are:

- monochrome laser printer
- monochrome and colour inkjet printer
- colour laser printer.

A laser printer uses magnetic toner to produce text and images on paper whereas inkjet printers work by squirting small drops of ink onto the page. They can provide both black and white and colour printing. Laser and inkjet printers are widely used in the workplace and at home. Colour printers are more expensive than monochrome ones but the price of colour inkjets is now in reach of most computer users.

Printers are manufactured in a variety of sizes and shapes. Two key features of any printer are the on-switch and the paper holder. The on-switch can be positioned in a range of locations including the back corners, front panel and the sides of the printer. In a similar way, the paper can be fed into a pull-out drawer or pushed into an opening. Each manufacturer has their own design and it is important to study the printer's manual before using it.

Exercise 11

Printers

1 It is important to familiarize yourself with the printer you are going to use, so in this exercise you are going to explore your printer.

2 First make sure it is not connected to the power supply. Inspect the printer and see if you can locate the on-switch and where the paper is loaded.

3 Remove the paper and inspect it. In most cases the paper is A4 size and is loaded as a block. Replace the paper carefully. When you load paper it is useful to fan the edges of

continued

the block since this will help stop it sticking together. A problem with all printers is that the paper will sometimes jam inside (rather like a photocopier).

4 Connect the printer to the power supply and switch it on. Each printer will start in its own individual way but you are likely to hear some noise and see any control lights flash. If you are using a large laser printer it will have a display panel and you will probably see a message appear, such as Warming Up. When the printer is ready this message will change (e.g. Ready). Smaller laser and inkjet printers will often have only a few lights. Inspect the labels near the lights and you may see error, paper and data lights. The meaning of the lights being illuminated depends on the type and model of your printer.

5 Observe the printer's start-up process.

6 Some printers have a demonstration or test function. This is indicated by a button labelled Demo or Test. If your printer provides this function press the button and see what happens. Often a short document will be printed. In some cases this provides background information about the printer.

7 Once you are confident that you know how to switch the printer on and load the paper, switch the printer off if you are not going to use it.

Exercise 12

Create, save and print a document

1 Open Microsoft® Word by clicking on Start , highlighting the All Programs option to reveal a menu of options and single-clicking on Microsoft Word . The application will open (Figure 1.22). Maximize the window using the control buttons in the top right-hand corner of the window if the display does not fill the screen.

2 When the application is open you will notice that in the work area there is a small flashing vertical line in the top left-hand corner. This is called a cursor and it is here that your text will appear when you begin to enter it.

3 Enter the following:

This is a short passage to help me understand how to create, save and print a document. The keyboard has many keys to enter text and numbers. The number keys are 1,2,3,4,5,6,7,8 and 9. The symbol keys are =-/#.,:@?!£&%+*.

Observe the movement of the cursor and how the text wraps around at the end of each line. Remember to use the Shift key to access symbols on the top of keys and to insert upper case letters.

4 Once you have created a document you can save it as a file by selecting the File menu and the Save option. The Save As window (dialog box) opens (Figure 1.25). This shows a view of a folder called Documents and Settings in which is stored a variety of folders.

To save your work you need to enter a file name in the File name: box and then click on the Save button. Windows® inserts a filename based on the text you have entered (i.e. This is a short passage to help me understand how to create). You can use this name or enter a new one by clicking in the File name: box and entering a name. You may have to delete the automatic name. Your file will then be

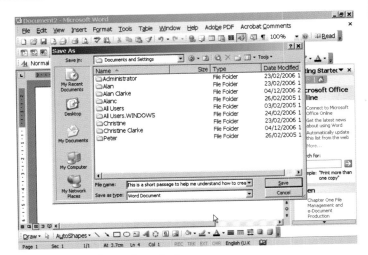

Figure 1.25 Save As window

saved in the Documents and Settings folder. If you would like to save your file elsewhere you have to change the name in the Save in: box. You change this box by clicking on the down arrow button at the end of the box, and a list of other choices where you can store your file appears (Figure 1.26).

In many of the exercises you are instructed to save your file to a floppy disk. However, you are free to save them to any drive or folder.

5   Notice that below the File name: box is another called Save as type. This allows you to save your file as a particular file format. Since you are saving from the Microsoft® Word application, it automatically defaults to this.

6   Insert a floppy disk into the drive. Enter your filename as Document, select Save in as Floppy (A:) and click on the Save button. You will hear the disk drive and see the mouse pointer turn into an hourglass for a few moments. This tells you that Windows® is working on a task.

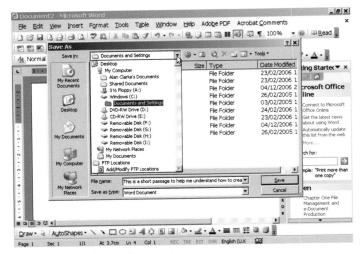

Figure 1.26 Save As locations

7   If you now change your document by adding more text and want to update your saved file all you need to do is select the File menu and option Save. The Save As window will not appear since the system assumes you want to update your file Document stored in the same place (i.e. floppy disk).

8 Add extra text in order to test saving again. Your passage should now read:

> This is a short passage to help me understand how to create, save and print a document. The keyboard has many keys to enter text and numbers. The number keys are 1,2,3,4,5,6,7,8 and 9. The symbol keys are =-/#.,:@?!£&%+*. This is extra text to test saving again.

9 Select the File menu and the Save option. You may hear the drive start up but the Save As window will not appear. It is good practice to save your document early and then update it at regular intervals. Some applications can be set to save your work automatically every few minutes. However, you should establish the habit of saving at regular intervals. There are few things worse than losing all your work due to a problem with the computer or an electricity failure because you have not saved your work for a few hours.

(Microsoft® Word will automatically save your work – select the Tools menu, Options item to reveal the Options window. Choose the Save tab and consider the choices).

10 Another useful feature of saving in Windows® is that you can save the same document many times under different names. If you select the File menu and the Save As option then the Save As window will appear and you can choose to save the document again under another name and in another folder. In this case save your document as Document2 in the floppy disk. You should see the original Document file (Figure 1.27).

11 You can repeat this operation as many times as you like and it is useful as a means of keeping an original document while revising its contents for another purpose (e.g. using a letter to the electricity company as a template for one to the gas supplier).

12 Having created a document you can print it by selecting the File menu and the Print option. A Print window will appear and you can print immediately if your printer is connected by clicking on the OK button. This will print your document using the printer's default settings. These are the standard settings which establish factors such as the number of copies, which pages to print if your document is longer than a single page, orientation of the paper (i.e. portrait or landscape) and quality of the printing. In many cases the defaults produce a perfectly acceptable printed document.

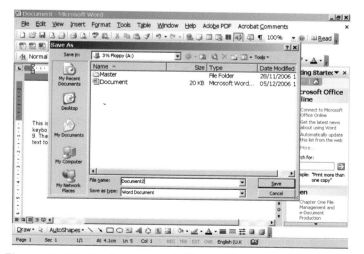

Figure 1.27 **Saving several files with different names**

continued

13 Print your short document using the default settings. Repeat the printing actions until you are confident you understand the process.

14 Close Microsoft® Word by selecting the File menu and the Exit option.

Figures 1.25, 1.26 and 1.27, how an optional PDF-maker Toolbar. Your version of Microsoft Word® may not show this option.

Spelling

Microsoft® Word provides you with a function to check your spelling and grammar. This is carried out by selecting the Tools menu and Spelling and Grammar option. This opens the Spelling and Grammar window. In the window are displayed mistakes and suggested corrections that you are asked to decide on. You can choose to ignore them or accept the change.

The spell-checker is often selected to work automatically when you are creating a document. In this case the word processor underlines words and phrases with either red or green lines. Red indicates a spelling mistake while green shows a grammatical error.

Spellcheckers have limitations. They can only detect spelling mistakes but if you have used the wrong word but spelt it correctly then it will not be identified (e.g. see and sea; fill and full; so and sow). It is therefore important not to rely only on the spelling checker but also to proofread your documents.

Retrieving a file

Once you have saved a file, you can use the application you used to create it to retrieve it in order to print extra copies or change its contents.

Exercise 13

Retrieving a file

1 Open Microsoft® Word by clicking on Start, highlighting All Programs and single-clicking on Microsoft Word. The application will open. Maximize the window using the control buttons in the top right hand corner of the window if the display does not fill the screen. Insert your floppy disk into the drive.

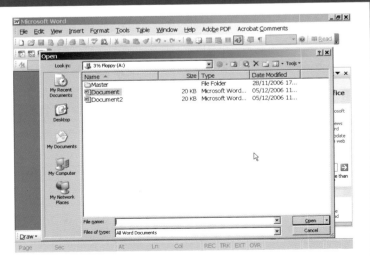

Figure 1.28 Open window

continued

2 Select the File menu and Open option. This will reveal the Open window. Choose the floppy disk by using the down arrow button at the end of the Look in box. This should reveal the files stored on your floppy disk (Figure 1.28).

3 Highlight the file you want to retrieve by single-clicking on it. Click on the Open button and you will see the contents of the file appear in the Microsoft® Word work area.

4 Close the application by selecting the File menu and the Exit option.

5 Repeat this exercise until you are confident that you can retrieve files.

Exercise 14

Introducing Editing

1 Load Microsoft® Word by selecting the Start button, highlighting the All Programs option and clicking on the Microsoft® Word item or by double-clicking on the Word icon on the desktop.

2 Using the keyboard, enter:

Titan is the largest satellite of Saturn and was discovered by Christiaan Huygens in 1655. It is a large moon with a radius of 2575 km and is the largest moon in the solar system. Titan has a nitrogen- and methane-rich atmosphere. This makes observing the surface of the satellite difficult. The Voyager spacecrafts used a variety of methods to investigate Titan. These suggest that Titan has an atmospheric pressure greater than the Earth's and possibly has methane clouds which rain ethane.

3 Observe that the text starts a new line when it needs to without your doing anything. This is called word-wrapping. If you have been trained as a typist it can often be difficult to stop yourself trying to create a new line.

4 Move your mouse pointer to the start of the text on the T of Titan. Click there and you will see that the cursor (flashing line) has moved to the start of the text. If you enter text now it will appear at the cursor. This is the way you insert text into a document. If you press the Enter key you will create a new line. Press the Enter key twice and using the up arrow key on the keyboard move up the two lines you have just created. Enter the word Titan and you will have added a heading to your passage. The Enter key is sometimes known as the Return key.

The text will look similar to Figure 1.29 which has been entered into Microsoft® Word. Do not worry if in your work area you are not able to get the same number of words per line as in the example. This is a result of the settings within the word processor which you can change later.

5 When entering text you will sometimes make a mistake. It is therefore important to always proofread any text that you enter in order to remove errors.

6 There are two main ways to remove or delete text. Using the above example, the cursor should be flashing at the end of Titan. If you press the Backspace key then the cursor moves left and deletes the last character. If you continue to tap the key, you can delete your entry.

7 The other way to remove text is to use the Delete key which is located in the bottom-right corner of the keyboard near the number pad. The Delete key works by removing the characters to the right of the cursor.

8 Enter Titan again to replace your heading.

9 We will now save this passage onto a floppy disk as the file Titan. This procedure is the same as in Exercise 12 (i.e. insert a floppy disk into drive A: and select the File menu and click on the Save option to open the Save As window).

10 You can close Microsoft® Word now by clicking on the File menu item and selecting the option Exit. An alternative way is to click on the close button in the top right-hand corner of the application window (Figure 1.29).

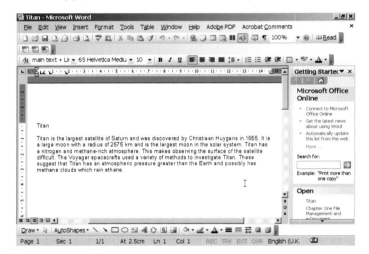

Figure 1.29 Text

Manipulating text

You have already entered a short passage and saved it to your floppy disk. Microsoft® Word and other word processors provide you with tools to insert, delete, move and replace text. There are three tools called Cut, Copy and Paste which are especially useful. They are available on the Standard toolbar (Figure 1.30) and on the Edit menu (Figure 1.31). You can choose either option. Both figures show an additional toolbar PDFMaker, this is an optional toolbar and may not be available to you.. You can add or remove toolbars using the View menu and Toolbar option.

The three tools operate in similar ways. The first step is to highlight the text you want to manipulate. To do this, you move your pointer to the start of the text you want to work on and click, holding down the mouse button and moving the pointer over the words that you want to manipulate. You will see them highlighted (i.e. the background colour changes). When you have highlighted all the words you need, release the mouse button. If you have made an error simply click the mouse away from the highlighted area and the highlighting will disappear so you can try again.

An alternative way of highlighting a line or a paragraph is to move the pointer into the page margin next to a line of text and it will change into an arrow shape. If you click the mouse when the pointer is arrow-shaped then the whole line will be highlighted. If you hold down the left button when the pointer is arrow-shaped then if you move the pointer you will continue to highlight the text. In this way you can highlight a whole passge.

If you click on the Copy tool or the menu option, the text you have highlighted will be copied to a special area of the computer's memory – the Clipboard. You can now paste it in another part of the passage. This process does not change the original text. You add the copied text by pointing to where you want to place it and clicking there. The cursor is now at the new location. If you then click on the Paste tool or the menu option, the highlighted text is inserted into the new location. You can see that the Copy and Paste tools work together. You cannot paste until you have copied.

The Cut tool or the menu option works in the same way but with one difference: when you select Cut , the highlighted text is removed.

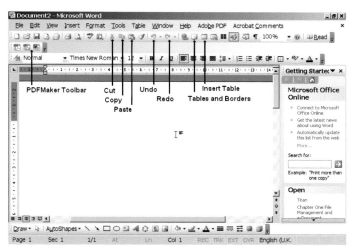

Figure 1.30 Standard toolbar

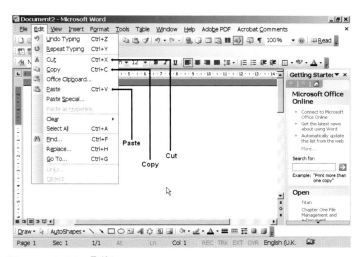

Figure 1.31 Edit menu

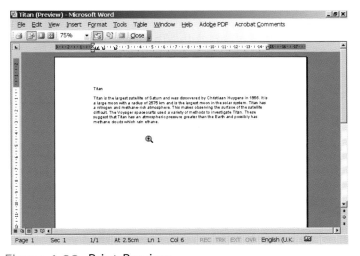

Figure 1.32 Print Preview

An alternative to Cut is to highlight the text and continue to hold down the left mouse button. You can then drag the words to a new location using the mouse pointer.

A common error when moving text is to leave behind a full stop or comma. It is always important to check that you have copied or cut the text you intended and have not left behind any parts of it.

The standard toolbar contains two important tools for when you make an error – Undo and Redo (Figure 1.30). If you make a mistake you can reverse it by clicking on Undo . If you make an error in using Undo then you can turn the clock back with Rndo . We will practise these functions in the next exercise along with Cut , Copy and Paster .

Printing

Printing documents is an important function of a word processor. However, it is important to always proofread your documents to ensure they are free of mistakes before printing them. Microsoft® Word offers a range of functions linked to printing, including an option to preview your text as a printed document without wasting any paper. Within the File menu, Print Preview opens up the window shown in Figure 1.32. This allows you to check if the document is presented in the way that you want it to be. When you have completed the preview, click on the Close button to return to the document.

When you are ready to print, click on the File menu then choose the Print option to open the Print window (Figure 1.33).

You must first select the printer on which your document is to be printed. This is shown in the Printer area at the top of the window in the box entitled Name. The Microsoft® Windows operating system allows you to link several printers to a single stand-alone computer. The list of printers is shown when you click on the down arrow next to the Name box. You select your printer by clicking on it.

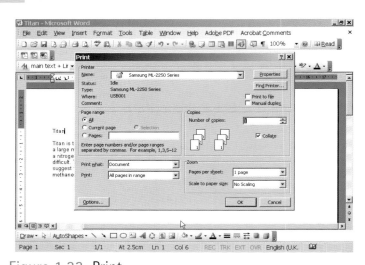

Figure 1.33 Print

You can choose what you want to print.

- All – whole document
- Current Page – only the page on which your cursor is flashing
- Pages – you enter the page range you want to print (e.g. 23–34)
- Number of copies – how many copies you want to print.

When you are ready you click on the OK button to start the printer.

Exercise 15

Manipulating and printing text

1 In the previous exercise you saved a file called Titan. We are now going to load this file into Microsoft® Word.

2 Load Microsoft® Word either by selecting the Start button, highlighting the All Programs option and clicking on the Microsoft Word item or by clicking on the Microsoft Word icon on the desktop.

3 You can load a file by single-clicking on the File menu item to open up the menu which has an option called Open. Click on Open and a window called Open will appear (Figure 1.28). An alternative approach is to click on the Open icon on the standard toolbar (Figure 1.30).

4 The Look in: box tells you what drive the window is looking at. You need to aim it at the floppy disk. You do this by clicking on the small button with the down arrow at the end of the Look in: box. A menu will appear. Click on the floppy disk option and the details of the Titan file will appear in the main working area. To open the file click once on the file to highlight it and then on the Open button on the right-hand side of the window. An alternative way is to double-click on the Titan file. In either case the text of the file should now appear in the working area of Microsoft® Word.

5 Enter the following text as new paragraphs below the previous text.

The Voyager spacecraft were not simply on a mission to survey Titan. They were taking advantage of the outer planets (e.g. Jupiter, Saturn, Neptune and Uranus) being aligned in the 1970s so that it was possible to visit several in one space trip. Two Voyager spacecraft were launched a few weeks apart in 1977.

The Voyager-1 was to fly past Jupiter, Saturn and their moons while Voyager-2 was to visit Jupiter, Saturn, Uranus and Neptune and their moons. Both spacecraft had two cameras and took thousands of digital photographs of the outer planets and their satellites. The pictures were sent to Earth as radio signals containing the digital information.

6 Practise using the Undo and Redo icons so that you become familiar with how they work.

7 Practise using the Delete and Backspace keys. Remember that the Delete key removes text to the right while the Backspace key removes text to the left.

8 When you are confident about Undo, Redo, Delete and Backspace keys then attempt these tasks:

a) Highlight

The Voyager spacecraft were not simply on a mission to survey Titan.

This is achieved by positioning the mouse pointer immediately in front of the 'The' and holding down the left mouse button then moving the pointer over the sentence until it is all highlighted (i.e. background changes colour). You will see the sentence gradually highlight as you move over the text.

b) Copy

With the sentence highlighted click on the Copy icon. (If you place your mouse pointer over the Copy icon you will see it animate and a small label will appear telling you it is the Copy icon. This works with all the icons to help you identify their different functions.) You can also copy the text using the Edit menu which includes the Cut, Copy and Paste functions. When you click on Copy nothing will change and the sentence will remain highlighted.

c) Paste

To paste the text you have copied (i.e. the sentence highlighted) you need to move the mouse pointer to where you want to copy the text to. In this case move your pointer to the end of the passage and click once and you will see the cursor flashing in the new position and the highlighting will disappear. Now click on the Paste icon and you will see the sentence appear at the end of the passage (Figure 1.34).

....and took thousands of digital photographs of the outer planets and their satellites. The pictures were sent to Earth as radio signals containing the digital information. The Voyager spacecraft were not simply on a mission to survey Titan.

Figure 1.34 **Paste**

9 If you click on the Undo icon the pasted text will be removed and you can practise pasting again. Continue copying and pasting until you feel confident.

10 Now try the Cut function.

a) Highlight the sentence below:

The pictures were sent to Earth as radio signals containing the digital information.

b) Cut

Click on the Cut icon and the sentence will disappear. You have not lost the text. It is simply saved to a special area of the memory called the Clipboard. Copied text is also saved here. Normally you can only paste the last item you have cut or copied. The Clipboard does hold up to twelve items but to paste them you need to use the Clipboard toolbar (select the Edit menu and then click on Office Clipboard to reveal the Clipboard window). Figure 1.35 shows the contents of the Clipboard.

c) Paste

Position your cursor at the location you would like to paste the cut text to by clicking once. If you click on the Paste icon then the text will now appear at the new position.

An alternative to using Cut is to employ the drag and drop technique. If you highlight the text you want to move and then click on it and hold down the mouse button you can drag the text to a new position. The pointer changes during the move to provide a guide bar to accurately position the text.

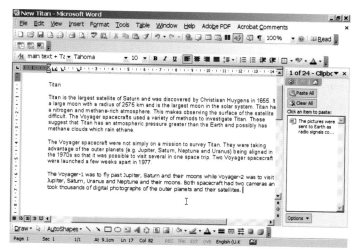

Figure 1.35 **Clipboard**

11 Practise using the Copy , Cut and Paste functions. If you use the Undo , Redo , Delete and Backspace functions you will be able to return to the original passage.

12 Practise using the drag and drop technique. If you use the Undo function you will be able to return to the original passage.

13 When you have finished save your text to the floppy disk. The file should be called New Titan.

14 Print your text after proofreading it and checking its appearance using the Print Preview option in the File menu.

15 You can close Microsoft® Word now by clicking on the File menu item and selecting the option Exit . An alternative way is to click on the Close button in the top right-hand corner of the application window.

Tables

Microsoft® Word can help you to insert tables of information into your document. The Table function is located in the Table menu. If you highlight the Insert option then a menu is revealed which includes the Table option. If you select the Table option then the Insert Table window appears. This allows you to chose the number of rows and columns your table will contain. Figure 1.36 shows the Insert Table window.

Alternatively you can select the Insert Table icon on the Standard toolbar. This opens a grid of rows and columns. You need to highlight the number of rows and columns that you want in your table by moving your pointer over the cells.

Borders and Shading

Microsoft® Word provides you with functions to enclose your documents or parts of them in a wide variety of borders. You can also shade your text to make it stand out. These functions are designed to help you produce quality documents but over-use of them can lead to the opposite. Shading is effective if the contrast between the text and background colours is sharp but if the colours chosen do not sufficiently contrast then the text can be difficult to read. Readability depends to a large extent on the degree of contrast between the colours.

The Borders and Shading option can be found in the Format menu and when it is selected the Borders and Shading window is opened (Figure 1.37). Across the top are three tabs – Borders , Format Page Border and Shading . The first tab provides a variety of ways of enclosing text while the third offers ways of shading text (Figure 1.38).

Alternatively you can select the Tables and Borders icon on the Standard toolbar.

Headers and Footers

On many documents you will have noticed that at the top and bottom are standard words which appear on every page (e.g. author's name, date and page numbers). These are called headers and footers. You will sometimes be asked to add them as part of your assessment tasks in order to identify the work as your own.

If you select the View menu and the Header and Footer option then an area enclosed in a dashed line will appear at the top

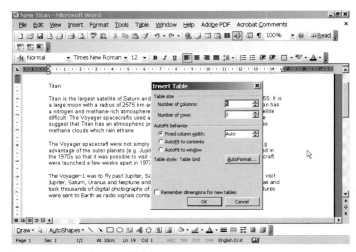

Figure 1.36 Insert Table

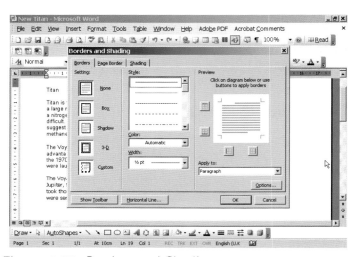

Figure 1.37 Borders and Shading

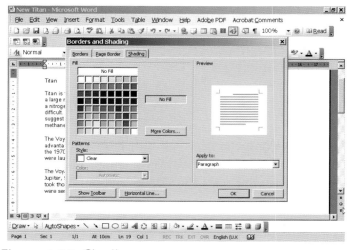

Figure 1.38 Shading

and bottom of your page with a toolbar containing a range of tools (Figure 1.39). Your page of text has a faded appearance. You can enter text from the keyboard into the dashed area or use the tools to insert items (e.g. date and file names). The tool Insert AutoText provides a range of items that you can enter into the header or footer such as Author, Page and Date.

Bullets and Numbering

Word provides a variety of ways of producing lists. You can have many different sorts of bullets and numbers using the Bullets and Numbering option within the Format menu. This displays the Bullets and Numbering window (Figure 1.40) which has four tabs across the top – Bulleted , Numbered , Outline Numbered and List Styles . he first offers you a choice of different bullets. The second tab offers a selection of numbers including letters of the alphabet and brackets. The third tab provides access to more complex numbering and bullet systems and the fourth offers a range of list styles.

Alternatively you can choose the Numbering and Bullets icons on the Format toolbar.

Word Count

When writing, you will often want to achieve a specific length of document. If you are studying then assignments are often limited to a precise length (e.g. no more than 1000 words). Microsoft® Word lets you count the words within a document by

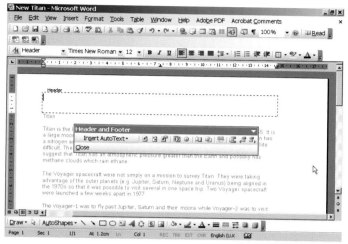

Figure 1.39 Header and Footer

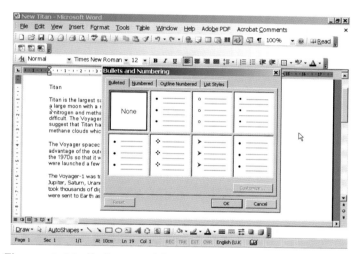

Figure 1.40 Bullets and Numbering

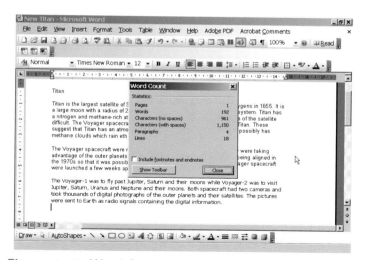

Figure 1.41 Word Count

selecting the Tools menu and the Word Count option. This opens the Word Count window. Figure 1.41 shows the number of pages, words, characters and lines for the whole document or a highlighted section. If you highlight a section Word Count will focus only on that area.

Exercise 16

Tables, Bullets, Borders and Shading

1 In the previous exercise you saved a file called New Titan. We are now going to load this file into Microsoft® Word.

2 Load Microsoft® Word either by selecting the Start button, highlighting the All Programs option and clicking on the Microsoft® Word item or by clicking on its icon on the desktop.

3 You can load a file by single-clicking on the File menu which has an option called Open. Click on Open and a window called Open will appear (Figure 1.28). An alternative approach is to click on the Open icon on the standard toolbar (Figure 1.30).

4 The Look in: box tells you what drive the window is looking at. You need to aim it at the floppy disk. You do this by clicking on the small button with the down arrow at the end of the Look in: box. A menu will appear. Click on the floppy disk option and the details of the New Titan file will appear in the main working area. To open the file click once on the file to highlight it and then on the Open button on the right-hand side of the window. An alternative way is to double-click on the New Titan file. In either case the text of the file should now appear in the working area of Microsoft® Word.

5 Enter the introductory text and table below at the end of the passage (select the Table menu, highlight the Insert option and click on the Table option).

The four main Moons of Saturn are shown below:

Moons	Size (radius)
Titan	2600
Rhea	760
Iapetus	720
Dione	560

6 Highlight the table and select the Format menu and Borders and Shading option to display the window. Select the triple line style. Notice that the preview changes to show you what effect it will have on the table. Figure 1.42 shows the table with triple line style

7 Explore some other borders for the table. Try highlighing a paragraph and enclosing it in a border.

8 Highlight the title Titan and select the Borders and Shading option then the Shading tab. Choose a colour to shade the title. I selected red. Now highlight the second

paragraph and shade it another colour. I selected yellow. Use the Undo option to remove shading.

9 An alternative way of displaying the information about the four largest moons of Saturn is a list. Highlight the table and select the Table menu, highlight the Delete option and click on Table . The table will be removed. Place your cursor one line below 'The four main moons of Saturn are shown below'. Now select the Format menu and the Bullets and Numbering option to open the window. Choose the Bulleted tab and any of the bullets that you prefer. After the bullet enter the name of the moon and then press return. A new bullet will appear on the line below. Figure 1.43 shows the results of the bullets.

10 Now save your file with the name New Titan Extra.

11 The next step is to give the new document a header and footer. Select the View file and the Header and Footer option. The header dashed area and the toolbar will appear. Click on the Insert AutoText down arrow and a list of options will appear. Select the Author, Page # and Date item. You

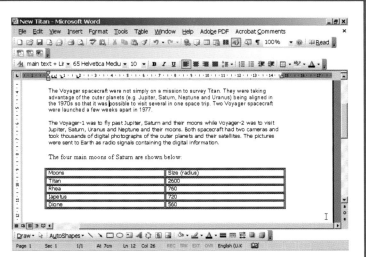

Figure 1.42 Triple line style

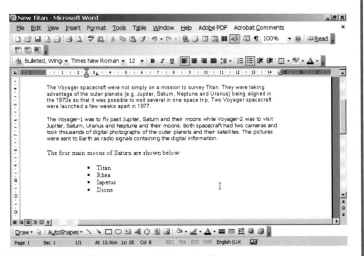

Figure 1.43 Bullets and Numbering

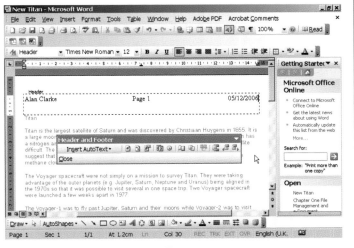

Figure 1.44 Headers and Footers

File Management and e-Document Production

37

continued

should see that they appear in the header (Figure 1.44). Now scroll down the page and you will see a dashed area at the bottom for the footer. Click inside the area and select `Insert AutoText` and chose the filename. I called the file New Titan Extra. Alternatively you could insert date and filename using the toolbar bottoms. CLAiT 2006 only requires you to enter a filename and date.

12 The next step is to use the Word Count function to measure how many words are in our passage. Finally check your document for errors by proofreading it.

13 When you have finished save your file on to the floppy disk and print your document (remember to use `Print Preview` to check before printing).

14 You can close Microsoft® Word now by clicking on the `File` menu and selecting the option `Exit`. An alternative way is to click on the `Close` button in the top right-hand corner of the application window.

Replacing words and phrases

Obviously you can replace a word or phrase by simply deleting what you wish to replace and entering the new word or phrase. However, Microsoft® Word provides an automatic way to find and replace a word or a phrase. This is available within the `Edit` menu (Figure 1.31) as the `Replace` option. If you select this option by clicking on it then the window shown in Figure 1.45 will appear.

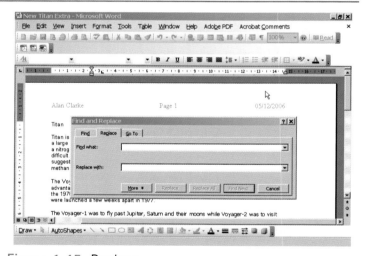

Figure 1.45 Replace

Type the text you want to replace in the Find what: box and the replacement text in the Replace with: box. The function will search for the text and either automatically replace it throughout the document (Replace All) or allow you to select which ones to change (Replace). In either case you start the function by clicking on the `Find Next` button.

Appearance and layout

Word processors (e.g. Microsoft® Word) have many functions that allow you to change the layout and presentation of text. These include altering the margins, changing the line spacing, aligning (justifying) the text and emphasizing words, phrases or whole passages. When you enter a passage of text there is no need to get the appearance right first time since these functions let you change it until you are satisfied.

Many organizations have a house style or a standard way of presenting their letters, documents and reports. This is intended to provide a common look and feel to all documents. If you begin working for a new employer it is important to know if they have a house style.

Margins

The margins of a word processor document are controlled by the Page Setup item under the File menu. If you click on File and then on Page Setup, the window shown in Figure 1.46 will be opened.

Figure 1.46 shows you that you can change all four margins (i.e. Top, Bottom, Left and Right). You change the settings for each margin by clicking on the up or down arrow buttons. As you change the margin you can see the overall effect on your document by watching the Preview area. The changes take effect as soon as you click on the OK button. If you make a mistake you can always use the Undo icon to reverse the changes.

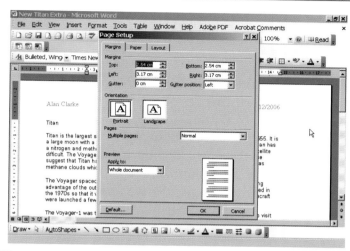

Figure 1.46 Page Setup

The Page Setup window also provides access to functions that allow you to select the orientation of the page. Figure 1.46 shows the choice between landscape and portrait orientation. You select the orientation by clicking on your choice.

Line spacing

Word processors let you adjust the line spacing of your document allowing you to double-space either a single paragraph or a whole document. The line spacing functions are provided within the Paragraph option of the Format menu. When you click on the Paragraph option, the window shown in Figure 1.47 will appear. Towards the middle of the window you will see the Line spacing box which, if you click on the down arrow at the end of the box, will display a range of options.

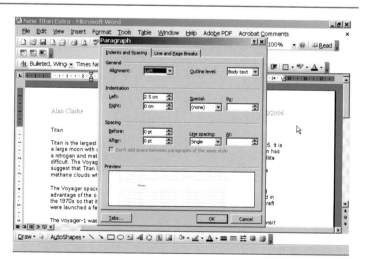

Figure 1.47 Paragraph option

These are selected by clicking on the one you want. When you enter text it will follow the new line spacing. To change existing text you need to first highlight the material you want to alter.

Tabs and Indents

When you are writing you may want to indent text (e.g. at the start of a new paragraph) to provide emphasis or provide a visual clue for your readers. The Paragraph window (Figure 1.47) provides you with the means of controlling indents.

The Tab key on the keyboard allows you to indent text. The size of a tab (i.e. single press of the key – called a tab stop) is set by the Tabs option within the Format menu which opens the Tabs window. This controls the size and justification of tabs. Figure 1.48 shows the Tabs window.

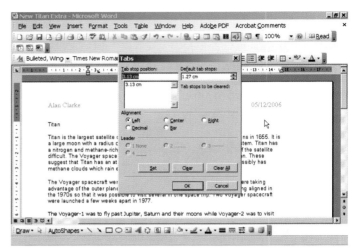

Figure 1.48 Tabs

Inserting a new paragraph

To add a new paragraph break you need to position the cursor by clicking with the mouse pointer at the desired position and then pressing the Enter key twice. The first key press moves the start of the new paragraph to the next line while the second press inserts a blank line between the paragraphs.

Emphasize text

Microsoft® Word provides you with a range of tools to emphasize your words. These include:

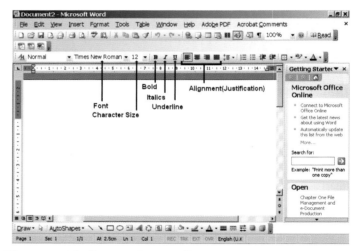

Figure 1.49 Formatting toolbar

- changing the font and character size of your text
- emboldening your words
- underlining your words
- changing your text into italics.

These functions are available on the Formatting toolbar (Figure 1.49) and also in the Format menu (Figure 1.50) within the Font item. If you select one of the toolbar options it will change to indicate that it is active and everything you now enter is in the emphasized form (e.g. underlined). You need to click on the option a second time to de-select it. It can also be used to change existing text. The normal process of changing text, from a single character to a whole document, is to highlight your selection and then choose the function's icon or menu option.

Alignment (Justification)

There are four ways of aligning (justifying) a document. These are:

- Left – the left text edge is parallel with the margin and the right is ragged
- Right – the right text edge is parallel with the margin and the left is ragged
- Centred – the text is aligned down the centre of the page with both edges ragged
- Double – both the left and right text edges are parallel with the margins (this is called Justify on the Formatting toolbar).

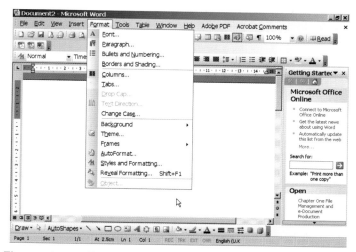

Figure 1.50 Format menu

Alignment (justification) functions are provided in the Paragraph option (Figure 1.47) of the Format menu (Figure 1.50) and on the formatting Toolbar (Figure 1.49). If you select one of the toolbar options it will change to indicate it is active and then everything you now enter will be in the new line alignment (justification) (e.g. centred). You need to click on the option a second time to de-select it. The process can be used to change existing text by highlighting the section and selecting the desired alignment (justification) icon or menu option.

Exercise 17

Appearance and layout

1 Load Microsoft® Word either by selecting the Start button, highlighting the All Programs option and clicking on the Microsoft® Word item or by double-clicking on its icon on the desktop.

2 Enter the passage below in Times New Roman and character size 12.

(Hint – select the font and character size from the Formatting toolbar before entering text)

Invasion of Russia – 1812

In 1812 Napoleon invaded Russia with one of the largest armies that had ever been assembled. Over 600,000 men had been brought together from all parts of Europe that formed the French Empire. Italians, Dutch, Belgians, Germans and Frenchmen marched across the frontier and the vast majority never returned. It was 700 miles to Moscow and the army had to march across a desolate landscape of forest and marsh where villages were days apart.

In past campaigns French armies had relied upon living off the countries they had attacked. Russia was not a rich land and a large force would not be able to subsist from pillage. The French knew that they could not use their old tactics so they had gathered stores to transport into Russia. Each soldier was heavily loaded with flour, bread, rice and biscuits to last many days. The army staff had planned to transport huge quantities of supplies to last through the normal fast and furious French assault to knock out the Russian armies.

Napoleon's army entered Moscow less than three months later having fought several major and minor battles but it had not destroyed the Russian army. In past campaigns the occupation of the capital city had followed the destruction of the opposing army. It was not long before the French army had to retreat through winter weather with a supply system that had completely failed.

3 Save the passage on your floppy disk as a file called 'Invasion' (there is a `Save` icon on the Standard toolbar – a picture of a floppy disk – or select the `File` menu and the `Save` option). It is good practice to save your text as soon as you can and then to update the file as you make changes. When you select `Save` later you will not be shown the Save As window since the application assumes that you simply want to update your original file. If you want to save the altered text as a different file you need to select the `Save As` option in the `File` menu. The procedure is then the same as you earlier undertook for saving a new file.

The `Save As` option also allows you to change the filename of your document. This is useful if you want to create a master document for a whole series of publications or if you want to keep copies of the document at the different stages of its development.

4 Change the margins of your documents so that:

left and right are 3 cm

top and bottom are 3.5 cm.

Select the `File` menu and the `Page Setup` option.

5 Change the line spacing to 1.5 by highlighting the text and selecting the `Format` menu and the `Paragraph` option.

6 Change the title Invasion of Russia so that it is in the Arial font and in character size 14 and embolden the text (i.e. highlight the text, choose the Arial font, the character size and bold option on the Formatting toolbar).

7 Change the alignment (justification) of the title to centred (i.e. highlight the title and select the `Center` icon on the Formatting toolbar).

8 Change the alignment (justification) of the rest of the passage to double (i.e. highlight the text and select the `Justify` icon on the Formatting toolbar).

9 Insert a new paragraph at

Each soldier was heavily loaded with flour, bread, rice and biscuits to last many days.

continued

Position your cursor before Each and press Enter twice to break the text and insert a blank line between the paragraphs.

10 Remember to save your finished text and print the document (select the File menu, Print Preview and then the Print icon). Check that the text is correct and correct any errors.

11 Close Microsoft® Word by selecting the File menu and the Exit option or use the Close button in the top right-hand corner of the window).

Templates

Many organizations base their correspondence and other documents on templates. These are standard documents in which the structure and layout is determined centrally. Users enter the content of the document but the rest is pre-determined. This is to allow the organization to present a consistent look and feel to the wider world. It allows the quality of documents to be more easily maintained.

Templates can be created to meet any document need such as:

■ Letters
■ Faxes
■ Reports
■ Minutes of meetings.

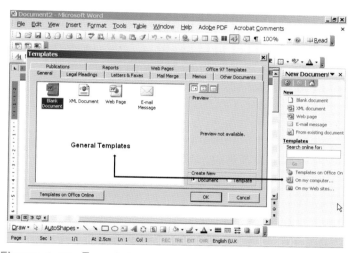

Figure 1.51 Template

To create a template you need to select the File menu and the New option to reveal the New Document task pane to the right of the work area. Select the On my computer option in the Templates section of the New Document task pane. This will open the Templates window. This has many tabs across the top. If you choose the General tab then a range of templates provided by Microsoft® Word are displayed (Figure 1.51). You can also create your own by selecting a document, clicking on the Template button in the Create New area in the bottom right-hand corner of the window and on the OK button. You can amend the templates provided by Microsoft® Word or create new ones.

Changing a password

Computer security is extremely important for both office and home users. In the office, making sure systems are secure through the use of passwords is important for protecting data from unauthorized access. At home, although you may not have data that you wish to keep secret, good security protects against misuse be it accidental or malicious. Viruses are a continual threat to all computers so that it is vital to ensure access to them is controlled. It requires a major effort to remove a virus infection and can result in a considerable loss of data, waste a large amount of your time and require technical assistance to remove. It is now established practice to maintain virus protection systems and an important part of this is to regulate access through passwords.

Microsoft® Windows and many other suppliers offer a wide range of security systems. Whatever security software you use it is important to understand the need to use original passwords and to change them regularly. Try not to use your name or anything obvious. Good practice is to pick a word at random from a dictionary and add some numbers either within or at the end of the word, or to use a completely random series of numbers and letters.

To change your Windows® password you need to access the Control Panel. This involves clicking on the Start button and clicking on Control Panel to reveal the Control Panel window. In this window there is an icon called User Accounts , shown as two people. When you

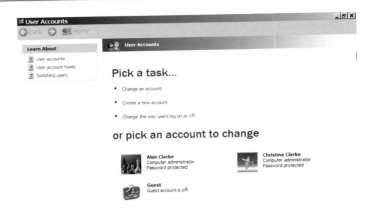

Figure 1.52 User accounts

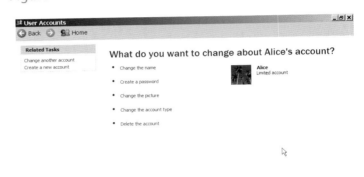

Figure 1.53 Alice's Account

Figure 1.54 Create password

double-click on this icon it will open the User Accounts window (Figure 1.52). This allows you to:

- Change an account
- Create a new account
- Change the way users log on and off.

Each user has their own account. If you click on Create a New Account then you can add a new user to the computer system by following the sequence of choices. Alice is an example of a new user (Figure 1.53) and if you click on a new user's name then her User Account appears, which allows you to create her password (Figure 1.54).

Other Control Panel options

The Control Panel provides ways of changing system settings. You can adjust:

- the sound volume of your system by selecting the Sounds and Audio Devices icon to display the Sounds and Audio Devices Properties window
- the date and time of the system by selecting the Date and Time icon to reveal the Date and Time Properties window.

You can alter various other settings such as adjusting the display, mouse, keyboard and printers.

Screen prints

Windows® provides you with a standard function to capture an image of the screen display (i.e. a screen print). This is available from the keyboard by pressing the PrtSc key. You can then open a blank document and use the Paste option to insert the image into a document. As part of the New CLAiT assessment you will occasionally be asked to use the screen print to provide evidence of your work. It is therefore worth practising.

Safe working practice

There are a number of straightforward actions you can take to reduce the risk of injuring yourself when you are using a computer. One of the key problems is Repetitive Strain Injury (RSI) in which by using the computer incorrectly you place a strain on your body (e.g. hands, wrists and arms) which may result in permanent harm.

Here are some things you can do to keep yourself safe:

Space

It is important to give yourself plenty of space. You must have plenty of room for your legs and body. There should be enough space around the computer for your papers and books so that you can reach them without stretching. You can use a paper stand to hold your papers to help you copy text without turning. You should be comfortable. Even a tiny need to twist or turn your body can be harmful over a long period.

Breaks

It is good practice to take regular breaks away from the computer.

Chairs

Your chair should be adjustable so that you can alter the height and backrest. It should support your lower back. Your feet should either be placed squarely on the floor or on a foot rest with your knees slightly higher than the chair to ensure good circulation of blood. Again it is important to be comfortable.

Your eyes should be aligned slightly below the top of the monitor and you should be positioned about 18 inches from the display.

Reduce strain

When you are using the computer you must avoid placing any strain on hands and wrists by:

1 Keeping your wrists straight while typing (e.g. by using a rest)
2 Not resting on your wrists
3 Typing gently without excessive force
4 Taking frequent breaks and avoiding typing for long periods.

Light

Computer monitors are very susceptible to reflection. It is therefore important to position your screen so it does not reflect light from the sun or the room lights. You will probably need to experiment. Monitors and other types of screen are normally designed to allow you to change their angle and their brightness and contrast.

Cables

Because computers often have a large number of cables to link them to other equipment, there is always a risk of tripping over them. It is good practice to inspect the general area around your computer to identify and remove any risks.

Shortcuts

You may have observed that when you are using Windows® or WordPad some of the menu options have a letter underlined. This is a keyboard shortcut. They provide you with an alternative way of selecting the option other than clicking on the option with the mouse pointer. You press the Alt key and, holding it down, press the letter that is underlined (e.g. File). This has the same effect as clicking on the option. It is useful if you are entering text as you can therefore select the option without taking your hands away from the keyboard.

Help

Microsoft Windows® has a help function, accessed by selecting the Start button and clicking on the Help and Support option. The Help and Support Center window will appear (Figure 1.55). This provides help with many topics (e.g. What's new in Windows XP) and ways of gaining assistance. You may wish to explore the topics. Click on the options which will reveal sub-topics and so on. You can return to the original display by clicking on the Back button in the left-hand top corner.

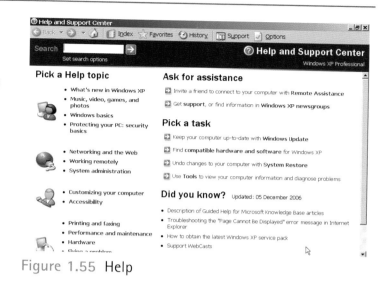

Figure 1.55 Help

More Practice

Activity 1

1 Load Microsoft® Word either by selecting the Start button, highlighting the All Programs option and clicking on the Microsoft Word item or by clicking on its icon on the desktop.

2 Enter the passage below in Tahoma font and character size 10 by selecting the font and character size from the Formatting toolbar before entering text.

3 Set the margins as follows (File menu, Page Setup and Margins tab):

Left and right – 4 cms

Top and bottom – 3 cms.

The page orientation should be portrait (File menu and Page Setup).

For many people guinea pigs are the perfect pet. They are small friendly animals who rarely bite and are easy to keep healthy. Guinea pigs are rodents and are not from Guinea so the name is a little misleading. They actually originate from Peru. There are several different breeds including selfs which are smooth-haired animals, Himalayans, Abyssinians and Crested.

Guinea pigs are herbivores. They need to be given fresh vegetables every day since they cannot make their own vitamin C. Their teeth grow all the time so they need to be given food which they need to grind so that their teeth do not get too long. Dry food is available which has been enriched with vitamin C. Guinea pigs are enthusiastic about their food and will tell you when they are hungry. They will talk to you when you are late just to remind you they like their food on time.

Guinea pigs can be kept indoors or outdoors. If they are in an outside hutch they need to be secured against both the cold and the local cats. A frosty night can leave pigs very distressed while they have few defences against cats. Indoor animals need the opportunity to exercise in the open air in a run or other secure enclosure. All guinea pigs love eating grass.

4 Create a header by selecting the View menu and the Header and Footer option. Enter your own name as the header and add a date to the footer and the filename Guinea Pig.

5 Once you have entered the text, carefully check it for mistakes and use the spellchecker (Tools menu and Spelling and Grammar option) to ensure it is free from spelling mistakes. Save the passage on your floppy disk as a file called Guinea Pig by selecting the File Menu and then Save .

6 Insert a title 'Guinea Pig – Cavies' separated by one blank line from the rest of the passage in Arial font and character size 14. (Use the mouse to move the cursor, select the font and character size from the Formatting toolbar before entering the title.)

7 Underline the title by highlighting the text and selecting the Underline icon from the Formatting toolbar.

8 Insert the new paragraph below so that it becomes the third one.

These little animals enjoy each other's company so should be kept together. Female pigs are called sows and males are boars. The young animals are born with their eyes open and will be running around their hutch soon after birth. They are suckled by their mothers but will soon eat vegetables and can be separated from them within a few weeks.

9 Change the line spacing to double (by highlighting the passage, selecting the Format menu and the Paragraph option).

10 Change the alignment (justification) of the passage to left (by highlighting the text and selecting the Align Left icon on the Formatting toolbar).

11 Replace 'guinea pigs' with 'guinea pigs (cavies)' throughout the passage – you should find six occasions (use the Edit menu and the Replace option). Proofread your final document to ensure it is free from mistakes.

12 Save your changed file (File menu and Save option or Save icon on the Standard toolbar).

13 Print your document by selecting the File menu, the Print Preview and Print options (or the Print icon from within Print Preview).

14 Close Microsoft® Word (by selecting the File menu and the Exit option or click on the Close button).

Activity 2

1 Create a folder called Hobbies on your floppy disk by clicking My Computer , choosing 3½ Floppy (A:), selecting the File menu, New and Folder options. Enter the name Hobbies to replace New Folder title.

2 Create a subfolder called Pets in the folder Hobbies by opening the folder and selecting the File menu , New and Folder options. Enter the name Pets to replace New Folder title.

3 Create another subfolder called Extra in the folder Hobbies.

4 Rename the folder Hobbies as your name (e.g. Alan Clarke) by highlighing the folder, selecting the File menu and the Rename option.

5 Copy the file Guinea Pig from Activity 1 into the subfolder Pets (highlight the file and copy and paste).

6 Delete the subfolder Extra (highlight the file and select delete option from the File menu).

7 Take a screen print of the folder that has your name (e.g. Alan Clarke) by pressing the Shift and Print Screen (PrtSc) keys.

8 Take a screen print of the file Guinea Pig in the subfolder Pets.

9 Paste your screen prints into a Microsoft® Word document.

10 Add a header and footer to your document and enter your name and date in the footer.

11 Save the document with the filename Screen Print on your floppy disk.

12 Print the document.

13 Close your files.

The screen print method is sometimes required as part of the assessment process to provide evidence that you have completed the tasks.

SUMMARY

1 **What is a computer?** A computer consists of two main components: hardware and software.

2 **Hardware** Hardware is the physical elements of the equipment that you can see when you look at a computer. These include a monitor, main box (containing the Central Processing Unit), printer, keyboard and mouse.

3 **Software** Software is the instructions that control the hardware. Software is divided into two main types which are operating systems and applications.

4 **Serial, Parallel and USB ports** Ports are the means of connecting peripheral equipment to the main computer.

5 **DVD and CD–RW drives** These are different types of drives which allow disks to be used with a computer. DVD disks allow the computer to read very large amounts of information which are stored on the disk. DVD disks are often used to hold the contents of an entire movie. CD–RW drives allow you to save information onto a special type of CD–ROM and to read the information stored on the disk.

6 **Memory Stick** A memory stick is a portable device that allows you to store files and folders by plugging it into a computer's USB port. It is also called a flash or pen drive or even a dongle.

7 **Mouse** The mouse enables you to carry out a series of actions including single-clicking with left and right mouse buttons, double-clicking and dragging and dropping.

8 **Keyboard** The keyboard allows you to enter text and numbers into computer applications.

9 **Window controls** In the top right-hand corner of the window are three control buttons. These are minimize , maximize and close .

10 **Storing files** Information is stored on disks (e.g. floppy and hard disks) in the form of files which are placed in folders to help organize them. Files have different formats depending on the nature of the information they store (e.g. documents and images).

11 **Windows Explorer** Explorer provides the functions to search the disks for files and folders. Other functions include deleting and renaming files.

12 **Search** Click on the Start button and Search option to reveal the Search Results window.

13 **Accessories** Windows® contains several applications which come bundled with the operating system. These include WordPad (word-processing), Paint and Calculator.

14 **Load Microsoft® Word** Open Microsoft®Word either by clicking on the Start button, highlighting All Programs and single-clicking on the Microsoft Word option or double-clicking on its icon on the Windows® desktop.

15 **Insert text** You must position the cursor where you need to insert the text. Move your mouse pointer to the new position and click there. The cursor will appear as a flashing line and you can now enter your text.

16 **Save** Select the File menu and the Save option. The Save As window (dialog box) opens. Select the location (Save in: box) and name your file (File name: box) then click on the Save button.

17 **Save As** Select the File menu and the Save As option. The Save As window opens. Select the location (Save in: box) and name your file (File name: box) then click on the Save button.

18 **Save a file on a floppy disk** Insert a floppy disk into drive A: and click on the File menu and the Save option to reveal the Save As window. Select the drive (3½ Floppy (A:)) and enter a filename. Having saved a file once, you can update it by clicking on the File menu and Save without the Save As window appearing again. It simply overwrites the original file. An alternative is to click on the Save icon on the Standard toolbar to update the file.

19 **Close** Click on the File menu and the Exit option or click on the Close button in the top right-hand corner of the application window.

20 **Delete text** You have two different keys which both work from the position of your cursor.
Backspace key – this removes text, character by character to the left of the cursor position.
Delete key – this removes text, character by character to the right of the cursor position.
There is also Undo and Redo. Undo removes the last action you have undertaken while Redo carries out actions removed by Undo.

21 **Move text** Highlight the text you want to move. Select either the Copy or Cut icons on the Standard toolbar or alternatively the Edit menu and the Cut or Copy options. Reposition the cursor at the place you want to move the text to and then select the Paste icon on the Standard toolbar or the Edit menu and the Paste option.

22 **Drag and drop** Highlight the text. Click on it and hold down the mouse button. Drag the text to the new position using the mouse. The pointer changes during the move to provide a guide bar to position the text accurately.

23 **Tables** Use the Table menu. Highlight the Insert option and Table option to open the Insert Table window.

24 **Borders and Shading** Select the Format menu and the Borders and Shading option to open the window with three tabs – Borders, Page Border and Shading – across the top.

25 **Headers and Footers** Use the [View] menu and the [Header and Footer] option.

26 **Bullets and numbering** Use the [Format] menu and the [Bullets and Numbering] option.

27 **Word Count** Use the [Tools] menu and the [Word Count] option.

28 **Replace text** Use the [Edit] menu and the [Replace] option to open the Replace window. Enter the text you want to replace in the Find what: box and the replacement text in the Replace with: box.

29 **Change margins** Use the [File] menu and the [Page Setup] item to open the window which controls the four margins (i.e. left, right, top and bottom).

30 **Orientation** Select the [File] menu and [Page Setup] option. This presents you with the choice between the landscape and portrait orientation of the page.

31 **Alter line spacing** Using the [Format] menu and the [Paragraph] option. The Paragraph window will open with the Line spacing function box.

32 **Alignment** (Justification) Select the [Format] menu and the [Paragraph] option or the Formatting toolbar. Select one of the toolbar options ([Align Left] , [Align Right] , [Center] or [Justify]). It will change to show it is active and then everything you now enter will be in the new alignment (justification) (e.g. centred). You need to click on the option a second time to de-select it. To change existing text, highlight it and then select the alignment (justification) icon or the menu option.

33 **Printing** Select the [File] menu, click on the [Print] option and the [OK] button.

34. **Retrieve** Select the [File] menu and the [Open] option. This will reveal the Open window. Use the down arrow button at the end of the Look in: box and select the file to be retrieved.

35 **Change password** Select the [Start] button, highlight the [Settings] option to open a menu and click on the [Control Panel] to reveal the Control Panel window. Double-click on the [Users and Passwords] icon.

36 **Safe working practice** The straightforward issues to reduce the risk of harm are sufficient space, regular breaks, eliminating strain and reducing light reflections.

37 **Shortcuts** Press the [Alt] key and, holding it down, press the letter that is underlined (e.g. Edit).

38 **Print Screen** Press the [Alt] and [Print Screen] (PrtSc) keys. Paste the image of the screen into a Microsoft® Word document by opening a new document and selecting the [Edit] menu and [Paste] option.

39 **Help** Select the [Start] button and click on the [Help and Support] option.

40 **Spelling and Grammar Checker** Select the [Tools] menu and [Spelling and Grammar] option. This opens the Spelling and Grammar window.

The spellchecker can be set work automatically so that spelling mistakes are undelined in red while green shows a grammatical error. It is always important to proofread the text and not to rely only on the spellchecker to identify mistakes.

Unit 2

Creating Spreadsheets and Graphs

This chapter will help you to use spreadsheets and charts and graphs applications. You will be able to:

- identify and use spreadsheet as well as charts and graphs software correctly

- use an input device to enter and edit data accurately

- insert, replicate and format arithmetical formulae

- use common numerical formatting and alignment

- manage and print spreadsheets and charts and graphs

- develop pie charts, line graphs and bar/column charts

- select and present single and comparative sets of data

- set numerical parameters and format data.

Assessment

This unit does not assume any previous experience of spreadsheets. However, it may be useful to have studied Unit 1 (File Management and e-Document Production). You will be assessed through a practical realistic assignment which is designed to allow you to demonstrate your knowledge and skills against each objective. Your tutor can provide you with more guidance.

Spreadsheet applications

Figure 2.1 and Figure 2.2 show Microsoft Excel® 2003. Figure 2.1 shows Excel® with the Getting Started task pane open. The task pane is intended to help you undertake some frequent tasks, in this case to open an existing workbook (spreadsheet) or start a new one. If you prefer to have the task pane closed you need to select the Close button in the top right-hand corner of the task pane or select the View menu and the Task Pane option to remove the tick icon next to the option. To open the task pane repeat the operation (i.e. View menu and Task Pane option to insert the tick).

Figure 2.2 shows that Microsoft Excel® 2003 is similar to other Microsoft® Office applications in that it comprises a menu and toolbars (e.g. Standard toolbar), work area and status bar at the bottom of the display. In the top right-hand corner are the three control buttons – minimize, maximize and close, which are displayed in all Microsoft® application windows. However, there are some differences, which are:

1   The work area is divided into a grid of rows and columns to form many individual cells. The active cell illustrated in Figure 2.2 is in row 1 and column A and is known as A1. When you are developing formulae it is important to identify particular cells and this is done by stating the column and row intersection.

2   At the bottom of the work area is an extra bar with tabs indicating Sheet 1, Sheet 2 and Sheet 3. This shows which worksheet is being used and Excel® allows you to group sheets together to form a workbook. Figure 2.2 shows that Sheet 1 is being displayed.

3   Beneath the Formatting toolbar is a row called the Formula bar which shows A1 at the left-hand end followed by a greyed-out area and *fx* symbol. A1 indicates the cell in which the cursor is currently placed and therefore this changes as the cursor moves. After the *fx* symbol, any formulae which are in the current cell are displayed. We will discuss formulae later in this chapter. There are several ways of loading an application such as Microsoft Excel®. The two most common are using:

- the Start button
- the Microsoft Excel ® icon on the Windows® desktop.

In the bottom left-hand corner of the Windows® desktop is a button called Start. This allows you to access various applications and standard features of the operating system. If you single-click on Start , a menu will pop up. If you place the mouse pointer over the All Programs item it will become highlighted (i.e. the background will change colour) and a new menu will appear alongside. If you click on the item shown as Microsoft Excel then the application will load. In a similar way if you double-click on the Excel icon shown on the desktop then Excel® will again load.

The exercises included in the chapter are intended to help you understand how to use

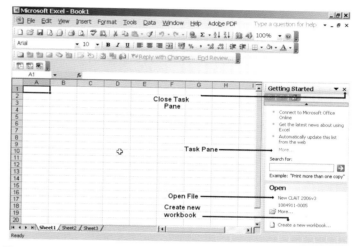

Figure 2.1   Microsoft Excel® 2003 with task pane open

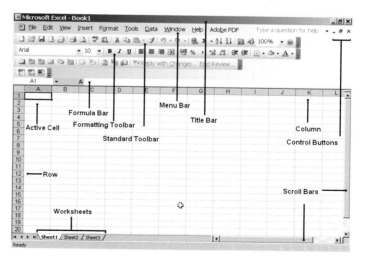

Figure 2.2   Microsoft Excel® 2003

spreadsheets as well as graphs and charts. They are simplified representations of the world and are not intended to be tutorials on accountancy but explanations of Excel®.

Exercise 18

Load and use Microsoft Excel®

1 Load Microsoft Excel® using either the All Programs menu or the Excel icon on the desktop.

2 Enter the table of information below to form your first spreadsheet. It shows a simple breakdown of the costs of operating the Acme Newsagent. Position your pointer in cell C3 and you will see the cell is highlighted by its borders becoming emboldened. Now enter Acme Newsagent. Repeat this, entering Newspapers in B8, Groceries in B9, Stationery in B10, Wages in B11, Total in B12, Costs in C6, Overheads in D6 and Total Costs in E6. Now add the numeric cost data to form the column of figures in column C in rows 8, 9, 10 and 11.

Acme Newsagent			
	Costs	Overheads	Total Costs
Newspapers	12,000		
Groceries	10,000		
Stationery	8,000		
Wages	6,00		
Total			

3 To select an individual cell you need to click within it and it will be highlighted. However, you can also select a whole row or column. To select a row or column click in the letter (e.g. A) or number (e.g. 1) which is at the end of the row or the top of the column. The row or column will then be highlighted. To remove the highlighting you need to click in another part of the sheet.

4 If you make a mistake when entering text or numbers then you can delete the characters using the Backspace key. However, if you have moved to a new cell then you can either overwrite your original entry by clicking on the cell with the error and entering the correct text or numbers or edit the text as it appears on the Formula bar. If you highlight the cell which contains the error you will see its contents appear on the Formula bar and you use your mouse pointer to position your cursor in order to amend the text.

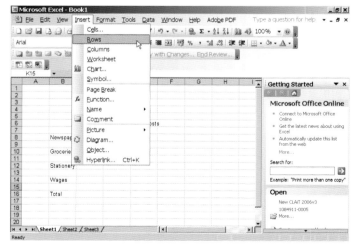

Figure 2.3   Insert menu

5 This table is perhaps a little crowded so you need to separate the rows with a blank row. Excel® allows you to insert new rows and columns. To insert a row click on Groceries to tell Excel® where you want to insert the row (it is inserted above the row the cursor is in) and on the Insert menu (Figure 2.3) then on the Rows item. A new row will be inserted between Groceries and Newspapers.

6 Now add a row between Groceries and Stationery; and Stationery and Wages; and finally Wages and Total.

7 Enter headings 'Income' starting in cell F6, 'Total Profits' in cell G6 and the information shown in Figure 2.4. Insert a column of information by highlighting column F, selecting the Insert menu (Figure 2.3) then the Columns item. A new column will be created. The menus in all Microsoft® Office applications are sometimes presented in a shortened form ending with two arrows. If you click on the arrows the rest of the menu options are displayed.

8 Save the spreadsheet you have created onto a floppy disk. This procedure is the same in all Windows® applications – you save a spreadsheet, database or graphic image in exactly the same way. Insert a floppy disk into drive A: and click on the File menu which will open to show a list of options. Select Save and a window will open.

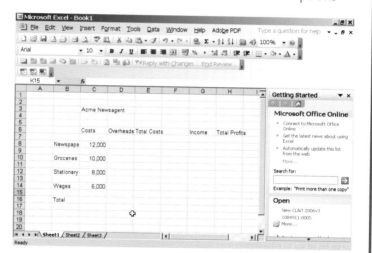

Figure 2.4   Spreadsheet

9 Click in the File name: box and enter A:\Acme Newsagent. Now click on the Save button on the right of the window. You have now saved the table as a file called Acme Newsagent. You may hear drive A: working during this process.

10 It is possible to save the spreadsheet again under a different filename so that you have two identical files, but because they have different filenames, they are treated as individual files. In order to do this you need to select the File menu and the option Save As.

11 You can close Excel® now by clicking on the File menu and a menu will appear with a list of options. At the bottom of the list is the option Exit. If you click on Exit then Excel® will close. An alternative way is to click on the Close button in the top right-hand corner of the application window.

New

On occasion you will want to start a new spreadsheet once you have completed one. Select the File menu and the New option. This opens the New Workbook Task Pane which is divided into a number of sections. These provide access to many standard templates for spreadsheets. Select the Blank Workbook option. A new blank spreadsheet will appear.

Delete, Clear and Hide

Excel® provides three useful options linked to deleting the contents of cells, rows and columns. These are:

- Delete (Figure 2.5)
- Clear (Figure 2.5)
- Hide (Figure 2.6).

The first step in using the options above is to identify the row, column, cell or area of the spreadsheet by highlighting or placing the mouse pointer in the cell or row or column. The Edit menu provides access to the Delete and Clear options. If Delete is selected, then a small Delete window appears providing different options for removing the item. Delete permanently removes the item and adjusts the spreadsheet layout. If Clear is selected then another menu of options appears (e.g. if All is chosen the contents of the selected area are removed but not the spreadsheet structure/layout).

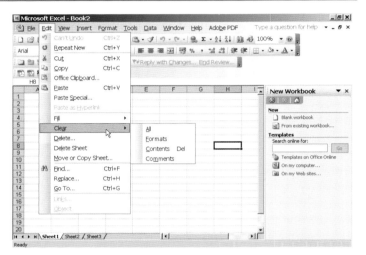

Figure 2.5   Edit menu

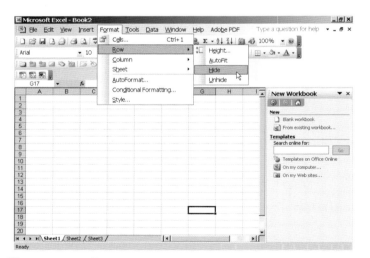

Figure 2.6   Format menu

The difference between Delete and Clear is that Delete removes the contents and the spreadsheet structure, while Clear simply removes the contents. Clear also provides some extra options such as removing the formatting of an entry while leaving contents behind. You would probably use Clear to amend an area in the heart of a spreadsheet and Delete if you wanted to start again.

The Hide function is accessed by selecting the Format menu, then the options Row, Column or Sheet (Figure 2.6). Again you identify the area you want to hide by highlighting or placing the mouse pointer in the particular row or column. By selecting Hide, that area of the spreadsheet will disappear. It can be returned by selecting the Unhide option. Hide does not delete the items but only hides them from view. This is useful if you do not want to disclose confidential information.

Exercise 19

Delete, Clear and Hide

1 Load Microsoft Excel® using either the All Programs menu or the Excel icon on the desktop.

2 Enter the table of information below to form your first spreadsheet. It shows a family budget:

	January	February	March
Food and drink	300	320	270
Clothes	80	75	145
Travel	160	400	140
Leisure	60	110	95
Services	25	42	67
Council Tax	105	105	105

3 Save the spreadsheet you have created onto a floppy disk. Insert a floppy disk into drive A: and click on the File menu and a menu will open showing a list of options. Select Save and a window will open.

4 Click in the File name: box and Enter A:\Budget. Now click on the Save button on the right of the window. You have now saved the table as a file called Budget. You may hear drive A: working during this process.

5 If you make a wrong choice you can retrace your steps by using the Undo option in the Edit menu. This is also useful when you want to explore the effects of different options without making any permanent changes.

6 Explore the three options delete, clear and hide. Highlight the February column (i.e. from the February title to 105) and then select the Delete option on the Edit menu. The column will disappear and the cells will move to the left. You should observe that the gap between January and March closes (i.e. the structure of the spreadsheet is removed). To change the movement click on a cell away from your information. Click on Delete again and another menu with four options will open – the Shift cells left is the default setting but the menu allows you to select other options. Don't change the default just review the other options.

7 Now select the Edit menu and the Undo Delete option and the column will reappear.

8 Highlight February again and select the Edit menu and highlight Clear to reveal a menu with four options – click on All. Observe what happens – the content disappears but the gap between January and March does not close (i.e. the structure is not removed).

9 Now select the Edit menu and Undo Clear and the content will reappear

10 Highlight February once more and select the Format menu and highlight the Column

continued

option to reveal a menu of five choices. Select the Hide option. Observe what happens – the column disappears and a line of highlighting is left between January and March.

11 Now select the Format menu and highlight the Column option to reveal the menu of options. Select the Unhide option and you will see the column reappear.

12 Explore the three options using Undo or Unhide to return to the original spreadsheet until you understand the different effects of delete, clear and hide.

13 You can close Excel® now by clicking on the File menu; a menu will appear with a list of options. At the bottom of the list is the option Exit . If you click on Exit then Excel® will close. An alternative way is to click on the Close button in the top right-hand corner of the application window.

Spreadsheet Formulae

Figure 2.7 shows a spreadsheet of the costs and income of the Acme Newsagent. This spreadsheet employs a number of formulae to:

- add up columns and rows of figures
- calculate overheads
- calculate the total profit of the business.

Fomulae are used by spreadsheets to calculate numerical values. They allow you to add up columns of figures to produce a total, subtract the contents of different cells,

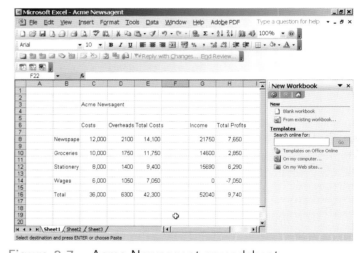

Figure 2.7   Acme Newsagent spreadsheet

multiply, divide and undertake more complex calculations. One of the most important features of a spreadsheet is that you can build formulae within the sheet to calculate almost anything.

The mathematical operators used in Microsoft Excel® are:

- + add
- − subtract
- * multiply
- / divide.

Brackets are also important because they tell Excel® to calculate anything in the brackets first before going on with the remaining parts of the calculation.

Formulae are based on giving each cell a reference (e.g. A1, D12, M7) made up of the column letter and the row number.

Example

B8 Column B and Row 8

In Figure 2.7 you can see the column letters and row numbers. Cell C8 (Column C and Row 8) contains the number 12000. To calculate overheads (i.e. contents of D8) of the newspapers this number needs to be multiplied by 0.175 which represents the current rate of overheads (17.5% or 0.175). The formula is C8*0.175 (i.e. contents of cell C8 multiplied by the overhead rate). By using a formula referring to the cell's unique address C8 each time the number placed in the cell changes the new value of overheads is automatically calculated.

Example

C8 = 12000   D8 = 2100 (Overheads)
C8 = 8000   D8 = 1400 (Overheads)
C8 = 6000   D8 = 1050 (Overheads)

It is possible to have a formula based on the actual number so that our example of an overhead formula could be 12000*0.175. This would give the correct value but each time the cost of newspapers changed you would also need to change the formula.

Figure 2.7 shows four examples of formulae. These are:

1 Cell D8   = C8*0.175

   Overheads on newspapers are the cost of the newspapers (cell C8) multiplied by 0.175 which produces 17.5% of the cost (the current rate of overheads). To avoid confusion with the letter x, spreadsheets use the symbol * as the multiplication sign.

2 Cell E8   = C8+D8

   To produce the total cost of newspapers requires the cost of the papers (C8) to be added to the overheads (D8).

3 Cell H8   = G8−E8

   Total profit is income minus cost, so the profit on newspaper sales is the total income from the newspapers (cell G8) less their total cost (cell E8).

4 Cell C16   = SUM(C8:C14)

   To total or add up a column or row of figures, the Microsoft Excel® spreadsheet provides a standard function called SUM. This function means that all the contents of cells between C8 to C14 are added together (i.e. C8+C9+C10+C11+C12+C13+C14).

These four examples show that a spreadsheet is able to add, subtract and multiply the contents of any cell or combination of cells. It is also possible to divide the contents of any cell. If we want to know what the profit was likely to be in a quarter (three months) we could divide the total profit (cell H16) by 4 (H16/4). The use of brackets tells Excel® to calculate anything inside them first. This is important since it changes the result.

Example

C8=5 and D8=8   C+D8/2 = 9   but (C8+D8)/2 = 6.5

Replication

Formulae can be copied to new locations in a similar way to other Microsoft® Office applications. However, there is an important difference. In most cases when you copy a formula to a new location it changes to allow for the new position in the spreadsheet. However, before you replicate a formula check that it is correct or you will be spreading an error across the spreadsheet.

Example

A formula to total three cells A1+A2+A3 is in cell A5. Copy the formula to B5 and the formula will change to B1+B2+B3 so that it carries out the same function but in the context of the new row. Copying in a spreadsheet is called replication to show this change in formula. In order to replicate information or a formula, highlight the area or cell to be copied and then use the Edit menu and the Copy option. The Paste option is then employed to copy the information or formula to the new location.

Exercise 20

Formulae

1 In the previous exercise you saved a file called Acme Newsagent and we are now going to load this file into Microsoft Excel®.

2 Using either the All Programs menu or the Excel icon methods, load Microsoft Excel®.

3 You can load a file by single-clicking on the File menu item to open up the menu which has an option called Open . Click on Open and a window called Open will appear.

4 The Look in: box tells you which drive the window is looking at. You need to aim it at drive A:. You do this by clicking on the small button with the down arrow at the end of the Look in: box. A menu will appear. Click on the Floppy (A:) option and the details of Acme Newsagent will appear in the main working area. To open the file, click on the file once to highlight it and then on the Open button on the right-hand side of the window. An alternative way is to double-click on the Acme Newsagent file. In either case the text of the file should now appear in the working area of Excel®.

5 The first step is to enter a formula to calculate the Overheads on the Costs. Overheads is 17.5% of the costs so if you multiply costs by 0.175 you will calculate the Overheads. Enter = C8*0.175 into cell D8. To enter the other Overheads amounts you can use a technique called replication. Highlight cell D8 by single-clicking on the cell and clicking on the Copy icon on the Standard toolbar or the Edit menu and the Copy option. Now click on the cell you want to copy the formula to (e.g. D10) by highlighting the cell and clicking on Paste on the Standard toolbar or the Paste option in the Edit menu. The formula is copied into the new cell but will change to adapt to its new location so it will now read =C10*0.175. Paste the formula into D12 (= C12*0.175) and D14 (= C14*0.175).

6 The second step is to enter the formula to total Costs and Overheads. Excel® provides a standard function called Sum, available on the Standard toolbar (Figure 2.8). You highlight both cells C8 and D8 by clicking on C8 and holding down the left mouse button then dragging the pointer over D8 and E8 and releasing. The three cells should now be highlighted. By clicking on

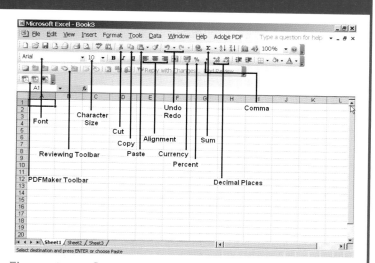

Figure 2.8   Standard and Formatting toolbars

the AutoSum icon on the toolbar you will see the formula appear in E8 (=SUM(C8:D8)). The AutoSum is shown by the symbol Σ. Repeat this action for rows 10, 12 and 14. This will produce formulae in E10 (=SUM(C10:D10)), E12 (=SUM(C12:D12)) and E14 (=SUM(C14:D14)).

7 Now enter the formula to calculate Total Profits. This is equal to Income minus Total Costs. In cell H8 enter =G8-E8 and then replicate the formula in H10, H12 and H14. If you make a mistake you can delete all the formulae by highlighing the area (i.e H10 to H14) and selecting the Delete key or Edit menu and Delete option. It does not matter that you are deleting some blank cells. It will not have any effect.

8 Now total each column using the Sum function (i.e. highlight C8 to C16 and click on the Sum function to enter the formula in cell C16 =SUM(C8:C15)). Replicate the formula in D16, E16, G16 and H16.

9 Save the new file on your floppy disk as file A:\Acme Newsagent Formula. Select the File menu and the Save As option which will reveal the Save As window and you can save the file under a new name. If you select the Save option you will overwrite your original file. The Save As function allows you to save files under different names.

10 Close Microsoft Excel® by selecting the File menu and the Exit option or click on the Close button in the top right-hand corner of the application window.

Presentation

Microsoft Excel® provides the normal presentation options that are available in many Microsoft® Office applications. You can therefore:

■ change or select font (Figure 2.8) and character size (Figure 2.8) using options on the Formatting toolbar

- embolden, italicize and underline text using options on the Formatting toolbar
- align (justify) text (align left, align right and centre text – Figure 2.8) using options on the Formatting toolbar
- change the format of numerical data (Figure 2.8) using options on the Formatting toolbar
- change the width and depth of rows and columns (Format menu – Figure 2.6).

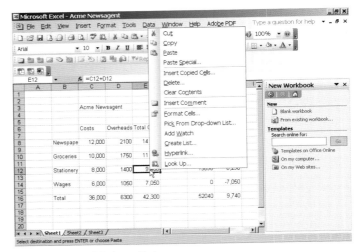

Figure 2.9   Right-click menu

These presentation options work in a similar way to other Microsoft® Office products. You can either select the option (e.g. font) before you enter text or numbers or change the option later. You change the formatting by highlighting the area that needs to be changed (e.g. cell, row or column) and then selecting the desired option.

Spreadsheets have extra formatting options to allow numerical information to be presented in a variety of ways. These include (Figure 2.8 – Formatting toolbar):

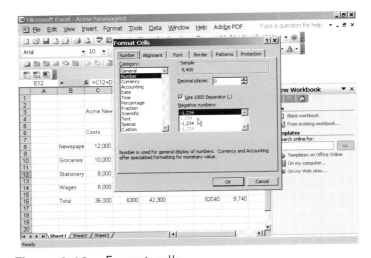

Figure 2.10   Format cells

- Currency – to display numerical information with a £ sign in a currency format
- Percent – to display data in percentage style
- Comma – to format numbers with commas in appropriate places
- Decimal places – to increase and decrease the number of decimal points shown.

An alternative approach to changing the formatting is to use a pop-up menu that appears if you right-click on the item or highlighted area you want to change. This opens a menu (Figure 2.9) with the option Format Cells which, if selected, opens a window of format options (Figure 2.10). This allows you, among other options, to change the format of numbers (i.e. decimal points, currency, etc.) by selecting the Number tab or, using the Font tab, to select fonts, character size, bold, italics and underline.

Calculation

When you change data in a spreadsheet it will recalculate other values that are dependent upon the item. This may be carried out automatically so it can be confusing if you are unaware that it has happened.

The calculation takes account of the true value of the item, not simply what is displayed. If the display has removed or limited the number of decimal places then the values displayed will reflect the formatting. However, the calculation will be based on actual values with all decimal places. The example below shows that this can be confusing faced with a spreadsheet calculation that adds 20 to 34 to produce 55. This looks wrong if you have forgotten that the actual values are 20.2 and 34.4 and that by selecting no decimal places you round up the result (i.e. 54.6 becomes 55 when rounded up).

Example

Actual Value: 20.2 plus 34.4 = 54.6

Excel Spreadsheet format without any decimal places: 20 plus 34 = 55 (the decimal value is rounded up to the next whole number).

Exercise 21

Formatting

1   In the previous exercise you saved a file called Acme Newsagent Formula and we are now going to load this file into Microsoft Excel®.

2   Using either the All Programs menu or the Excel icon methods load Microsoft Excel®.

3   You can load a file by single-clicking on the File menu to open up the menu which has an option called Open . Click on Open and a window called Open will appear.

4   The Look: in box tells you what drive the window is looking at. You need to aim it at drive A:. You do this by clicking on the small button with the down arrow at the end of the Look in: box and a menu will appear. Click on the Floppy (A:) option and the details of Acme Newsagent Formula will appear in the main working area. To open the file, click on the file once to highlight it and then on the Open button on the right-hand side of the window. An alternative way is to double-click on the Acme Newsagent Formula file. In either case the text of the file should now appear in the working area of Excel®.

5   The title of the spreadsheet is not prominent. Enhance Acme Newsagents by selecting a new font and a new character size. Highlight the title then click on the arrow button on the font box (Formatting toolbar) and a list of fonts will appear. You select one by single-clicking on the item. Explore the fonts until you find one that you like. Now select the character size by using the down arrow next to the size box (the title must still be highlighted). Another list will appear from which you can choose a size. Pick one that emphasizes the importance of the title.

6   The headings of the rows and columns need to be emboldened. Highlight the row or column and click on the Bold icon on the toolbar. Now centre the row headings by highlighting them and selecting the Center justification icon.

7   Some of the headings are too wide for their columns. The columns can be adjusted by placing the mouse pointer over the row or column headings' edge on the line that

divides the row or column. The mouse pointer will change shape (to double-headed cross arrows) and if you hold down the left mouse button you can drag the column wider or narrower. The same is true of adjusting the height of the rows. An alternative approach is to use the Format menu (Figure 2.6). Select Row or Column and Height or Width respectively.

8 Adjust the column widths so that the headings fit their columns better (e.g. Newspapers, Total Costs and Total Profits).

9 It is important in a spreadsheet to be able to format the numerical data. In Acme Newsagents we are dealing with money so the data should be formatted as currency. This is achieved by highlighting the data and clicking on the Currency icon on the toolbar. Observe the change – a pound (£) sign will be added and a decimal point and two zeros added to show pence. If the result is too wide for the column then a series of hash marks (i.e. ####) will be shown.

10 This spreadsheet does not have data which include pence so we could remove the decimal point. Highlight the numerical data and click on the Decrease Decimal icon (Formatting toolbar – Figure 2.8). Click twice on the icon to remove the two digits after the point. Experiment with adding decimal places using the Increase Decimal icon, but finish with a display without decimal places (i.e. no pence). Figure 2.11 shows the final spreadsheet.

11 Save the new file on your floppy disk as file A:\Acme Newsagent Presentation. Select the File menu and the Save As option which will reveal the Save As window and you can save the file under a new name. If you select the Save option you will overwrite your original file. The Save As function allows you to save files under different names.

12 Close Microsoft Excel® by selecting the File menu and the Exit option or click on the Close button in the top right-hand corner of the application window.

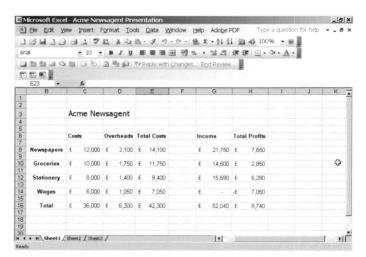

Figure 2.11   Acme Newsagent presentation

Page Setup

Microsoft Excel®
provides a range of
functions to allow you
to select the overall
appearance of the page
presenting the
worksheet, for example
the orientation of the
page. There are two
options – portrait or
landscape. Figure 2.12
compares the two
orientations and
illustrates that you can
set the four page
margins at the top,
bottom, right and left
of the page.

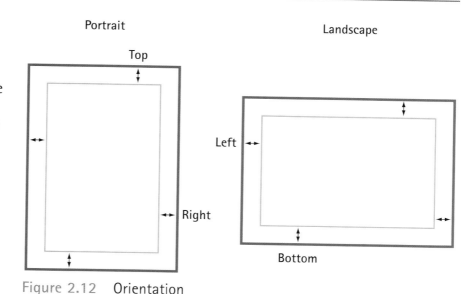

Figure 2.12   Orientation

To select the orientation and margins
you need to choose the ⌐File menu⌐
and the ⌐Page Setup⌐ option to reveal
the Page Setup window (Figure 2.13).
This has four tabs across the top.
They are:

- ■ ⌐Page⌐ (Figure 2.13)
- ■ ⌐Margins⌐
- ■ ⌐Header/Footer⌐
- ■ ⌐Sheet⌐.

Each tab provides access to a
number of options. The Page tab
(Figure 2.13) offers you the means to:

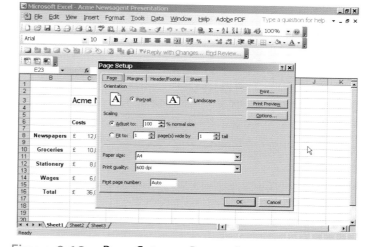

Figure 2.13   Page Setup – Page tab

- ■ choose orientation (i.e. landscape and portrait)
- ■ scale the sheet to fit the printing paper
- ■ select the print paper size
- ■ print the sheet
- ■ preview what the sheet will look like when printed.

The Margins tab offers you the means to (Figure 2.14):

- ■ set all four page margins (i.e. left, right, top and bottom)
- ■ set the size of the header and footer
- ■ centre the sheet
- ■ print the sheet

- preview what the sheet will look like when printed.

The Header/Footer tab offers you the means to (Figure 2.15):

- enter a header
- enter a footer
- enter custom headers and footers (e.g. date, filename and page number)
- print the sheet
- preview what the sheet will look like when printed.

The Sheet tab offers you the means to (Figure 2.16):

- choose how the sheet is printed including if the gridlines and row and column headings appear
- print the sheet
- preview what the sheet will look like when printed.

Find and Replace

You will occasionally need to change an entry in a spreadsheet. You can obviously do that by deleting what you wish to replace and entering a new item. However, Microsoft Excel® provides an automatic way to find and replace an entry. This is available within the Edit menu as the Replace option. This is very useful if you need to make several identical changes since it removes the risk of making a mistake in entering the replacement. A related function is the Find option in the Edit menu which will locate an entry. This is useful in large or complex spreadsheets.

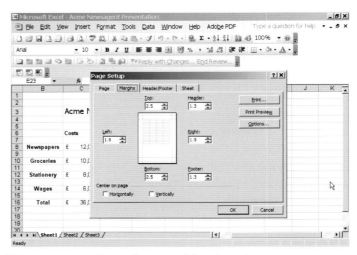

Figure 2.14   Page Setup – Margin tab

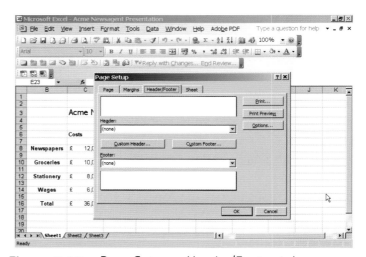

Figure 2.15   Page Setup – Header/Footer tab

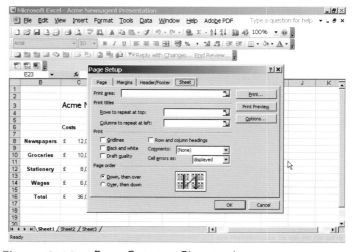

Figure 2.16   Page Setup – Sheet tab

Exercise 22

Presentation

1 Load Microsoft Excel® using either the All Programs menu or the Excel icon on the desktop.

2 Set the page orientation to landscape using the File menu and Page Setup option.

3 Enter the table of information below to form your first spreadsheet. It shows the operating costs of three different cars.

	January	February	March	April	May	June	Total
Model A	88	93	90	89	92	96	
Model B	102	108	101	99	105	111	
Model C	65	71	70	64	67	64	
Total							

4 Create a header using the File menu and Page Setup option. Use the Custom Header button to enter your name and insert an automatic date.

5 Save the new file on your floppy disk as A:\Operating Costs. Select the File menu and the Save option which will reveal the Save As window and you can save the file.

6 Use the SUM function to calculate the total for January column.

7 Replicate the formula to display the total for all the months (i.e. February to June).

8 Use the SUM function to calculate the total for the Model A row (i.e. January to June).

9 Replicate the formula to display the total for all the remaining Models (i.e. Models B and C).

10 Insert the rows Model D and E between Model C and Total. Enter the information below:

	January	February	March	April	May	June
Model D	128	132	138	126	129	135
Model E	35	39	31	37	41	33

11 Insert the column Price between Model and January.

	Price
Model A	12235
Model B	14679
Model C	8980
Model D	17568
Model E	6950

12 Replicate the total formula to rows Model D and E and the column Price.

13 Develop a formula to calculate the mean price of the five car models (i.e. divide the total of the prices by 5). Figure 2.17 displays the spreadsheet.

14 Save the file on your floppy disk as file A:\Operating Costs.

15 Close Microsoft Excel® by selecting the File menu and the Exit option or click on the Close button in the top right-hand corner of the application window.

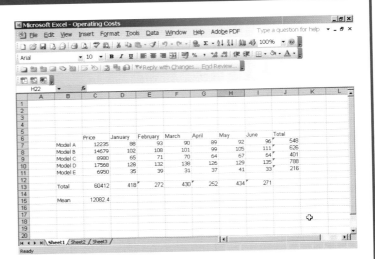

Figure 2.17   Operating Costs totals

Borders and Shading

Borders and shading can be added to spreadsheets to improve their appearance and focus users' attention on key aspects. This is important if you are preparing numerical information for your manager or a client. People often judge quality on appearance so, even if you have developed a sophisticated mathematical model, if it is poorly presented it may be regarded with suspicion.

Microsoft Excel® offers the Borders function on the Formatting toolbar

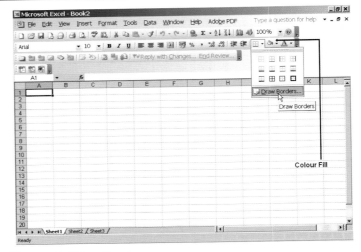

Figure 2.18   Borders

which, if selected, opens a small window with a variety of options. These are shown in Figure 2.18. You can choose to enclose a whole sheet, draw an individual line or provide borders around each cell. This allows you to select the areas of the sheet you want to emphasize.

On the Formatting toolbar next to the Borders icon is the Fill Color function with which you can add colour shading to the sheet. When you choose Fill Color it will reveal a palette of colours. For both Borders and Fill Color highlight the area you want to affect and then choose the type of border or colour you want. If you highlight a row and select red then you will see that the row gains a red background colour.

Printing

It is important to be able to print out a sheet or workbook. Microsoft Excel® offers a range of functions linked to printing. These include previewing your sheet as a printed document. Within the File menu, Print Preview opens up the window shown in Figure 2.19. This lets you check if the printed sheet is presented in the way that you want it to be. When you have completed the preview, click on the Close button to return to Excel®. If you want to print the spreadsheet immediately there is a Print button to link you to the Print window (Figure 2.19).

Usually, the default is to print in portrait mode, that is, with the narrow edge of the paper at the top, so that when you preview your sheet you may discover that it flows over two pages. If you would prefer it to

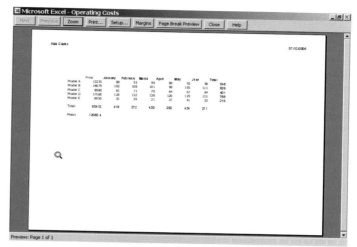

Figure 2.19   Print Preview

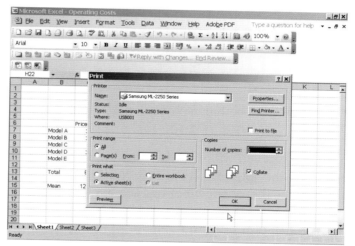

Figure 2.20   Print

be presented on a single page, you need to change the default to landscape (i.e. the long edge across the top). This can be carried out from the Print preview window by selecting the Setup button, which opens the Page Setup window. Select landscape by clicking in the radio button near the Landscape label and then clicking on the OK button to confirm the change. When you print now it will be in landscape mode. The example shown in Figure 2.19 would be printed in landscape.

When you are ready to print click on the File menu and the Print option. The window shown in Figure 2.20 appears. You are presented with a number of options which people initially may find puzzling.

1   You must first select the printer on which your document is to be printed. This is shown in the Printer area at the top of the window in the box entitled Name. The Microsoft Windows® operating system allows you to link many different printers to a single stand-alone computer. The list of printers is shown when you click on the down arrow next to the Name box. Select your printer by clicking on it. The printer shown is the default printer.

2 You need to decide how much of the document you want to print (Print range). The choices are:

- $\blacksquare$ All – whole document
- $\blacksquare$ Pages – you enter the page range you want to print (e.g. 23–34)
- $\blacksquare$ The default setting is All .

3 You can select what to print (Print what). The choices are:

- $\blacksquare$ Selection (a highlighted area of the sheet)
- $\blacksquare$ Active sheet(s) (whole sheet)
- $\blacksquare$ Entire workbook (multiple related sheets)
- $\blacksquare$ The default is Active sheet(s) .

4 You can select how many copies to print (Copies).

When you are ready, click on the OK button to start the printer. If you change none of the settings the default ones will be used.

When printing a spreadsheet, it is important to decide whether you want to include the gridlines or not. This has to be set in the Page Setup option of the File menu within the Sheet tab. The box next to the Gridlines item must be clicked, which will put a tick in the box. Gridlines will be inserted in the spreadsheet printout. Another important option is to print the sheet showing the heading. This can be achieved through the Page Setup option within the Sheet tab. The box next to the Row and Column headings must be clicked, which will put a tick in the box (Figure 2.16).

In some cases you will want to print the formulae rather than their results. Select the Tools menu and the Options item. This opens the Options window. Click on the View tab and look for the Window options section and the Formulas. You need to click in this box. A tick will appear and then you can click on the OK button to confirm the change. You should notice that you can also select options for printing row and column headers and gridlines. This is an alternative to using the Page Setup function.

To return to printing with the actual numbers or without gridlines you will have to repeat the operation and click once more in the Formulas or Gridlines boxes. This will remove the tick. Confirm the change by clicking on the OK button.

When you choose to print the formulae, your spreadsheet format will change to accommodate their different lengths. It will change back when you de-select this option.

As part of your assessment you will need to be able to print a spreadsheet showing the formulae.

Exercise 23

Borders, Shading and Printing

1 In the previous exercise you saved a file called Operating Costs and we are now going to load this file into Microsoft Excel®.

2 Using either the All Programs menu or the Excel icon on the desktop load Microsoft Excel®.

3 You can load a file by single-clicking on the File menu and then the Open option to display the Open window.

4 The Look in: box tells you what drive the window is looking at. You need to aim it at drive A:. You do this by clicking on the small button with the down arrow at the end of the Look in: box and a menu will appear. Click on the Floppy (A:) option and the details of Operating Costs will appear in the main working area. To open the file, click on the file once to highlight it and then on the Open button on the right-hand side of the window. An alternative way is to double-click on the Operating Costs file. In either case the text of the file should now appear in the Excel® working area.

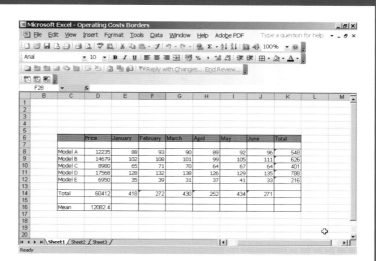

Figure 2.21   Borders and Shading

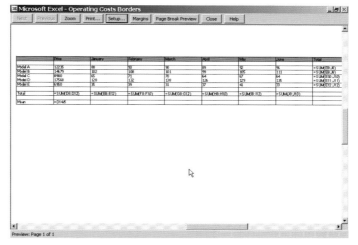

Figure 2.22   Displaying formulae

5 Insert a new row to form the new top line of the sheet and then insert a new column to the left of the Model column. This is to allow you to enclose the whole area in a border.

6 Highlight the whole area of the spreadsheet you have entered. Select the Borders function. Explore the different options using the Undo function (Edit menu) to return your sheet to its original state. When you are confident that you understand the different options highlight the whole area and choose the option that provides a border around each cell (Figure 2.21).

7 Highlight the top row of the sheet (i.e. Price to Total) and select the Fill Color function and choose the colour red. The top row should now have a red background colour (Figure 2.21).

8 Save the file on your floppy disk as A:\Operating Costs Borders. Select the File menu then the Save As option which will reveal the Save As window and you can save the file.

continued

9 Print the sheet in landscape orientation showing the data with gridlines but without row and column headings (i.e. select the File menu and Page Setup with the Sheet tab; alternatively select the Tools menu and Options). Ensure that the sheet prints onto a single page.

10 Print the sheet in landscape orientation showing the formulae (select the Tools menu and the Options item) with gridlines and row and column head (i.e. select the File menu and Page Setup with Sheet tab). Ensure that the sheet prints onto a single page.

11 Figure 2.22 displays the formulae in Print Preview.

12 Close Microsoft Excel® by selecting the File menu and the Exit option or click on the Close button in the top right-hand corner of the application window.

Graphs and chart applications

When presenting numerical information, it is sometimes difficult even for highly numerate people to understand the relationship between the different elements. However, if you can convert the information into visual images then it is far easier to see the trends and relationships. There are several forms of visual representations such as pie charts, line graphs and bar or column charts. Microsoft Excel® has a number of functions to turn numerical information into graphs and charts. There are other applications which allow you to model live data, that is, systems which take data as it is created (e.g. output from a processing plant) and show it in the form of a chart or a graph. These charts and graphs continuously change because the data they are modelling is altering all the time. This type of continuous output is often printed on a special printer called a plotter. Excel® graphs and charts are, by comparison, static representations of data.

Nevertheless, if the spreadsheet information changes then you can produce new graphs and charts. This allows you to monitor the information visually and would be useful if you were producing a monthly spreadsheet of sales figures, salary costs or staff absences. Charts and graphs also provide opportunities to compare numerical information.

Spreadsheets allow you to create models of information so that you can see the consequences of changes (e.g. price rises, decreased costs, changes in interest rates and pay increases). These changes can also be converted into graphs and charts to help you analyse the changes and their effect on other factors. A visual presentation of data (i.e. a graph or chart) may enable you to identify effects which are not easy to see in a table of numbers.

Figure 2.17 shows a comparison of the running costs of five models of cars. Although the table helps you to see the relationships, visual representation adds another dimension, helping people to identify connections between the models that may not otherwise be obvious.

Pie charts

A pie chart is used to represent numbers as slices of a circle so that the size of each slice is proportional to the whole. In Figure 2.23 the pie chart shows the comparison of the price of the five models.

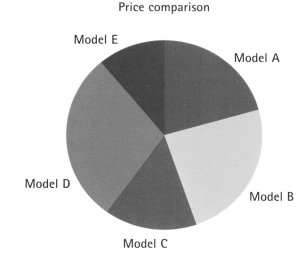

Figure 2.23   Price comparison

Line graphs

A line graph helps you to compare different factors. The graph in Figure 2.24 compares the running costs of the five models over six months.

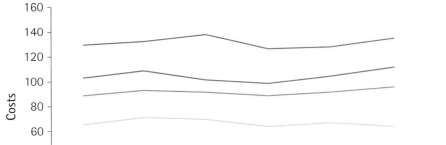

Figure 2.24   Running costs line chart

Column charts

A column chart represents numbers as columns of different height. Figure 2.25 shows the column chart for the running costs of the five models. In the mathematics a column chart may be shown in a different way to an Microsoft Excel® column chart.

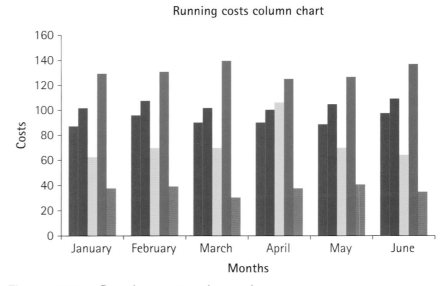

Figure 2.25   Running costs column chart

Bar chart

A bar chart is similar to a column chart except that the data are represented as bars rather than columns. Figure 2.26 shows a bar chart comparing the running costs of the five models. In mathematics a bar chart may be shown in a different way to a Microsoft Excel® bar chart

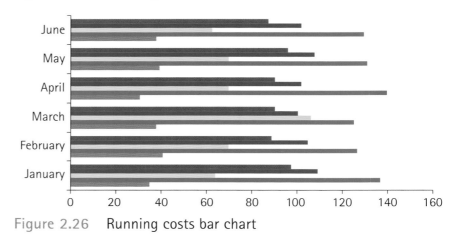

Figure 2.26   Running costs bar chart

Comparison

Figures 2.23, 2.24, 2.25 and 2.26 are based on the same numerical information (Figure 2.17) in the form of pie, line, column and bar charts. You should review and compare the different visual presentations. How effective do you feel the displays are in showing the information? You need to consider what purpose the different forms of charts and graphs serve.

Creating a chart in Microsoft Excel®

Microsoft Excel® contains a range of functions to present numerical information in the form of graphs and charts. These are available in the Chart function of the Insert menu. Alternatively you can select the Chart icon on the Standard toolbar (Figure 2.27).

The first step is to insert data into the spreadsheet in the normal way. The data is highlighted, the Insert menu is selected and then Chart or alternatively the Chart icon . This opens up the Chart Wizard (Figure 2.28). On the left-hand edge is a list of <u>C</u>hart types from which you choose the type of chart or graph you wish to use. This is done by clicking once on the one you select. On the right-hand side of the window the charts will change to show you examples of your chosen chart. Again you need to select the example you want to use. This is achieved by a single click. A description of the chart is given below the examples. If you want to see what your actual chart will look like then you click on the

Press and Hold to <u>V</u>iew Sample
button holding the left mouse button down. When you release the mouse button the chart will disappear.

At the top of the Chart Wizard window you will see that it states that it is Step 1 of 4. Figure 2.28 shows Step 1 of the process. You move between the steps by clicking on the Next button. The second Step is shown in Figure 2.29 which illustrates a column chart. The data range is shown in this display as =Sheet1!$E$8:$J$12. This may look confusing but if you ignore the $ signs it reads E8:J12, that is, the data is drawn from sheet 1 and the area E8 to J12.

It is vital to check that the Wizard has used the correct data range. It does not always get the range right and therefore your chart may be wrong. You should check the data range is correct each time you create a graph or chart. Each exercise will ask you to check your data range. In the middle of the window is an area called Series in. This offers two options, <u>R</u>ows and Co<u>l</u>umns. If you change the option you will see the chart change. It is worth considering the two options to identify which one serves your purpose best.

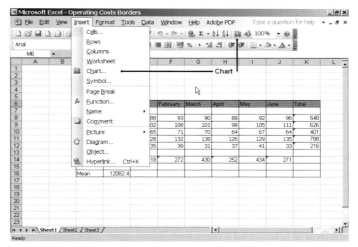

Figure 2.27   Chart function

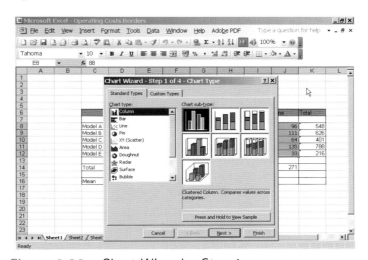

Figure 2.28   Chart Wizard – Step 1

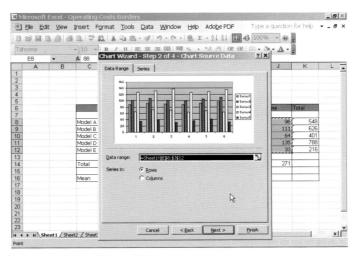

Figure 2.29   Chart Wizard – Step 2

When the Next button is clicked again the display will change to Step 3 (Figure 2.30). This dialog box allows you to label your chart. You can enter an overall title for the chart or graph, label the axes of the graphs and add a legend. The options available in Step 3 will depend on the chart or graph you have selected. For example, a pie chart does not have axes so there is no point in providing options to label them. Figure 2.32 shows the column chart with the different labels identified. The legend is essentially an explanation of the colour coding of the chart. In this case it is needed since five colours are employed. You can use Step 3 to remove the legend.

If the Next button is clicked again then the display will change to Step 4 (Figure 2.31). This window determines whether the chart is placed on a new sheet or as an additional object in an existing sheet (i.e. a chart placed alongside the data). A chart placed on a separate sheet allows you more freedom to present your chart or graph in the way you want while placing a chart alongside its related data does help to illustrate their inter-relationship. The exercises will ask you to create your graphs or charts on a separate sheet. However, you may wish to experiment with the other option. Once you have made this decision you can complete the process by clicking on the Finish button. At each step you can return to the previous step by clicking on the Back button. This allows you to correct errors.

Once the Finish button is selected the chart or graph appears. Figure 2.32 displays the column chart overlaying the related data and can be dragged around using the mouse to show that the data and the chart can be seen side by side.

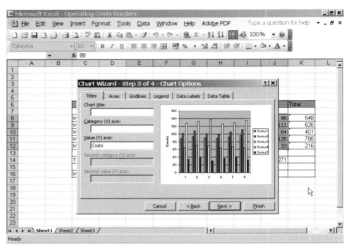

Figure 2.30   Chart Wizard – Step 3

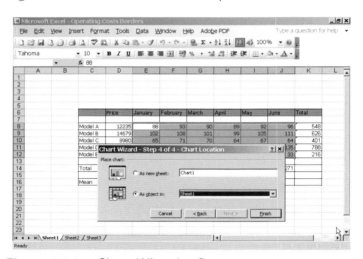

Figure 2.31   Chart Wizard – Step 4

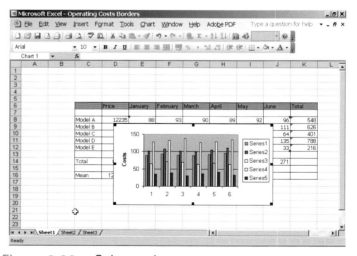

Figure 2.32   Column chart

To create the titles and labels for your charts and graphs does require that you understand the terms. Figure 2.33 displays the main titles and labels. The only one missing is the data label since it was not appropriate for this particular chart. You can add data labels to your charts. In Figure 2.33 you could show the value (i.e. the X axis value, e.g. 100) against the actual column.

Editing a chart or graph

Once you have finished a chart or graph you can move it around the display, adjust its size and change the layout. This is done by single-clicking on the chart. The chart's surrounding rectangle (enclosure) changes to show small black squares on each corner and in the middle of the lines (Figure 2.32). These are called handles. If the pointer is clicked within the chart's enclosure and the mouse button held down and dragged then the whole chart can be moved to a new location. If the same approach is used with individual objects within the chart they too will be enclosed in a rectangle (Figure 2.34). You must click on the chart object itself, not on the surrounding white space. They can then be dragged to a new position within the chart's overall enclosure.

The mouse pointer changes shape when dragging the chart enclosure to new positions and when the mouse is being used to change the shape and size of the chart. If you place the mouse over the small black squares (handles) either in the middle of the lines or on the corners then they change to double-headed arrows and by holding down the mouse pointer you can drag the side or corner of the enclosure to expand the chart or push the line in to reduce the chart's size.

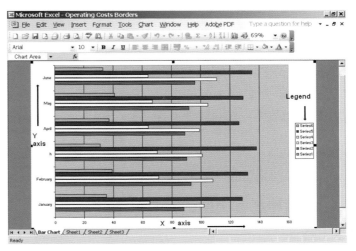

Figure 2.33   Parts of a Chart

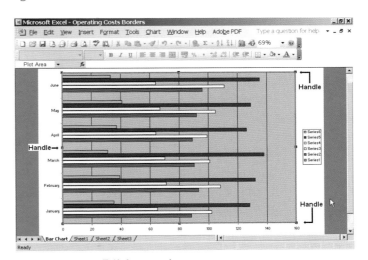

Figure 2.34   Editing a chart

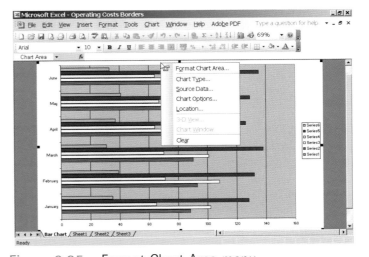

Figure 2.35   Format Chart Area menu

Once you have created a chart you can still make changes and amend it by right-clicking on the enclosure. This reveals a menu of options, shown in Figure 2.35. This is the Format Chart Area menu which allows you to access the options available during the Chart Wizard process and edit the chart or graph.

If you right-click on the individual chart objects different menus of options appear such as Format Legend , Format Plot Area , Format Data Series and Format Axis .

Exercise 24

Creating a column chart

1 Load Microsoft Excel® using either the All Programs menu or the Excel icon on the desktop.

2 Enter the table of information below. It shows a simple breakdown of the sales of motor cars over a six month period.

January	35,000
February	47,500
March	21,000
April	32,900
May	16,000
June	34,780

Start your sheet in cell A1 (with January) with the sales information in B1 (35,000) so that the table covers the area A1 to B6.

3 Highlight the table (i.e. A1 to B6) by clicking once in A1 and holding down the mouse button, dragging the pointer to B6. The whole table will be highlighted and you can then release the button.

4 Select the Chart Wizard (i.e. Insert menu and Chart option). Explore the options of Column, Bar, Line and Pie charts by clicking on each in turn and then considering the different options and their descriptions.

5 Finally select Column Chart type and the default sub-type, which is in the

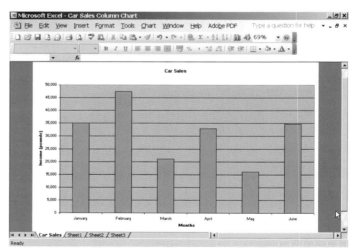

Figure 2.36   Car Sales column chart

top left-hand corner. Using the Press and Hold to View Sample button review the chart. Remember that you must hold down the left mouse button to see the chart. If you release it the image will disappear.

6   Select the Next button to move to Step 2 and review the data range to ensure it is correct. Click on the Next button again to move to Step 3.

7   In Step 3 select the Titles tab and enter:

Chart title – Car Sales
Category (X) axis – Months
Value (Y) axis – Income (pounds)

8   In Step 3 select the Legend tab and remove the tick from the radio button Show legend. In this case there is no need for a legend since there is only one set of data.

9   Click on the Next button to move to Step 4. Select As new sheet and enter the Car Sales column chart. When you are ready, click on the Finish button. The chart will appear on a separate sheet from the data it relates to (Figure 2.36).

10 Save the spreadsheet you have created on to a floppy disk. This procedure is the same in all Windows® applications so you can save a spreadsheet, database or graphic image in exactly the same way. Insert a floppy disk into drive A: and click on File menu and a menu will open showing a list of options. Select Save and a window will open.

11 Click in the File name: box and enter A:\Car Sales Column Chart. Now click on the Save button on the right of the window. You have now saved your chart as a file called Car Sales Column Chart. You may hear drive A: working during this process.

12 You can now close Excel®. Either click on the File menu and a menu will appear with a list of options. At the bottom of the list is the option Exit . If you click on Exit then Excel® will close. An alternative way is to click on the Close button in the top right-hand corner of the application window.

Exercise 25

Creating a Line chart/graph

1   Load Microsoft Excel® using either the All Programs menu or the Excel icon on the desktop.

2   Enter the table of information below. It shows a breakdown of the travel expenses claimed by an employee of a large company.

	Mileage	Subsistence	Other
April	230	85	56
May	450	120	32
June	80	16	6
July	167	45	14
August	144	23	7

continued

Start your sheet in cell C8 (with April) with the final item of Other (i.e. 7) in F12 so that the table covers the area C7 to F12.

3 Highlight the months and mileage part of the table entered (i.e. C8 to D12) by clicking once in C8 and, holding down the mouse button, dragging the pointer to D12.

April	230
May	450
June	80
July	167
August	144

4 Select the Chart Wizard (i.e. Insert menu and Chart option). Explore the Column, Bar, Line and Pie charts by clicking on each in turn and then considering the different options and their descriptions.

5 Finally select Line Chart/Graph type and the default example. Using the Press and Hold to View Sample button review the chart. Remember that you must hold down the left mouse button to see the chart. If you release it the image will disappear.

6 Select the Next button to move to Step 2 and review the data range to ensure it is correct. Then click on the Next button again to move to Step 3.

7 In Step 3 select the Titles tab and enter:

Chart title – Expenses
Category (X) axis – Months
Value (Y) axis – Claim
(pounds)

8 In Step 3 select Legend tab and remove the tick from radio button Show legend. In this case there is no need for a legend since there is only one set of data. Select Gridlines and tick the box Category (X) axis Major gridlines and Value (Y) axis Major gridlines. Watch the addition of gridlines.

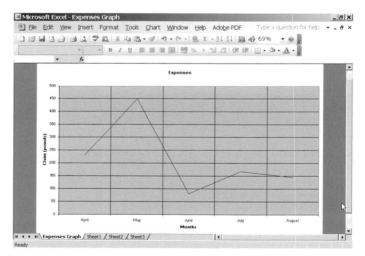

Figure 2.37   Expenses graph

9 Select the Next button to move to Step 4. Select As new sheet and enter Expenses Graph. When you are ready click on the Finish button. The chart will appear on a separate sheet from the data it relates to (Figure 2.37).

10 Save the spreadsheet you have created on to a floppy disk. This procedure is the same in all Windows® applications. You can save a spreadsheet, database or graphic image in

continued

exactly the same way. Insert a floppy disk into drive A: and click on the $\boxed{\underline{\text{File}}}$ menu. A menu will open showing a list of options. Select $\boxed{\underline{\text{Save}}}$ and a window will open.

11 Click in the File name: box and Enter A:\Expenses Graph. Now click on the $\boxed{\underline{\text{Save}}}$ button on the right of the window. You have now saved your graph as a file called Expenses Graph. You may hear drive A: working during this process.

12 You can now close Excel®. Either click on the $\boxed{\underline{\text{File}}}$ menu and a menu will appear with a list of options. At the bottom of the list is the option $\boxed{\underline{\text{Exit}}}$. If you click on $\boxed{\underline{\text{Exit}}}$ then Excel® will close. An alternative way is to click on the $\boxed{\text{Close}}$ button in the top right-hand corner of the application window.

Exercise 25A

Creating a line chart/graph – non-continuous data

1 In Exercise 25 you created a line chart for the mileage expenses of an employee. This exercise offers you the opportunity to repeat the exercise and create two additional line charts for subsistence and other expenses. This involves selecting data that is not continuous.

2 Load Microsoft Excel® using either the $\boxed{\text{All Programs}}$ menu or the $\boxed{\text{Excel}}$ icon on the desktop.

3 Highlight the months and subsistence parts of the table by first clicking once in C8 and, holding down the mouse button, drag the pointer to C12 and releasing. Now hold down the Ctrl key and click in the E8 cell and, holding down the mouse button, drag the pointer to E12. You should now have:

April   85
May   120
June   16
July   45
August   23

4 Select the Chart Wizard (i.e. $\boxed{\underline{\text{Insert}}}$ menu and $\boxed{\text{Chart}}$ option). Select the $\boxed{\underline{\text{Line}}}$ Chart/Graph type and the default example. Using the $\boxed{\text{Press and Hold to } \underline{\text{V}}\text{iew Sample}}$ button review the chart. Remember that you must hold down the left mouse button to see the chart. If you release it the image will disappear.

5 Select the $\boxed{\underline{\text{Next}}}$ button to move to Step 2 and review the data range to ensure it is correct. Then click on the $\boxed{\underline{\text{Next}}}$ button again to move to Step 3.

6   In Step 3 select the Titles tab and enter:

Chart title – Expenses Subsistence
Category (X) axis – Months
Value (Y) axis – Claim (pounds)

7   In Step 3 select Legend and remove the tick from the radio button Show legend. In this case there is no need for a legend since there is only one set of data. Select Gridlines and tick the box Category (X) axis Major Gridlines and Value (Y) axis Major Gridlines. Watch the addition of gridlines.

8   Select the Next button to move to Step 4. Select As new sheet and enter Subsistence Expenses. When you are ready click on the Finish button. The chart will appear on a separate sheet from the data that relates to it.

9   Save the spreadsheet on the floppy disk with the filename Expenses Graph.

10   Now repeat the process but produce a line chart of the months and other expenses data. This will allow you to practise working with non-continuous data.

11   Highlight the months and other parts of the table by first clicking once in C8 and holding down the mouse button, dragging the pointer to C12 and releasing. Now hold down the Ctrl key and click in the F8 cell and, holding down the mouse button, drag the pointer to F12. You should now have:

April   56
May   32
June   6
July   14
August   7

12   When you have completed both charts close Excel® by selecting the File menu and Exit option. Alternatively click on the Close button in the top right-hand corner of the application.

Creating a pie chart

1 Load Microsoft Excel® using either the <u>All Programs</u> menu or the <u>Excel</u> icon on the desktop.

2 Enter the table of information below. It shows the number of books borrowed by type from a small branch library.

Library Books

Romance	126
Historical	34
Crime	87
Contemporary	12
Factual	95

Start your sheet in cell D4 (with Romance) with the final item (i.e. 95) in E8 so that the table covers the area D4 to E8.

3 Highlight the library data (i.e. D4 to E8) by clicking once in D4 and, holding down the mouse button, dragging the pointer to E8.

4 Select the Chart Wizard (i.e. <u>Insert</u> menu and <u>Chart</u> option). Explore the options of Column, Bar, Line and Pie charts by clicking on each in turn and then considering the different options and their descriptions.

5 Finally select <u>Pie</u> Chart type and the default example which is in the top left-hand corner. Using the <u>Press and Hold to View Sample</u> button review the chart (remember that you must hold down the left mouse button to see the chart. If you release it the image will disappear).

6 Select the <u>Next</u> button to move to Step 2 and review the data range to ensure it is correct and then click on the <u>Next</u> button again to move to Step 3.

7 In Step 3 select the <u>Titles</u> tab and enter:

   Chart title – Library Books

8 In Step 3 select <u>Legend</u> tab and change the placement of the legend to the left by clicking on the appropriate radio button.

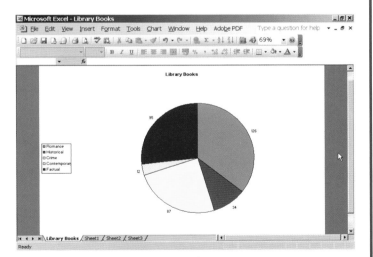

Figure 2.38   Library Books chart

9 In Step 3 select <u>Data Labels</u> tab and select <u>V</u>alue by clicking on the radio button. This will display the value of each sector on the Pie chart.

10 Select the [Next] button to move to Step 4. Select As new <u>s</u>heet. The chart will appear on a separate sheet (Figure 2.38). This chart has a legend which is appropriate since it is important to know what each colour relates to. In this pie chart we have also added data labels (i.e. the value of each segment).

11 Save the spreadsheet you have created on to a floppy disk. This procedure is the same in all Windows® applications. You save a spreadsheet, database or graphic image in exactly the same way. Insert a floppy disk into drive A: and click on the [File] menu and a menu will open showing a list of options. Select [Save] and a window will open.

12 Click in the File name: box and enter A:\Library Books. Now click on the [Save] button on the right of the window. You have now saved your chart as a file called Library Books. You may hear drive A: working during this process.

13 You can now close Excel®. Either click on the [File] menu and a menu will appear with a list of options. At the bottom of the list is the option [Exit]. If you click on [Exit] then Excel® will close. An alternative way is to click on the [Close] button in the top right-hand corner of the application window.

Comparative charts and graphs

Displaying a single set of data can be important but charts and graphs are very useful when comparing several sets of information. In Exercise 24 you created a line graph (Figure 2.37) showing the relationship between months and mileage claimed. The spreadsheet (Expenses Chart) included data on subsistence and other claims. It is possible to produce a chart comparing these different elements.

Exercise 27

Comparison

1 Load Microsoft Excel® using either the [All Programs] menu or the [Excel] icon on the desktop.

2 Load the Expenses Graph file by single-clicking on the [File] menu to show the [Open] option. Click on [Open] and a window called Open will appear.

The Look <u>i</u>n: box tells you which drive the window is looking at. You need to aim it at drive A:. You do this by clicking on the small button with the down arrow at the end of the Look <u>i</u>n: box. A menu will appear. Click on the Floppy (A:) option and the Expenses Graph will appear in the main working area. To open the file click on it once to highlight it and then on the [Open] button on the right-hand side of the window. An alternative way is to double-click on the file. In either case the spreadsheet and chart will appear in the working area of Excel®.

continued

3. The spreadsheet is on Sheet1 so click on the tab to locate it. Highlight the whole table of data (i.e. C7 to F12). This includes the row and column headings.

4. Select the Chart Wizard (i.e. Insert menu and Chart option). Select Bar Chart type and the default example which is in the top left-hand corner. Using the Press and Hold to View Sample button review the chart. (Remember that you must hold down the left mouse button to see the chart. If you release it the image will disappear.)

5. Select the Next button to move to Step 2 and review the data range to ensure it is correct. Then click on the Next button again to move to Step 3.

6. In Step 3 select the Titles tab and enter:

   Chart title – Comparing Expenses
   Category (X) axis – Months
   Value (Y) axis – Amount (pounds)

7. In Step 3 select Legend tab and explore the placement of the legend (top, bottom and right) by clicking on the appropriate radio buttons.

8. Select the Next button to move to Step 4. Select As new sheet and enter Comparing Expenses. When you are ready click on the Finish button. The chart will appear on a separate sheet from the data it relates to (Figure 2.39). The three coloured bars represent the different parts of the expenses claim.

9. Save the spreadsheet you have created on to a floppy disk. This procedure is the same in all Windows® applications. You save a spreadsheet, database or graphic image in exactly the same way. Insert a floppy disk into drive A: and click on the File menu and a menu will open showing a list of options. Select Save As and a window will open.

10. Click in the File name: box and enter A:\Comparing Expenses. Now click on the Save button on the right of the window. You have now saved your chart as a file called Comparing Expenses. You may hear drive A: working during this process.

11. Now repeat the process (remember that the data is on Sheet 1) but select a line graph instead of a bar chart. Call the new graph Comparing Expenses2. Figure 2.40 shows the line graph.

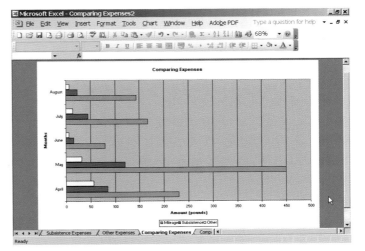

Figure 2.39   Comparing Expenses – bar chart

continued

Compare the bar chart with it and decide which you feel provides the more useful image. Try to identify which one helps you compare the three sets of data.

12 Save the spreadsheet you have created on to a floppy disk. This procedure is the same in all Windows® applications. You save a spreadsheet, database or graphic image in exactly the same way. Insert a floppy disk into drive A: and click on the File menu and a menu will open showing a list of options. Select Save As and a window will open.

13 Click in the File name: box and enter A:\Comparing Expenses2. Now click on the Save button on the right of the window. You have now saved your chart as a file called Comparing Expenses2. You may hear drive A: working during this process.

14 You can close Excel® now. Either click on the File menu item and a menu will appear with a list of options. At the bottom of the list is the option Exit . If you click on Exit then Excel® will close. An alternative way is to click on the Close button in the top right-hand corner of the application window.

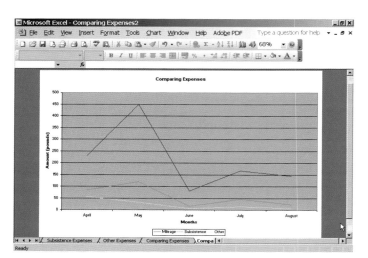

Figure 2.40   Comparing Expenses2

Set axes and upper and lower limits

With any chart and graph it is important to be able to set the axes because these provide you with the scale against which to judge the display. Microsoft Excel® provides functions to edit the scale. If you click on the corner of your axes then a handle will appear. Double-clicking on the value axis (notice a small label appears to help you identify the axis) will open up the Format Axis window.

To change the scale you enter new values in the boxes within the Scale tab (Figure 2.41). The range is set by changing the Minimum and Maximum values.

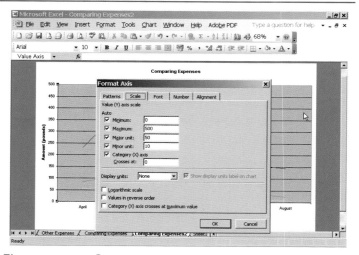

Figure 2.41   Set axes

Editing line graphs

Line graphs rely on the colour and thickness of the lines to distinguish them from the background. This is especially important when they are printed. The lines can be edited in a similar way to changing the scale of the axes. Double-click on the line and the Format Data Series Window will appear. Alternatively single-click on the line to reveal the handles and then right-click to reveal a menu with the option Format Data Series which, if selected, will display the Format Data Series window. Figure 2.42 shows the Format Data Series

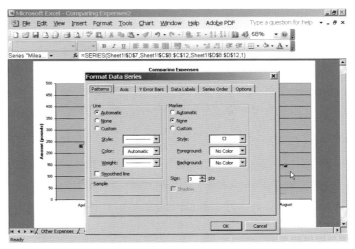

Figure 2.42 Format Data Series window

window. To change the colour, thickness or style of the line you need to select from the options revealed by clicking on the down arrow alongside the options.

Exercise 28

Edit Graph

1 Load Microsoft Excel® using either the All Programs menu or the Excel icon on the desktop.

2 Load Comparing Expenses2 by single clicking on the File menu to show the Open option. Click on Open and a window called Open will appear.

The Look in: box tells you which drive the window is looking at. You need to aim it at drive A:. You do this by clicking on the small button with the down arrow at the end of

the Look in: box. A menu will appear. Click on the Floppy (A:) option and Comparing Expenses2 will appear in the main working area. To open the file click on it once to highlight it and then on the Open button on the right-hand side of the window. An alternative way is to double-click on the Comparing Expenses file. In either case the spreadsheet and graph will appear in the working area of Excel®.

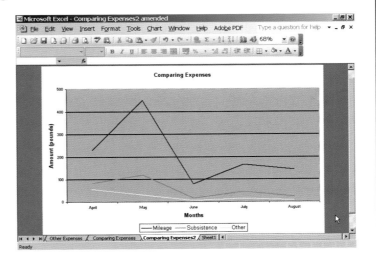

Figure 2.43 Comparing Expenses changes

3 The graph is on the Comparing Expenses2 tab so click on it to display it.

4 Change each of the lines to improve their visibility. Double-click on each line to open the Format Data Series window and explore the Style , Color and Weight options. Choose the options that you prefer.

5 Change the scale of the Y axis to 0 to 500 and the major unit to 100 by clicking on the axis to reveal the handles and then right-clicking to show a short menu with the Format Axis option. When this is chosen it will open the Format Axis window. Alternatively double-clicking the axis will open the Format Axis window. Change the values in the option boxes and confirm the changes by clicking on the OK button.

6 Change the character size of the title, Y axis, X axis labels and legend labels by double-clicking on them to reveal appropriate menus.

7 Figure 2.43 shows the outcomes of these changes.

10 Save the spreadsheet you have created on to a floppy disk. This procedure is the same in all Windows® applications. You save a spreadsheet, database or graphic image in exactly the same way. Insert a floppy disk into drive A: and click on the File menu and a menu will open showing a list of options. Select Save As and a window will open.

11 Click in the File name: box and enter A:\Comparing Expenses amended. Now click on the Save button on the right of the window. You have now saved your chart as a file called Comparing Expenses amended. You may hear drive A: working during this process.

12 You can close Excel® now. Either click on the File menu and a menu will appear with a list of options. At the bottom of the list is the option Exit . If you click on Exit then Excel® will close. An alternative way is to click on the Close button in the top right-hand corner of the application window.

Printing a chart

Charts are visual representations of data so it is appropriate to print them in order that they can be distributed. Colour is also employed to distinguish between the different components; it is useful to provide coloured printouts whenever possible. If you do not have access to a colour printer then it is important to check that the colours you are using are clear when reproduced using different shades of grey. You can do this by using the Print Preview option in the File menu. If your computer is connected to a colour printer the preview will be in colour but if your printer is black and white only then the preview will use different shades of grey.

To print a chart you need to select the File menu and then the Print option. Figure 2.44 shows the Print dialog box. The dialog box is divided into different areas. Printer shows the printer that your computer is connected to, Print Range allows you to select All or a page range, Copies allows you to print multiple copies of the chart and Print what allows you to select which sheet to print (i.e. the active sheet or the whole workbook). The Preview button allows you a final check to see if your chart is correct.

When your chart has been included in the sheet with the data (i.e. selected as an object within a sheet at Step 4 in the Chart Wizard) you can print the chart with the sheet data. This is obviously useful since you show the visual representation alongside the numerical information. However, there are also occasions when you need to print the chart separately. In order to print the chart or graph you need to highlight it and then select the File menu and Print option. The Print window will show in the Print what area that the Selection option has been selected (i.e. radio button filled). Alternatively you can choose the File menu and Print Preview option to review the chart or graph. The Print button on the Formatting toolbar will print on the default printer without opening the Print window. Figure 2.45 shows the Print Preview of the Comparing Expenses Bar Chart when the computer is linked to a colour printer.

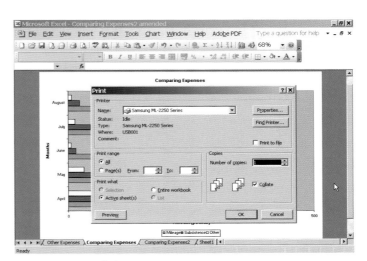

Figure 2.44   Print

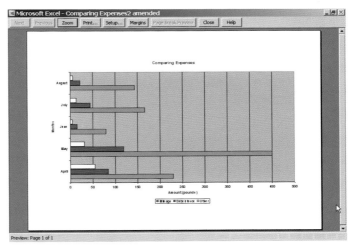

Figure 2.45   Printing a chart or graph separately

Exercise 29

Printing

1 Load Microsoft Excel® using either the All Programs menu or the Excel icon on the desktop.

2 Load 'Car Sales Column Chart' by single-clicking on the File menu to show the Open option. Click on Open and a window called Open will appear.

The Look in: box tells you which drive the window is looking at. You need to aim it at drive A:. You do this by clicking on the small button with the down arrow at the end of the Look in: box. A menu will appear. Click on the Floppy (A:) option and Car Sales Column Chart will appear in the main working area. To open the file click on it once to highlight it and then on the Open button on the right-hand side of the window. An alternative way is to double-click on the Car Sales Column Chart file. In either case the spreadsheet and graph will appear in the working area of Excel®.

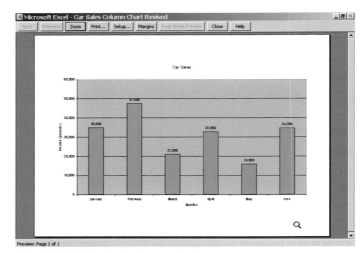

Figure 2.46   Print Preview

3 The graph is on the Car Sales Column Chart tab so click on it to display it.

4 Change the Y axis scale to 0 to 60,000 by double-clicking on it to open the Format Axis window and entering the new scale

5 Add the data value to each column by double-clicking on the bars to open the Format Data Series window and selecting the Data Labels tab and the Value radio button. Click on the OK Button to enact the changes.

6 Save the revised chart as the file Car Sales Column Chart Revised by selecting the File menu and the Save As option on your floppy disk.

7 Using Print Preview view the chart to check what Car Sales Column Chart Revised will look like when printed (Figure 2.46).

8 Print the chart on a single sheet by selecting the Print option from the File menu to open the Print window. Click the OK button to print the chart.

9 You can close Excel® now. Either click on the File menu and a menu will appear with a list of options. At the bottom of the list is the option Exit . If you click on Exit then Excel® will close. An alternative way is to click on the Close button in the top right-hand corner of the application window.

More practice

Activity 1

1 Load Microsoft Excel® using either the All Programs menu or the Excel icon on the desktop.

2 Enter the table of information below to form a spreadsheet with two decimal places. It shows a production plan of an engineering company called Tames Engineering. (Do not enter the information under potential profit. This shows how to calculate the formula).

	Volume	Cost	Price	Potential Profit
Nuts	6,000,000	0.03	0.04	(Price minus Cost) x Volume
Bolts	2,300,000	0.07	0.09	(Price minus Cost) x Volume
Bar	560,000	3.45	4.95	(Price minus Cost) x Volume
Sheet	76,000	12.87	15.32	(Price minus Cost) x Volume
Plate	17,000	36.80	39.50	(Price minus Cost) x Volume
Total				

3 Insert formulae to calculate potential profit, total volume and total potential profit (remember to replicate your formulae). You need to check if your formulae are correct. Once they are, you can change your numerical data many times with confidence that the calculations will be accurate.

4 Create a header and enter your name and an automatic date.

5 Improve the appearance of the sheet by:
   Adding the title Tames Engineering in Tahoma, size 14 and bold
   Centring all the column headings and changing their font size to 14 and making them bold
   Changing the column widths of Volume and Potential Profit so that they fit
   Emboldening all the row headings and changing their fonts to 14.

6 Change the format of the Cost, Price and Potential Profit columns to currency.

7 Reduce decimal places in the Potential Profit column to nil.

8 Print your spreadsheet showing gridlines and both formulae and actual values.

9 Investigate the effect on Potential Profit if you reduce prices to: 0.035, 0.08, 4.70, 14.85 and 38.50 respectively. A key advantage of spreadsheets is that they allow you to model what will happen if you make changes to increase output or prices or if costs change.

10 Print your spreadsheet showing gridlines and actual values.

11 Investigate what happens to the spreadsheet if you set the cost column to show only one decimal place. What you should observe is that the cost of nuts appears to be 0.0 while the profit remains the same. This is because the formulae operate on the real value not on what is presented. Change the cost column back to two decimal places.

12 Save the spreadsheet you have created with the filename Tames Engineering.

13 Close the file and exit Microsoft Excel®.

Activity 2

1 Load Microsoft Excel® using either the All Programs menu or the Excel icon on the desktop.

2 Enter the table of information below to form a spreadsheet with 2 decimal places. It shows the sales forecast of a printer, Jones Printing.

	April	May	June	Total	Price	Cash Flow
Books	6,000	7,500	5,600		1.84	(Total multiplied by Price)
Journals	11,000	9,890	7,600		0.37	(Total multiplied by Price)
Stationery	4,300	7,600	5,500		0.11	(Total multiplied by Price)
Catalogues	5,600	2,300	4,500		0.45	(Total multiplied by Price)
Total						

3 Insert formulae in the Total (April+May+June) and Cash Flow (Total multiplied by Price) rows as well as totals for the April, May, June, Total and Cash Flow columns (remember to replicate your formulae). You need to check that your formulae are correct. Once they are, you can change your numerical data many times with the confidence that the calculations will be accurate.

4 Create a header and enter your name and an automatic date.

5 Improve the appearance of the sheet by:

Adding the title Jones Printing in Arial, size 16 and bold

Changing all the column headings to centred Times New Roman, changing their font size to 14 and making them bold

Emboldening all the row headings and changing their fonts to Times New Roman, character size 14

Changing the column width of Cash Flow and the row headings so that they fit.

6 Change the format of the Price and Cash Flow columns to currency.

7 Print your spreadsheet showing gridlines and both formulae and actual values.

8 Investigate the effect on Cash Flow of increasing volumes during June to 6,000, 8,000, 6,000 and 5,000 respectively. A key advantage of spreadsheets is that they allow you to model what would happen if you make changes.

9 Print your spreadsheet showing gridlines and actual values.

10 Save the spreadsheet you have created on to a floppy disk with the filename Jones Printing.

11 Close the file and exit Microsoft Excel®.

SUMMARY

1 **Load Microsoft Excel®** Select the `Start` button, highlight the `All Programs` menu and click on the `Microsoft Excel` item or double-click on the `Excel` icon on the desktop.

2 **Close Microsoft Excel®** Select the `File` menu and the `Exit` option or click on the `Close` button in the top right-hand corner of the application window.

3 **New** Select the `File` menu and the `New` option. This opens the New Workbook task pane which is divided into sections. These provide access to many standard templates for spreadsheets. Select the `Blank workbook` option. A new blank spreadsheet will appear.

4 **Enter text or numerical data** Click on the chosen cell and enter text or numbers from the keyboard.

5 **Open the Task Pane** Select the `View` menu and the `Task Pane` option. To close the task pane repeat this operation or click on the `Close` icon in top right-hand corner of task pane.

6 **Delete, Close and Hide** Select the `Edit` menu and either the `Delete` or `Clear` options. Each will provide you with a range of choices.

   Select the `Format` menu, one of the options `Row`, `Column` or `Sheet` and the `Hide` option. The `Unhide` option is also available.

7 **Undo** Select the `Edit` menu and the `Undo` option.

8 **Insert rows and columns** Select where the row or column should be inserted and then the `Insert` menu and either the `Rows` or `Columns` item.

9 **Delete rows or columns** Select the row or column to be deleted by clicking in headings and then choose `Edit` menu and `Delete` option.

10 **Cell references** Each cell has a unique reference which is made up of the column letter and row number (e.g. A7, P16 and F12).

11 **Enter formulae** Formulae are used to calculate numerical values (e.g. total columns of figures). Formulae start with = sign (e.g. =F5-F9).

   Mathematical operators:
   +   add
   −   subtract
   *   multiply
   /   divide.

   A standard function (SUM) adds together the contents of a highlighted row or column of numbers (e.g. = SUM (C3:C6) =C3+C4+C5+C6).

   Brackets – operations inside brackets are carried out first.

12 **Change presentation** Highlight the text or item and select the font, character size, bold, italics, underline and justifying (align) icons from the Formatting toolbar.

Numerical formatting is also based on highlighting the item or area and then selecting the icon from the Formatting toolbar:
Currency – to display numerical information with a £ sign in a currency format
Percent – to display data in percentage style
Comma – to format numbers with commas in appropriate places
Decimal points – to increase and decrease the number of decimal points shown.

Change the width and depth of a row:
Place the mouse pointer over the row or column heading edge until the pointer changes shape. Hold down the left mouse button and drag the edge to widen or narrow the row or column.
Alternatively, right-click on the chosen item or highlighted area to reveal a pop-up menu. Select the Format Cells option to open the Format Cells window.

13 **Page Layout** Select the File menu and the Page Setup option.

14 **Headers and Footers** Select the File menu and the Page Setup option to open the Page Setup window. Chose the Header/Footer tab.

15 **Borders** Select the Borders icon on the Formatting toolbar.

16 **Preview printing** Select the File menu and the Print Preview option.

17 **Printing** Either select the Print button within the Print Preview window or Select the File menu, the Print option and the OK button.

18 **Print gridlines** Either select the File menu, the Page Setup option, the Sheet tab, click in the Gridlines box and the OK button, or Select the Tools menu, the Options item, the View tab, click in the Gridlines box and the OK button.

19 **Print Formulae** Select the Tools menu, the Options item, the View tab, click in the Formulas box and the OK button.

20 **Print Row and Column headings** Either select the File menu, the Page Setup option, the Sheet tab, click in the Row and column headings box and the OK button or select the Tools menu, the Options item, the View tab, click in the Row and column headings box and the OK button.

21 **Open the Chart Wizard** Insert data into the spreadsheet. Highlight the data then select the Insert menu and the Chart option. This opens up the Chart Wizard.

22 **Column, bar, line and pie charts** At the left-hand edge of the Chart Wizard is a list of Chart types. Click once on the type of chart. On the right-hand side of the window are displayed samples of your chart. Select the sample with a single click and a description of the chart is given below.

23 **Preview charts** Click on the Press and Hold to View Sample button holding the left mouse button down. If you release the mouse button then the chart will disappear.

24 **Data range** The second step of the Chart Wizard shows the data range in the form of =Sheet1!$B$8:$C$14. Removing the $ signs, the data range is sheet1 B8:C14. It is crucial to check that the chart or graph is based on the correct data range.

25 **Titles, legends and labels** Step 3 of the Chart Wizard provides options depending on the type of chart being developed.

26 **Correct errors** Use the Back button to move back through the Chart Wizard steps.

27 **New sheet** Step 4 of the Chart Wizard provides you with the options to present your graph or chart on a new sheet or as an additional object in an existing sheet (e.g. the one containing the data it relates to).

28 **Change display** Single-clicking on the chart will reveal handles which allow you to move and change the size of the chart using the mouse.

29 **Edit chart** Right-click in the chart enclosure. The Format Plot Area menu will appear allowing you to access the options available during the Chart Wizard process and make any changes.

30 **Alter axes** Double-clicking on the value axis (a small label appears to help you identify the axis) will open up the Format Axis window. The Scale tab allows you to change the scale of the chart axes.

31 **Save a file on a floppy disk** Insert a floppy disk into drive A: then click on the File menu and Save . Select the drive (Floppy (A:)) and enter the filename. Having saved a file once, you can update it by clicking on the menu and without the Save <u>A</u>s window appearing again. This simply overwrites the original file.

32 **Find and Replace** Select the <u>Edit</u> menu and then Re<u>p</u>lace or <u>F</u>ind .

Creating Spreadsheets and Graphs

95

Unit 3

3

Database Manipulation

This chapter will help you to:

- identify and use database software correctly
- use an input device to enter data in an existing database and present and print database files
- create simple queries/searches on one or two criteria and sort data
- produce appropriate pre-defined reports from databases using shortcuts
- present data in full, sorted alphabetically and numerically.

Assessment

This unit does not assume any previous experience of using a computer. You may find it useful to have completed Unit 1: (File Management and e-Document Production). You will be assessed through a practical realistic assignment which is designed to allow you to demonstrate your knowledge and skills against each objective. Your tutor can provide you with more guidance.

New CLAiT Syllabus

New CLAiT does not require you to create a database table. You must only be able to add and edit its contents and query them. This chapter nevertheless offers you the opportunity to create small straightforward databases and then to practise adding and editing their contents. This is useful if you are planning to extend your studies to CLAiT Plus, which does require students to develop a database, or if you are studying on your own without any access to a database.

If you do not want to create a database (i.e. undertake the extra tasks) then the databases are available from the supporting website (www.hodderclait.co.uk) and you are free to download them. We suggest that you download and save them on to a floppy disk. Exercises which are not part of the New CLAiT requirements are marked as optional.

Database applications

Microsoft® Access 2003 is a database creation application. You can use it to design databases for your own personal use (e.g. records of your video collection) or for an enterprise (e.g. customer information). In this chapter you will learn how to create a table of information in which information can be entered, stored and presented. A database can have one or many tables depending on the complexity of the system. In our exercises we will concentrate on a single table, which is the basic building block of more extensive databases.

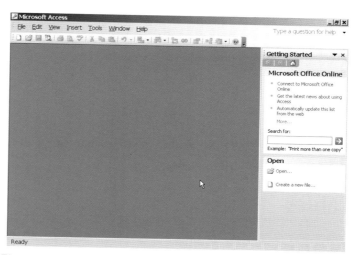

Figure 3.1 Microsoft® Access 2003

Figure 3.1 shows the opening display of Microsoft® Access 2003. The application window resembles other Microsoft® Office applications divided into:

- menu and toolbars at the top of the display
- a working area in which to develop the database
- status bar at the bottom of the window
- Getting Started task pane on the right side of the display.

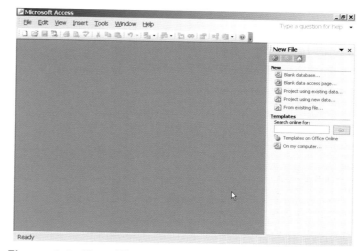

Figure 3.2 New File task pane

The Getting Started task pane offers a range of options including:
- Open an existing file
- Create a new file.

If you select the create a new file option the task pane changes to New File with the option Blank Database (Figure 3.2) which allows you to create a new database.

Spreadsheets versus databases

While both spreadsheets and databases create tables of information and so appear very similar, there are considerable differences between them.

A database can be designed so that:

- Data can be continuously changed in an efficient and effective way without the operator needing to know about the structure of the database

- Information held in the database can be presented in many different ways to meet a wide range of needs
- Information held in a database can be searched to locate any combination of data that it contains and the results of the search can be presented in a wide variety of ways.

Microsoft® Access provides:

- Forms – these offer different ways of entering, editing and viewing information
- Queries – these allow you to answer any questions you may have about the information contained in the database
- Reports – these enable you to present information combining data from several tables or from a single one.

Tables

The key feature of a database is a table. Figure 3.3 shows a Microsoft® Access table. Tables are groups of records. A record is a group of related fields, a field being a single item of the record, e.g. name, organization and telephone numbers.

In Microsoft® Access there are various different types of field which include: text, number, yes/no (i.e. can only contain a yes or a no), memo (i.e. a longer piece of text), date/time, currency (i.e. money), autonumber (i.e. automatically numbers the records in a table) and

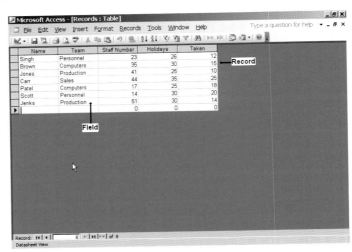

Figure 3.3 Microsoft Access table

hyperlink (i.e. links to a website). The number fields can be used as part of your calculations.

When you are creating a database table, you need to define the type of each field within the records. In Figure 3.3 Name, Team are text fields whereas Staff Number, Holidays and Taken are all number fields. The table illustrated is Holidays.

Creating a new database – optional

The first step in creating a database is to consider the information you may want it to contain. The example below shows the information that you might want to include in a staff holiday record table.

Example

Name – individual's name (i.e. text field)
Team – which team the individual works in (i.e. text field)
Staff Number – pay number (i.e. number field)
Holiday – number of days holiday entitlement (i.e. number field)
Taken – number of days taken (i.e. number field)

Name	Team	Staff Number	Holiday	Taken
Singh	Personnel	23	25	12
Brown	Computers	35	30	15
Jones	Production	41	25	10
Carr	Sales	44	35	25
Patel	Computers	17	25	18
Scott	Personnel	14	30	20
Jenks	Production	51	30	14

This table of information consists of seven records with each record composed of five fields.

Exercise 30

Optional
Creating a database table

1   Load Microsoft® Access by selecting Start , highlighting the All Programs menu and clicking on the Microsoft Access item or click on the Access icon on the desktop.

2   Microsoft® Access will load (Figure 3.1). Select Create a new file within the Getting Started task pane to open the New File task pane. Select the Blank database. The File New Database window opens to enable you to save your new database (Figure 3.4).
  -   You need to select a drive or folder in which to store your new database as a file. If you click on the arrow button next to the Save in: box, you can select floppy disk.
  -   Next you need to give the file a name. Insert the name Holidays in the File name box and click on the Create button (Figure 3.4). You will have saved your blank database as a file called Holidays on your floppy disk. The Holidays Database window is now shown (Figure 3.5).

3   The Holidays Database window shows three options with the Tables object on the left-hand side selected:
  -   Create table in Design view
  -   Create table by using wizard
  -   Create table by entering data .

  Double-click on Create table in Design view and the Table window opens (Figure 3.6).

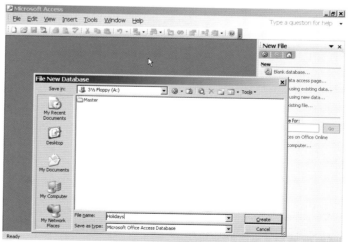

Figure 3.4 File New Database

4 You need to insert your field names and their types. If you enter Name in the Field Name box and click in the corresponding Data Type box, a small down arrow will appear revealing a list of types. Select text and click in the next Field Name box then enter Team. Complete the table as shown in Figure 3.6.

5 When you enter a type, observe that in Field Size a value (e.g. 50) will appear with a text type and Long Integer with a number type. The value 50 indicates the number of characters that the field can store while a Long Integer is a whole number (i.e. no decimal places). If you wanted to show real numbers (i.e. with decimal places) then you would need to click in the Long Integer box to produce a down arrow which, when clicked, gives you other options. In this case all our numbers are whole.

6 Close the window and you will be prompted to save your table (Figure 3.7). Indicate that you want to save the table and the Save As window will now appear allowing you to name your table. Call it Records and click on the OK button.

7 A warning message will now appear asking you to define a primary key. In this case

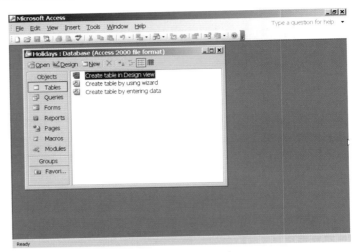

Figure 3.5 Holidays Database window

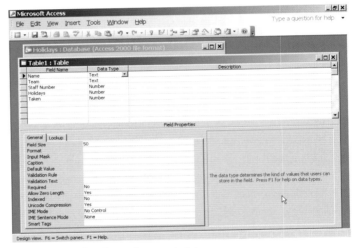

Figure 3.6 Design view – table

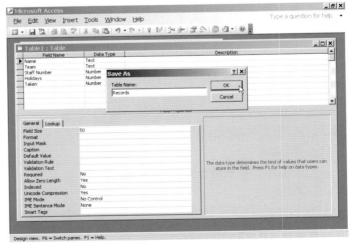

Figure 3.7 Save Table

continued

you do not need to define one so click on the No button. A primary key is a unique number which allows different tables to relate to each other.

8 You can now see the Holidays Database window but with an extra item added – Records (Figure 3.8).

9 Double-clicking on Records allows you to begin entering the data. We will return to this table to enter the data

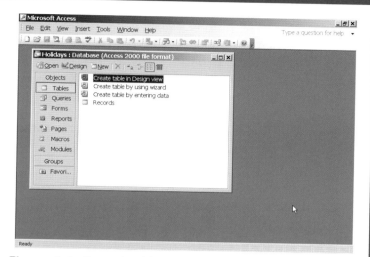

Figure 3.8 Record table

later. Close the window by clicking on the Close button in the top right-hand corner of the Holidays Database window.

10 Close Microsoft® Access by clicking on the Close button in the top right-hand corner of the main application window or select the File and the Exit option unless you wish to carry on immediately with the next exercise.

Exercise 31

The Holidays database is available on the supporting website (www.hodderclait.co.uk) if you would like to undertake this exercise without completing Exercise 30 (i.e. creating a database table).

Entering data

1 Insert your floppy disk into your drive. Load Microsoft® Access by selecting Start, highlighting the All Programs menu and clicking on the Microsoft Access item or click on the Access icon on the desktop.

2 Microsoft® Access will load (Figure 3.1). In the Getting Started task pane Open section will be the Holidays file. Double-click this item and the Holidays Database window will be displayed (Figure 3.5).

3 Double-click on Records and a blank table will appear. Complete the records, moving between the fields by clicking in each box. Alternatively use the arrow keys, Tab key or Enter key to move between fields.

4 When you have completed the table check each entry against the original data. It is vital that database information is correct since you will use this data later and often base decisions on it. If you find an error click into the field box to move the cursor into the box, and delete the mistake and insert the correct entry. Figure 3.9 shows the completed table.

continued

5 If you move your mouse pointer across the row or column heading you will see it change shape into an arrow (pointing to the right in the row heading and down in the column heading). If the pointer goes over the edge of the heading it changes into cross arrows. By holding down the left mouse button you can drag the column wider or row higher when the arrow's pointer is shaped as cross arrows.

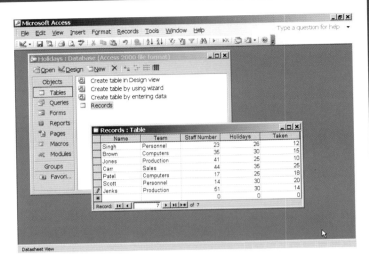

Figure 3.9 Records table

The down- or right-pointing single arrow will select (highlight) the row or column if clicked.

6 You now need to save the completed table. This is straightforward since it is saved automatically by closing the window. Click on the close button in the top right-hand corner of the window.

7 Close Microsoft® Access by selecting the File menu and the Exit option.

Editing data

Microsoft® Access has several tools to assist you with adding, deleting, amending and inserting records. You can insert new records (i.e. rows) and fields (i.e. columns). If you left-click with the pointer shaped as an arrow the row or column is highlighted (i.e. the pointer is over the column or row heading). By clicking the right mouse button a menu appears. Figure 3.10 illustrates the menu that appears when a row (i.e. a record) is highlighted. OCR New CLAiT requires that you are able to add and delete a record (i.e. a row).

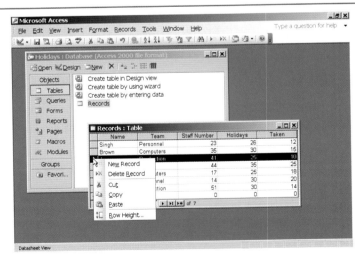

Figure 3.10 Right-button menu

To alter a single field, click into the field and delete the entry before entering the new content. If you have a large database and a number of changes to make then it is more efficient to use the Replace or Find functions in Microsoft® Access rather than change each one separately. In the example we have been working on you might want to change a team's name (e.g. from

Personnel to Human Resources). You could do this by going through all the records and manually changing them one by one, which is both time-consuming and also likely to produce errors. The more efficient way is to select the Edit menu and the Replace option to open the Find and Replace window. These options are only available if the Records table is open.

Exercise 32

Editing data

1 Insert your floppy disk into your drive. Load Microsoft® Access by selecting Start , highlighting the All Programs menu and clicking on the Microsoft Access item or click on the Access icon on the desktop.

2 Microsoft® Access will load (Figure 3.1). In the Getting Started task pane Open section will be the Holidays file. Double-click this item and the Holidays Database window will be displayed (Figure 3.5).

3 Double click on Records and the holiday data will appear.

4 The records need to be amended.

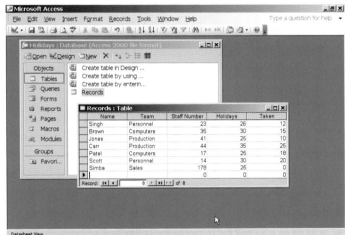

Carr has been transferred to Production. Change the Team field by clicking in the field, delete Sales using the Delete key and enter Production.

Jenks has left the company so this record needs to be deleted. Position the mouse pointer over the row heading and

Figure 3.11 **Amended table**

when the pointer has changed into an arrow, click on the right mouse button. The menu (Figure 3.10) will appear. By clicking on Delete Record you will remove the Jenks record. You may see a message appear asking if you are certain that you want to delete a record. Click on Yes to remove the record.

A new person has joined the company so you need to insert a record for Simba. The record is:

– Simba, Sales, 178, 25, 0

If you click in the bottom empty line of the table in the Name field you can begin to enter the new record. You move between fields by clicking or pressing the Tab or Enter keys.

5 When you have finished entering the new record and amending the others, carefully check the table. It is vital that databases contain no errors or the information you extract from them will be flawed. Figure 3.11 shows you the final table.

6 You now need to save your changes. Close the table by clicking on the Close button in the top right-hand corner of the table window. Your changes will be saved automatically.

7 Close Microsoft® Access by selecting the File menu and the Exit option.

Printing

An important aspect of all computer applications is the ability to print information. Microsoft® Access provides you with the functionality to print a table. This is available from the File menu and the Print option, which reveals the Print window, and you can print using the default settings by clicking on the OK button.

The Page Setup option in the File menu opens the Page Setup window which has two tabs: Margins and Page. Within Margins, you can

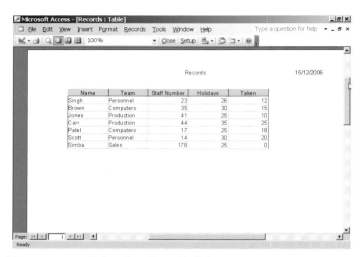

Figure 3.12 Print Preview Holidays

adjust the four margins and print using the Print Headings option. Within the Page tab you can choose the orientation of the page (i.e. either portrait or landscape).

Print Preview allows you to check the appearance of the printed document before you print it. Figure 3.12 shows the Print Preview Window of the Holiday table. If you are content with the appearance you can print it immediately by clicking on the Print icon and then on the OK button on the Print window, which will then appear.
Notice that the mouse pointer has changed into a magnifying glass which allows you to make the image larger or smaller.

Sorting, searching and querying

With a database, you can store a large amount of information and access it in any way you need to. Microsoft® Access lets you sort, query (i.e. question) and search the information.

Sorting lets you reorder the information and present it in a new sequence. You can sort the records into alphabetical, numerical or date order. This is useful if you wanted a list of the holidays information presented in the order of Staff Number, alphabetically by the name of the employee or the date of starting work. You can sort in ascending or descending order: A, B, C and D – ascending or D, C, B and A – descending; or 1, 2, 3 and 4 – ascending, or 4, 3, 2 and 1 – descending.

Searching is the term used for finding a particular piece of information within the database. By selecting the Edit menu and the Find option, you reveal the Find and Replace window which enables you to search the table for a particular field of information. This would be useful if, say, you wanted to find those employees who had not taken any holiday, those who had 25 days' holiday entitlement and so on.

Exercise 33

Simple sorting (alphabetically and numerically)

1 Insert your floppy disk into your drive. Load Microsoft® Access by selecting Start , highlighting the All Programs menu and clicking on the Microsoft Access item or click on the Access icon on the desktop.

2 Microsoft® Access will load (Figure 3.1). In the Getting Started task pane Open section will be the Holidays file. Double-click this item and the Holidays Database window will be displayed (Figure 3.5).

3 Double-click on Records and the holiday data will appear.

4 Highlight the Taken column by placing your mouse pointer over the column heading until the mouse pointer changes to an arrow. Click on the left mouse button and the column will be highlighted.

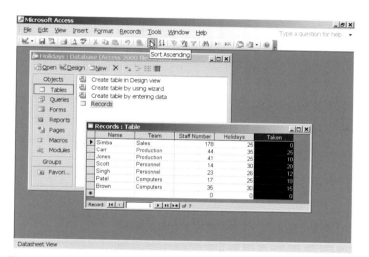

Figure 3.13 **Sort information**

5 With the column highlighted, you can sort the information in the Taken column using the Ascending and Descending icons on the toolbar. Figure 3.13 shows the column highlighted and the Sort Ascending icon (i.e. low to high).

6 Explore sorting this table using these icons and print each option (e.g. numerical ascending and descending). Select the File menu, the Print option and the OK button. To print a specific record, field or column of information you need to highlight the information and then select the Print

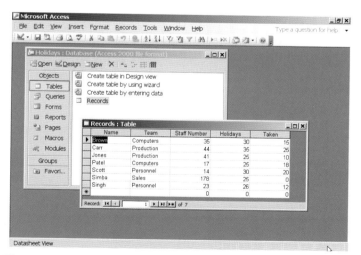

Figure 3.14 **Name sorted alphabetically**

option in the File menu. This will open the Print window in which you need to choose the Selected Records radio button and then the OK button. The highlighted fields will then be printed.

continued

7 Experiment with alphabetical sorting using the Name column (Figure 3.14) and again print each option. Figure 3.14 shows the Name column records sorted ascending.

8 Compare your printouts.

9 Close the table by clicking on the Close button in the top right-hand corner of the table window. You will be asked if you want to save the changes you have made (i.e. save the new format of your table). In this case click on the Yes button so that the new layout of the table is preserved.

10 Close Microsoft® Access by selecting the File menu and the Exit option unless you wish to continue with the next exercise in which case go to step 3 of the next exercise.

By using the Microsoft® Access functions, you can sort or search the database at any time but in each case you need to enter your requirements. These are useful for individual questions that you are unlikely to want to repeat. However, Microsoft® Access also provides a way of saving useful searches or sorts by using a Query.

Exercise 34

Creating a query

1 Insert your floppy disk into your drive. Load Microsoft® Access by selecting Start , highlighting the All Programs menu and clicking on the Microsoft Access item or click on the Access icon on the desktop.

2 Microsoft® Access will load (Figure 3.1). In the Getting Started task pane Open section will be the Holidays file. Double-click this item and the Holidays Database window will be displayed (Figure 3.5).

3 Select the Queries button in the list of Objects on the left-hand side of the window. Figure 3.15 shows the new view. Double-click on Create query in Design view . A new window will open with an overlaid window called

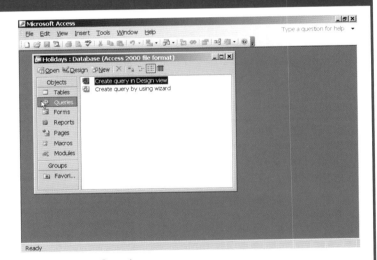

Figure 3.15 **Queries**

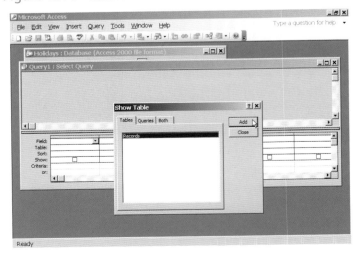

Figure 3.16 **Show Table**

Show Table (Figure 3.16). Click on the Add button on Show Table with the Records table highlighted and a small window will appear headed Records overlaying the Query 1 window.

4 Click on the Close button on the Show Table window to reveal Figure 3.17, the Query window.

5 In the Query window, a small box (Records) will have been added that shows the fields making up the Holidays table. The cursor will be flashing in the first Field box and a small down arrow will be shown at the end of the same box. Click on the down arrow and a list of the Records fields will appear. Select Name by clicking on it. Name will appear in the first box. Move to the next box (to the right) and repeat the operation selecting Team this time and so on until all the fields have been chosen.

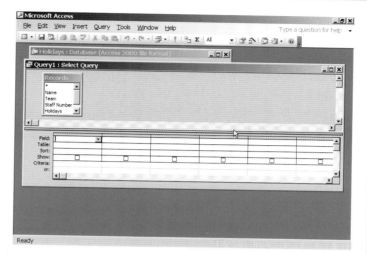

Figure 3.17 Query1: Select Query

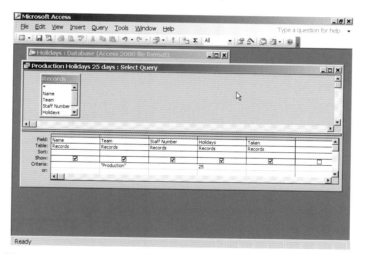

Figure 3.18 Production Holidays 25 Days query

6 In the Table row you will see the name of the table, Records, appear.

7 The third row is called Sort. If you click in any of the boxes you will see a down arrow appear which if you click on it reveals a list showing Ascending, Descending or Not Sorted. You can sort the table in this query in any way you choose. Let's create a new sort. Select the Holiday column Sort box and select Descending. The query will sort the table of information into the number of days of holiday from highest to lowest.

8 We can now save this query by selecting the File menu and the Save As option. The Save As window will appear and you need to enter Holiday Entitlement in the box entitled Save Query 'Query1' To: then click on the OK button.

9 We could now close the query window by clicking on the close button but instead we are going to create another query. First remove the sort from Holiday by clicking on the down arrow in the Holiday Sort field and selecting Not Sorted.

10 In the Show field you will have noticed that there is a tick in each field. This indicates that when the query is run the contents of this field will be shown. If you click on the tick, it will disappear and then that field will not be shown. The tick is replaced by clicking again in the tick box.

11 The query you are going to create will show the holiday records of all people working in the Production team.

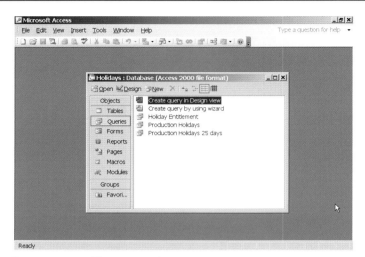

Figure 3.19 Three queries

12 In the Criteria field on the Team column enter Production. When you click away from this field you will see Production enclosed in inverted commas (i.e. 'Production'). If you make a mistake when entering Production then the query will not find any information since it cannot match the fields – your entry must be exact.

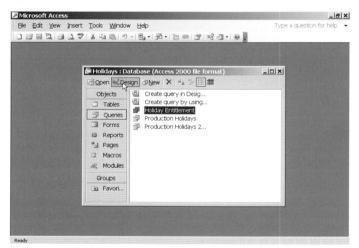

Figure 3.20 Amending a query

13 Save this query by selecting the File menu and the Save As option. Then enter Production Holidays as the name of the query and click the OK button.

14 Again, you could close this window but we will extend this query by adding a second criterion. In the Criteria field on Holiday enter 25. In this case the number is not enclosed in inverted commas. Your query will show all the Production employees who have 25 days' holiday entitlement. Figure 3.18 shows the final query.

15 Save this query by selecting the File menu and the Save As option and entering Production Holidays 25 days as the name of the query. Then click on the OK button.

16 Close the window by selecting the Close button in the top-right hand corner of the window. You will now see Figure 3.19 which shows the three saved queries. To run a query double-click it. Try the three queries to see if they are producing the results you desire. The results of the query are removed by clicking on the Close button.

17 If you find that the query is producing the wrong outcomes you can amend it by single-clicking the query to highlight it and then on the Design button on the toolbar (Figure 3.20). This will open the query to allow you to make the required changes.

18 When each query is run print the results by selecting the File menu, the Print option and the OK button.

19 Compare each printout and think about the queries you have created.

20 Close the Database window by selecting the Close button and then close Microsoft® Access by selecting the File menu and the Exit option.

Search criteria

In the last exercise we used numerical criteria. It is possible to qualify the numerical criteria using the following symbols:

>   greater than
<   less than
>= greater than or equal to
<= less than or equal to
<> not equal to

These symbols are available on the keyboard.

>   greater than (hold the Shift key down and then press the full stop key)
<   less than (hold the Shift key down and then press the comma key)
>= greater than or equal to (hold the Shift key down and then press the full stop key, release the keys and press the equals key)
<= less than or equal to (hold the Shift key down and then press the comma key, release the keys and press the equals key)
<> not equal to (hold the Shift key down, press the comma key and then the full stop key)

In your exercise you used the criteria of selecting records for Production employees with 25 days' holiday entitlement. With these symbols you could vary these criteria to select employees with less than 25 (i.e. <25), more than 25 (i.e. >25), greater than or equal to 25 (i.e. >=25), less than or equal to 25 (i.e. <=25) and not equal to 25 (i.e. <>25).

Exercise 35

Using numerical criteria

1 Insert your floppy disk into your drive. Load Microsoft® Access by selecting Start , highlighting the All Programs menu and clicking on the Microsoft Access item or click on the Access icon on the desktop.

2 Microsoft® Access will load (Figure 3.1). In the Getting Started task pane Open section will be the Holidays file. Double-click this item and the Holidays Database window will be displayed (Figure 3.5).

3 Select the Queries button in the list of Objects on the left-hand side of the window. Double-click on Create query in Design view . A new window will open with an overlaid window called Show Table. Click on the Add button on Show Table.

4 Click on the Close button on the Show Table window (Figure 3.17).

5 In the Query window a small box (Records) will have been added which shows the fields that make up the table. The cursor will be flashing in the first Field box and a small down arrow will be shown at the end of the same box. Click on the down arrow and a list of the table fields will appear. Select Name by clicking on it. Name will appear in the first box. Move to the next box and repeat the operation selecting Team this time and so on until all the fields have been chosen.

6 You are going to create a query that will identify the holidays for staff whose Staff Number is less than 40 and who have taken more than 5 days' holiday.

7 Click in the Staff Number Criteria field and enter <40 and then click in the Taken Criteria field and enter >5. Figure 3.21 shows the selections.

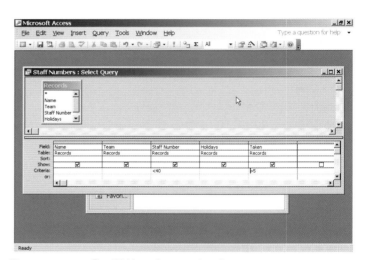

Figure 3.21 **Staff Numbers criteria**

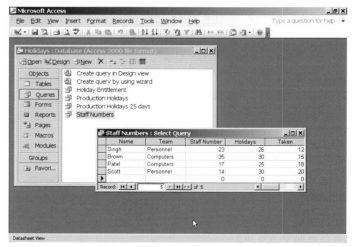

Figure 3.22 **Staff Numbers query**

continued

8   Save this query by selecting the File menu and the Save As option then enter Staff Numbers as the name of the query and click the OK button.

9   Close the window by clicking on the Close button in the top right-hand corner of the window.

10 Run the new query and check the results that it produces. Amend if necessary. Figure 3.22 shows the result of running the query.

11 Print the results of your query (select the File menu, the Print option and the OK button).

12 Close the Database window by selecting the Close button and then close Microsoft® Access by selecting the File menu and the Exit option.

Reports

Should you need to print out the results of a query or to display records from tables, the report function lets you do this. On the left-hand side of the Database window is the Reports button which will change the display to show two options:

- Create report in Design view
- Create report by using wizard.

The second option, shows the Report Wizard (Figure 3.23). You can create a report based on either a database table of information or the results of a query. You choose table or query using the down arrow at the end of the Tables/Queries box. This reveals a list of tables and queries. You can present the chosen information in both table and queries cases. The fields are shown in the left-hand column (Figure 3.23). The fields that you want to appear in the report need to be selected by highlighting them and clicking the single arrow button pointing to the right. The item is transferred into the right-hand column. If you want all the

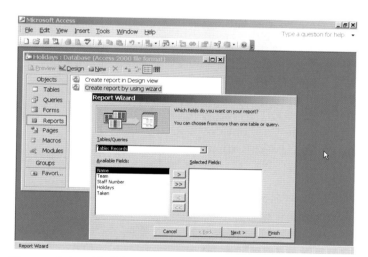

Figure 3.23 Holidays Database Report Wizard

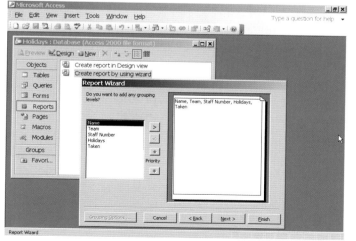

Figure 3.24 Data grouping

fields in the report then click on the double-arrow button. The process of selection can be reversed using the arrow button pointing to the left which removes the chosen fields.

Once you have selected your fields, click on the Next button and a new display appears providing you with the option to group your data. If you have not selected any fields then you will see an error message – 'You must select fields for the report before you continue'. Figure 3.24 shows the grouping display if you have selected some fields.

Having made your selections, click again on the Next button which allows you to sort the data. This is followed by options to choose the layout and page orientation of the report, select the style of the report from a set of templates and finally to name the report so that you can find it again. The final options also allow you to preview the report.

If you make a mistake then you can retrace your steps by using the Back button or use the Modify the report's design option on the final display (Figure 3.28). Figures 3.25 to 3.28 show the process.

With any printed report it is important that the data is displayed in full with records and headings completely shown. Your readers can easily be confused by only a partial display and you will be judged on the quality of the output rather than the excellent design of your database.

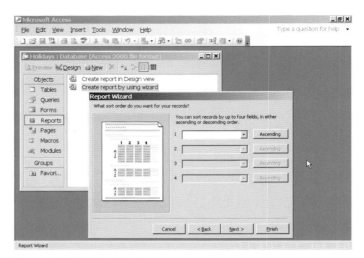

Figure 3.25 Sort data

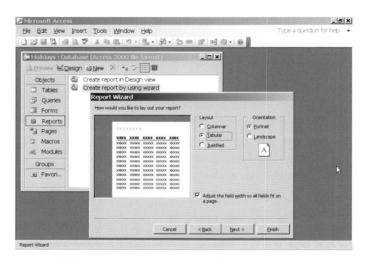

Figure 3.26 Layout and Orientation

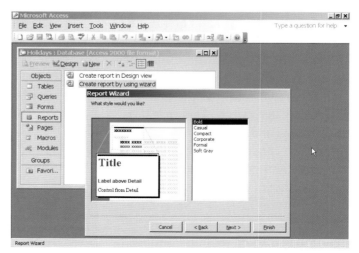

Figure 3.27 Style

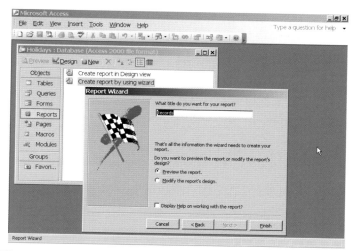

Figure 3.28 Preview report

Exercise 36

Report

1 Insert your floppy disk into your drive. Load Microsoft® Access by selecting Start , highlighting the All Programs menu and clicking on the Microsoft Access item or click on the Access icon on the desktop.

2 Microsoft® Access will load (Figure 3.1). In the Getting Started task pane Open section will be the Holidays file. Double-click this item

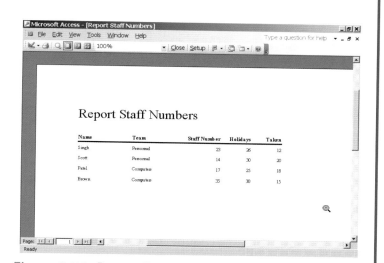

Figure 3.29 Report Staff Numbers

and the Holidays Database window will be displayed (Figure 3.5).

3 Select the Reports button in the list of Objects on the left-hand side of the window and the Create report by using wizard option. This will open the Report Wizard window.

4 Select the query Staff Numbers and all the fields in the query by using the double arrow button. Check that all the fields have been transferred and then click on the Next button. There is no need to select any groupings so click on Next .

5 Select the sort on Name so that the report is presented in descending order of staff names (i.e. Z to A) and then click on Next .

6 Select the tabular layout and landscape orientation and then click on Next .

7 Select the Formal style and then click on Next .

8 Give the report the title Report Staff Numbers, select the preview radio button and then click on the `Finish` button. The report will be shown since you have selected preview. Figure 3.29 shows the resulting report. It is important to check that you have displayed the data in full with complete field headings.

9 Print the report (select the `File` menu, the `Print` option and the `OK` button), check the contents are correct and that the data is printed in full.

10 Close the Database window by selecting the `Close` button and then Close Microsoft® Access by selecting the `File` menu and the `Exit` option.

More Practice

Activity 1

Creating a table – Optional activity

1 Load Microsoft® Access by selecting `Start`, highlighting the `All Programs` menu and clicking on the `Microsoft Access` item or click on the `Access` icon on the desktop.

2 Microsoft® Access will load (Figure 3.1). Select `Create a new file` within the Getting Started task pane to open the New File task pane. Select the `Blank database`. The File New Database window opens to enable you to save your new database (Figure 3.4).

You need to select a drive or folder in which to store your new database as a file. If you click on the arrow button next to the Save in: box, you can select floppy disk.

Next you need to give the file a name. Insert the name Customer Accounts in the File name: box and click on the `Create` button. You will have saved your blank database as a file called Customer Accounts on your floppy disk.

3 The Customer Accounts Database window shows three options with the Tables object on the left-hand side selected:
- `Create table in Design view`
- `Create table by using wizard`
- `Create table by entering data`.

Double-click on `Create table in Design view` and the Table window will open.

4 You are going to create the table below:

Customer Accounts

Name – company name (text field)

Address – address of the company (text field)

Contact – name of company customer contact (text field)

Credit – credit limit of the company (currency)

First Order – date of the first order from the company (Date/Time)

Size – size of the first order (number field)

Name	Address	Contact	Credit	First Order	Size
Deans	London	Anne	2500	01/10/90	500
Big Shop	Birmingham	Keith	1500	13/02/92	750
Mint	Sheffield	Jane	1000	26/06/96	250
Gordons	London	Stephanie	3000	19/08/95	250
Youngs	Manchester	David	2000	30/04/94	900
Palmers	Sheffield	Peter	3000	07/11/96	750

This table of information consists of six records with each record comprising six fields. You need to insert your field names and their types. If you enter Name in the Field Name box and click in the corresponding Data Type box, a small down arrow will appear revealing a list of types. Select Text then click in the next Field Name box and enter Address. Complete the table – Contact, Credit, First Order and Size. Both Credit and Size are currency type. First Order is type Date/Time.

5 When you enter a type you should observe that in Field Size a value (e.g. 50) will appear with a text type and Long Integer with a number type. The value 50 indicates the number of characters that the field can store while a Long Integer is a whole number (i.e. no decimal places). There is also a description box which allows you to enter additional information about the field. This is often useful when you need to amend the fields.

6 Close the window and you will be prompted to save your table. Indicate that you want to save the table and the Save As window will now appear allowing you to name your table. Call it Accounts and click on the OK button.

7 A warning message will now appear asking you if you need a primary key. In this case you do not need to define one, so click on the No button. The table window reappears and you should Close it by clicking on the close button in the top right-hand corner of the table window. You can now see the Customer Accounts Database window but with an extra item added – Accounts.

8 You can now enter the data by double-clicking on Accounts. Enter the text to produce Figure 3.30.

9 When you have completed the table, check each entry against the original data. If you find an error, click in the field box to move the cursor into the box. Delete the mistake and insert the correct entry.

10 Explore sorting the information using the Ascending and Descending icons on the toolbar. Sort the Name, Credit and First Order Fields. This will show you how to sort alphabetically, numerically and by date.

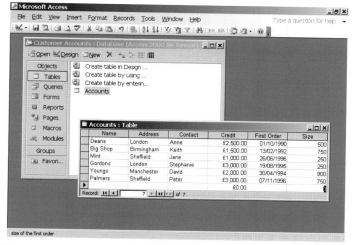

Figure 3.30 Accounts table

11 Close the window. The completed table will be saved automatically.

12 Click on the Close button in the top right-hand corner of the window.

13 Close Microsoft® Access by selecting the File menu and the Exit option.

Activity 2

The database Customer Accounts is available on the supporting website (www.hodderclait.co.uk) if you would like to undertake this exercise without creating the database.

Queries

1 Insert your floppy disk into your drive. Load Microsoft® Access by selecting Start, highlighting the All Programs menu and clicking on the Microsoft Access item or double-click on the Access icon on the desktop.

2 Microsoft® Access will load (Figure 3.1). In the Getting Started task pane Open section will be the Customer Accounts file. Double-click this item and the Customer Accounts Database window will be displayed.

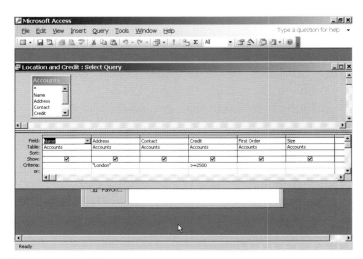

Figure 3.31 Query

3 Select the Queries button in the list of Objects on the left-hand side of the window. Double-click on Create query in Design view. A new window will open with an overlaid window called Show Table. Click on the Add button on Show Table and then on the Close button.

4 In the Query window a small box (Accounts) will have been added which shows the fields that make up the Accounts table. The cursor will be flashing in the first Field box and a small down arrow will

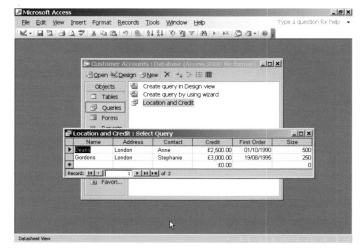

Figure 3.32 Location and Credit Query results

be shown at the end of the same box. Click on the down arrow and a list of the Customer Account fields will appear. Select Name by clicking on it. Name will appear in the first box. Move to the next box and repeat the operation selecting Address this time. Repeat the process adding Contact, Credit and Size fields.

5 You are going to create a query based on two criteria. These are:
Customers in London

Customers who have a credit limit greater than or equal to £2500.

6 Click in the Criteria box of Address and enter London.

7 Click in the criteria box of Credit and enter >=2500

8 Save this query (Figure 3.31) by selecting the File menu and the Save As option then enter Location and Credit as the name of the query and click on the OK button.

9 Close the window by selecting the Close button in the top right-hand corner of the window. You will now see that the Customer Accounts window shows the query. Double-click on the query to see if it produces the desired results (Figure 3.32). The results of the query are removed by clicking on the Close button.

10 If you find that the query is producing the wrong outcomes then you can amend it by single-clicking the query to highlight it and then on the Design button on the toolbar. This will open the query to allow you to make the required changes.

11 When the query is run, print the results by selecting the File menu, the Print option and the OK button. Check that the data is displayed in full.

12 You are now going to design a query to identify all customers who first placed an order on or after 30/04/94. The Customer Accounts Database window should be displayed.

13 Select the Queries button in the list of Objects on the left-hand side of the window. Double-click on Create query in Design view. A new window will open with an overlaid window called Show Table. Click on the Add button on Show Table and then on the Close button.

14 In the Query window a small box (Accounts) will have been added which shows the fields that make up the Accounts table. The cursor will be flashing in the first Field box and a small down arrow will be shown at the end of the same box. Click on the down arrow and a list of the Customer Account fields will appear. Select First Order by clicking on it. First Order will appear in the first box. Move to the next box and repeat the operation selecting Name this time. You simply want to identify the names of the customers.

15 You are going to create a query based on one criterion:
Customers who have placed orders on or after 30/04/94.

16 Click in the Criteria box of First Order and enter >=30/04/94.

17 Save this query by selecting the File menu and the Save As option then enter First Order as the name of the query and click on the OK button.

18 Close the window by selecting the Close button in the top right-hand corner of the window. You will now see that the Customer Accounts window shows the new query. Double-click on the query First Order to see if it produces the desired results (Figure 3.33). The results of the query are removed by clicking on the Close button.

19 If you find that the query is producing the wrong outcomes

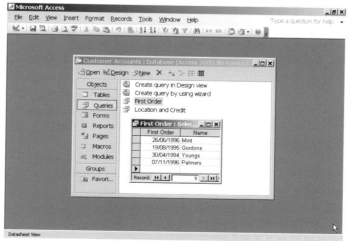

Figure 3.33 First Order results

then you can amend it by single-clicking the query to highlight it and then clicking on the Design button. This will open the query to allow you to make the required changes.

20 When the query is run, print the results by selecting the File menu, the Print option and the OK button. Check that the data is displayed in full.

21 Close the Database window by selecting the Close button and then close Microsoft® Access by selecting the File menu and the Exit option.

Activity 3

Reports

1 Insert your floppy disk into your drive. Load Microsoft® Access by selecting Start , highlighting the All Programs menu and clicking on the Microsoft Access item or double-click on the Access icon on the desktop.

2 Microsoft® Access will load (Figure 3.1). In the Getting Started task pane Open section will be the Customer Accounts file. Double-click this item and the Customer Accounts Database window will be displayed.

3 Select the Reports button in the list of Objects on the left-hand side of the window. Double-click on Create report by using wizard . The Report Wizard window will open. Select the table Accounts.

4 Select all the fields by clicking on the double arrows and transferring them to the right-hand column and then click on the Next button.

5 There is no need to group fields so click on the Next button.

6 Sort descending by Size and then click on the Next button.

7 Select the tabular layout and the landscape orientation and then click on the Next button. Remember that you need to display the data in full.

8 Choose the Compact style and then click on the Next button.

9 Give your report the title Size and select preview. Click on the Finish button.

10 The report will appear for you to check (Figure 3.34). It is important to check that the data is displayed in full.

11 When the report is run, print the results by selecting the File menu, the Print option and the OK button.

12 Close the Database window by selecting the Close button and then close Microsoft® Access by selecting the File menu and the Exit option.

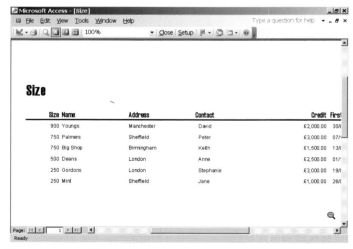

Figure 3.34 Size report

SUMMARY

1 **Load Microsoft® Access** Use either the Start button and the All Programs menu or double-click on the Access icon on the Windows® desktop.

2 **Close** Click on the File menu and the Exit option or click on the Close button in the top right-hand corner of the application or other window.

3 **Create a database – optional** Load Microsoft® Access. Select Create a new file within the Getting Started task pane to open the New File Task Pane. Select the Blank database. The File New Database window opens to enable you to save your new database.

Select a drive or folder in which to store your new database as a file. If you click on the arrow button next to the Save in: box you can select the floppy disk.

Give the file a name. Insert the name in the File name: box and click on the Create button. Your database is now saved.

The Database window is now revealed with three options with the Tables object on the left-hand side selected:

- Create table in Design view
- Create table by using wizard
- Create table by entering data .

Double-click on Create table in Design view and the Table window opens. Insert your field names and their types. You will be prompted to save your table when you close the window.

4 **Enter data** Load Microsoft® Access. Double-click on the database of your choice in the list displayed in the task pane. The Database window will appear.

Double-click on the table of your choice and the blank table will appear. Complete the records, moving between the fields by clicking in each box. Alternatively use the arrow keys, Tab key or Enter key to move between fields. Check each entry against the original data. To amend a single field, click on the field, delete its incorrect content and then re-enter the data.

5 **Delete a record** Highlight the record by positioning the mouse pointer over the row heading until the pointer changes shape. Click the left mouse button. Right-click in the highlighted row; the menu will appear and you select Delete Record .

6 **Add a record** Click on the blank row at the bottom of the table and insert data, moving between fields using the Tab or Enter keys or by clicking in the next field.

7 **Create a query** Select the Queries button in the list of Objects on the left-hand side of the Database window. Double-click on the Create query in Design view option. A new window will open with an overlaid window called Show Table. Click on the Add button on Show Table and then on the Close button.

In the Query window a small box shows the fields that make up the table. The cursor will be flashing in the first Field box and a small down arrow will be shown at the end of the same box. Click on the down arrow and a list of the table fields will appear. Select the field which will then appear in the box. Move across the boxes, entering the chosen fields.

Enter criteria in appropriate boxes.

Sort data by clicking in the sort boxes. Select the down arrow and choose Ascending, Descending or not sorted.

8 **Save a query** Save the query by selecting the File menu and the Save As option then enter the name of the query and click the OK button.

9 **Printing** Select the File menu and the Print option. This reveals the Print window and you can print using the default settings by clicking on the OK button. Alternatively select the File menu and Print Preview to check the appearance of the printed document before you print it. Click on the Print icon and then on the OK button in the Print window.

10 **Report** Select the Reports button in the list of Objects on the left-hand side of the Database window. Double-click on the Create report by using wizard . The window Report Wizard will appear. This will guide you through a series of choices about the content and presentation of your report. This includes saving the report so it can be used again.

Chapter 4

Producing an e-Publication

This chapter will help you to use desktop publishing to:

■ identify and use appropriate software correctly in accordance with laws and guidelines

■ use basic file handling techniques for the software

■ set up a standard page layout and text properties

■ use basic tools and techniques appropriately

■ import and place text and image files

■ manipulate text and images to balance a page

■ manage publications and print composite publications.

Assessment

This unit does not assume any previous experience of using a computer though you may find it useful to have completed Unit 1 (File Management and e-Document Production). You will be assessed through a practical realistic assignment which is designed to allow you to demonstrate your knowledge and skills against each objective. Your tutor can provide you with more guidance.

Microsoft® Publisher

Microsoft® Publisher 2003 is a desktop publishing application with which you create publications. These can be for your own personal use (e.g. a village newsletter) or for your business (e.g. an advertising leaflet). In this chapter you will learn how to create a publication using images and text. Many people find it difficult to understand the difference between word processing and desktop publishing (DTP). Word processing is about producing a document while a desktop publisher provides tools to control the precise presentation of text and images. DTP is more a tool for laying out text and pictures. It gives you control over the flow of text and the positioning and size of images.

Figure 4.1 shows the opening display of Microsoft® Publisher 2003. This consists of three areas:

■ Menus and toolbars that are similar to other Microsoft® Office applications

- New Publication task pane on the left of the display
- Work area on the right of the display showing 'To get started, select an option in the list'.

The New Publication task pane displays a list of options divided into sections (i.e. New from a design, New and Open). If you highlight any of the options (e.g. Design Sets, Web Sites and E-Mail and Blank Publications) in the New from a design section, then the left display changes to present you with more choices related to the type of publication you have selected. Microsoft® Publisher 2003 offers a wide range of standard publications on which to base your design.

Below the New from a design section is the New section which has three options:

- Blank Print Publication
- Blank Web Page
- From existing publication .

Finally at the bottom of the task pane is the section Open.

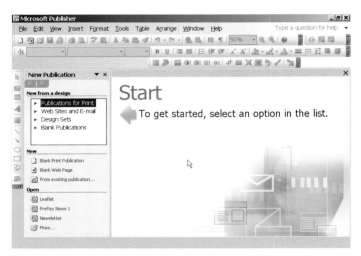

Figure 4.1 Microsoft® Publisher

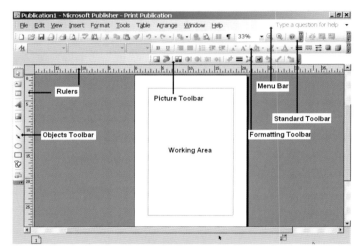

Figure 4.2 Publisher working area

If you select the Blank Print Publication option the display changes to show the working area. A blank full page publication is displayed with the Publication Designs task pane. You can close the task pane by clicking on the X symbol in the top right-hand corner of the task pane (Figure 4.2).

The application provides access to a range of tools through menus and toolbars. To the left of the window is the Objects toolbar offering a range of tools (e.g. to create WordArt, draw rectangles and access Clip Art). At the top of the window is a series of toolbars that let you print, save and format your publication. The Menu bar provides alternative routes to the same functions and other tools such as the selection of page sizes, margins and checking your spelling.

Exploring Microsoft Publisher

1 Load Microsoft® Publisher by selecting the `Start` button, highlighting the `All Programs` option and clicking on the `Microsoft Publisher` item or double-click on the `Publisher` icon on the desktop. Observe that it opens as shown in Figure 4.1.

2 Explore the different designs and options. In the New from a design section are four options:

    1   `Publications for Print`
    2   `Web Sites and E-mail`
    3   `Design Sets`
    4   `Blank Publications`

Highlight the different options and observe how the list of options in the section and also the choices on the right side of the display change. `Blank Publications` offers you a wide selection of different blank publications on which you can develop your design (e.g. web page, poster, business card and postcard). You select an option by double-clicking on it. Single-click on the `Full Page` option in the task pane and it will be highlighted. On the right side of the display the full page option will be enclosed in a blue rectangle to indicate it is also highlighted.

3 When you are ready, select the `Blank Print Publication` in the New section of the task pane. Figure 4.3 will appear.

4 The blank full page will occupy the working area and to the left is the Publication Designs task pane. You will see towards the right side of the Standard toolbar a percentage (e.g. 33%). This tells you the relative size of the document. The working area is enclosed in a ruler. If you move the mouse pointer you will see that on both the top and left-hand rulers a

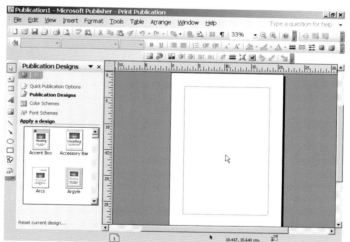

Figure 4.3 Blank Print Publication

faint line moves with respect to the mouse. This gives you guidance as to the position at which you are working on the document. If the ruler is not shown then select the `View` menu and `Rulers` option.

5 On the left-hand edge is a series of tools – Objects toolbar (Figure 4.2).

6 Explore the menus – what functions does each contain? Try to locate `Start` Page Setup which is on the `File menu`, `Layout Guides` (`Arrange` menu), `Copy` (`Edit` menu) and `Picture` (`Insert` menu).

continued

7 Explore the Publication Designs task pane. Click on each of the four options at the top of the Task pane (i.e. Quick Publication Options , Publication Designs , Color Schemes and Font Schemes) and observe the changes. Consider some of the options revealed and the sub-options linked to them.

8 When you are familiar with the different choices then close the task pane by clicking on the Close button in the top right-hand corner of the pane. This will change the display so that it appears like Figure 4.2.

9 Close Microsoft® Publisher by clicking on the Close button in the top right-hand corner of the window or by selecting the File menu and the Exit option. You may be asked if you want to save the changes that you have made; select the No button.

Designing

Microsoft® Publisher provides the tools to produce professional publications but it leaves the design to you. The critical factors in designing a publication are:

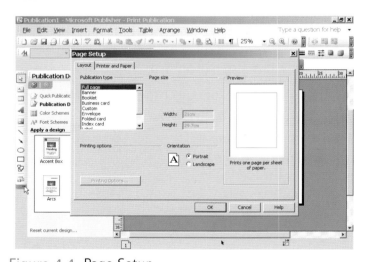

Figure 4.4 Page Setup

1 Modest use of variables – few things are worse than overuse of the desktop publishing features (e.g. too many colours, fonts (sometimes called typefaces), character sizes etc.). A useful rule is to use a feature for a distinct reason (e.g. using a different character size for each heading – main heading size 36, subheadings 20 and ordinary text size 12).

2 Consistency – in a way the design is a form of code that tells your readers how to understand the document so it is important that you follow a consistent design plan (e.g. the address always in the bottom right-hand corner of a page).

3 Attractiveness – initially your publications need to be visually attractive so that people will consider reading them. The use (not overuse) of pictures, colour and different fonts can provide an interesting publication. It is important for a document to be visually balanced.

4 Appropriateness – consider who your readers are and design for them.

5 Readability – a good publication is one which is easy to read. Readability is a combination of many factors but some simple tips are to provide plenty of white space (e.g. overcrowding text makes it difficult to read, so do not reduce line spacing unless you have no other choice), pictures relating to the text to increase the readers' interest and short sections which are often easier to understand than long ones.

6 Balance – a balance between text and images will make your publication attractive, pleasing on the eye and effective.

Standard Page Setup

The first task in designing a publication is to set the page size, orientation and margins.

Select the File menu then the Page Setup option to reveal the Page Setup window (Figure 4.4) which provides you with options to choose the publication type, paper size and orientation (i.e. either portrait or landscape). When you select a type, you are able to see your choice in the Preview area. Types are chosen by clicking on them. Click on the OK button to confirm your selections.

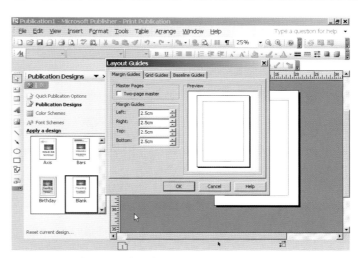

Figure 4.5 Layout Guides

Extra options will appear with some publication types, such as envelope where you will see an additional box appear allowing you to select from a range of different sizes of envelope (e.g. C3 and DL). Also the width and height boxes become active with some choices to allow you to change the dimensions of the publication.

To set the margins, select the Arrange menu then the Layout Guides option to reveal the Layout Guides window (Figure 4.5). This allows you to preview your choices. You can change each margin (left, right, top and bottom) by clicking on the up and down arrows. The window has three tabs. If you select the Grid Guides you can provide guidelines for a page divided into columns or rows.

Frames

Every item (e.g. images and text) that makes up a desktop publication is an individual object. Each object is enclosed in a frame which is invisible when printed unless you choose to create a border around it. Frames can be resized, rotated and moved using your mouse. They can be placed on top of each other so that a series of layers is created. Figure 4.6 shows a highlighted frame. The small empty circles, which form part of the enclosure and allow you to resize the

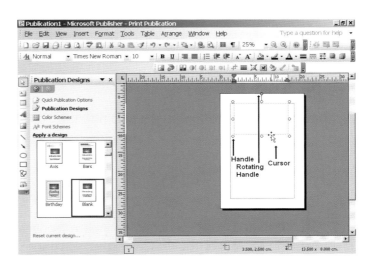

Figure 4.6 Frames

frame, are called handles. At the top of the frame is a green circle which, if you place the mouse pointer over it, changes into a circle with arrows. This allows you to rotate the object with movements of the pointer.

Figure 4.6 shows the shape of the mouse pointer when you place it over the frame in order to move the whole frame (i.e. object) to a new position. If you place the pointer over one of the handles it will change to a double-headed arrow. To move the object or resize it requires that you hold down the left mouse button and drag the object to a new location, or expand or contract its size.

Template

A template can save you a great deal of time and trouble. It is essentially a basic model of the publication which you use over and over again. Normally you will define the layout and format of the publication and then use this foundation to create new versions. This is useful if you are regularly publishing a document such as a monthly newsletter which you would like to have a standard appearance but with a variable content.

You create a template in the same way that you produce any other publication except that you save the layout and format before adding the detail content. The template is saved in the Microsoft® Publisher Template format. When you next want to create a similar publication you load the template and immediately begin to add the detail. In this way you save time and also produce a consistent documnt.

Master Page

The master page concept is similar to that of a template. You create a standard page which is reused throughout a multiple-page publication. This again provides a standard and consistent appearance to a document. There are no particular rules for the layout of a master page since it depends on what you are designing. A textbook, for example, will need a different master to a sales brochure.

A master page allows you to increase your productivity while maintaining a high standard of presentation. In addition, readers like a consistent presentation since it aids readability and helps them locate information.

Exercise 38

Page Setup

1 Load Microsoft® Publisher by selecting the `Start` button, highlighting the `All Programs` option and clicking on the `Microsoft Publisher` item or double-click on the `Publisher` icon on the desktop.

2 Select the `New` section and the `Blank Print Publications` option in the New Publication task pane.

3 The Microsoft® Publisher working area will appear with the Publication Designs task pane on the left of the display (Figure 4.3). Close the task pane by clicking on the `Close` button (i.e. X) in the top right-hand corner of the pane. This will change the display to show a blank full page in the centre of the working area.

4 Select the File menu, then the Page Setup option to reveal the Page Setup window (Figure 4.4). Explore the different layouts by considering their appearance in the Preview window before selecting the Full page option. Options are chosen by clicking on them. Change the page orientation to landscape and observe its appearance in the Preview window. When you are ready, click on the OK button to confirm the changes.

5 Select the Arrange menu then the Layout Guides to reveal the Layout Guides window (Figure 4.5). Explore changing the margins by observing the selections in the Preview area. When you are confident that you understand the choices, set the right and left margins to 4 cm and the top and bottom to 3 cm. Click on the OK button to confirm your selections. You can change the size of the margins by simply clicking on the up and down arrows or in the left, right, top or bottom boxes and entering the size from the keyboard.

6 You have now created a basic layout for a publication which might be useful as a newsletter or a handout in a presentation. This is a good time to save your outline publication. You could consider it as a master document or template. Microsoft® Publisher provides several master documents for you to choose from but you can also create your own. A master is simply a framework which serves a particular purpose that you can use over and over again to produce a particular type of publication. If you regularly produce a newsletter, it aids productivity and ensures they all follow a consistent design.

7 Insert a floppy disk into the computer's drive. To save your outline publication, select the File menu then the Save option to reveal the Save As window. You need to choose the location in which to store your publication by clicking on the down arrow at the end of the Save in: box. This will reveal a list. Click on the floppy disk option. You will then see this appear in the box. Now click in the File name: box and enter from the keyboard the name Landscape Column then click on the Save button. You will hear the drive working and the publication will be saved on the floppy disk as a file called Landscape Column.

8 It is good practice to save your work early and to update your saved file at regular intervals. This safeguards you against any problems with the application or computer. You will always have most of your work saved so that you can start again later without having to repeat all of it.

9 You have now established a basic layout. The next step is to consider where to place your text. Select the Text Box tool on the Objects toolbar. If you place the mouse pointer over a tool icon then a small label appears to tell you the name of the tool. When you have selected the Text Box the mouse pointer will change to a crosshair that allows you to accurately position your text. We are going to establish a text frame or area that will cover the top half of the page. You do this by positioning your pointer in the top left-hand corner of the column and then holding the mouse button down. Move the pointer down to form a rectangle at the top of the column. Your rectangle will be framed as shown in Figure 4.7. You can drag the rectangle to adjust the frame to your needs. Use the layout guides to help position the text frame.

10 If you move your mouse
pointer across the frame it
will change shape to show
its purpose:

- a double-headed arrow
  whenever you place the
  pointer on one of the
  small empty circles
  (called handles) at the
  corners or middle of the
  lines. This allows you to
  change the size of the
  text frame.
- a star will appear
  whenever you place your
  pointer near the lines but away from the handles. This lets you move the whole
  frame.
- an I bar indicates that you can insert text in this area.

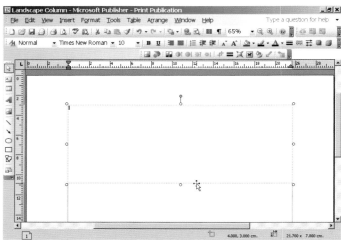

Figure 4.7 **Text frames**

11 Experiment with changing the size of the rectangle and moving it. When you have
finished, place the frame to cover the top half of the page. If you click away from the
frame, the heavy lines and handles will disappear (i.e. it is no longer highlighted) to
show you it is fixed. However, if you need to manipulate it, highlight it again by
clicking on the rectangle. If you make a mistake and need to delete the frame, you
must highlight it then press the Delete key or select the Edit menu then the
 Delete Object option.

12 Microsoft® Publisher provides you with tools to manipulate the text frame precisely.
With the text frame highlighted, select the Format menu then the Text Box option to
reveal the Format Text Box
window (Figure 4.8). The
window has a series of tabs
across the top which
provide access to more
options. Figure 4.9 shows
the options within the
 Text Box tab.

13 With the Format Text Box
window you can divide your
text frame into columns, set
the spacing between them
and set the four margins for
the text frame (Figure 4.9).
These may seem peripheral

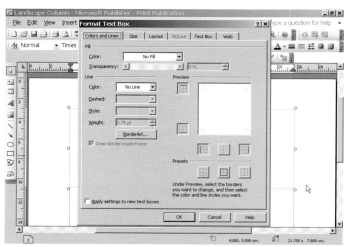

Figure 4.8 **Format Text Box**

matters but desktop publishing is about providing you with the tools to produce accurate and detailed publications. Microsoft® Publisher lets you produce publications equivalent to those of professional printers.

14 Select the Text Box tab (Figure 4.9). Set all the margins of your text frame to 0.5 cm. Click on the Columns button and create three columns with a spacing of 0.199 cm (Figure 4.10). This is the space between the three columns.

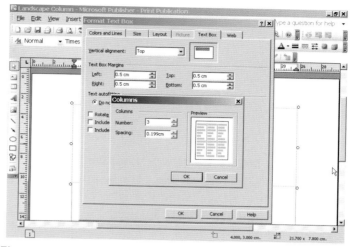

Figure 4.9 Format Text Box – Text Box tab – Columns option

15 You will notice that within your text box the cursor is flashing. This is the place where any text you enter will appear. Enter the heading Guinea Pigs. You may see a message appear to tell you the text is too small to be visible and offering you the option of zooming in on the text by pressing the function key F9.

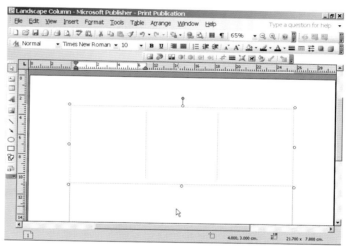

Figure 4.10 Three-column publication

The zoom option is also available on the toolbar box (i.e. minus and plus magnifying glasses).

16 You can resize the text by highlighting it (click on the start of the text and, holding the left mouse button down, move the pointer to the end of the text). Now select the character size box on the Formatting toolbar. The small down arrow button to the right of the character size box will reveal a list of sizes. In a similar way, the down arrow next to the font box will list fonts that you can select. Fonts are also called typefaces.

For this publication you are creating the initial heading so it is important to select a font and character size that is eye-catching. The list of fonts includes two different types called serif and sans serif. A serif-type font has small flags on the ends of the characters while a sans serif type font does not. You might say that serif fonts have more fancy characters or that sans serif fonts have plain characters. You need to experiment with your choice of fonts to find the ones that you like.

Serif Font Characters	Sans Serif Font Characters
F T	FT

17 Select a character size of 20 by clicking on that number in the list and then select the Arial font (or one of your own choice). Observe how your title now appears. While selecting your font, scroll down the list and you should notice many with similar names. These are likely to belong to the same family of fonts. Fonts are divided into families that vary in size from a single item to ones with many elements.

18 Save your publication by selecting the File menu and the Save option. The Save As window will not appear since the system assumes you are updating your previously saved file Landscape Column. If you want to create a new saved file you need to select the Save As option. This will reveal the Save As window and you can enter a new filename.

19 Close the application by clicking on the Close button in the top right-hand corner of the window or by selecting File and then the Exit option.

Manipulate fonts

An alternative way to manipulate the fonts and character sizes is available from the Format menu. Select the Font option, revealing the Font window (Figure 4.11). The text frame and the selected words need to be highlighted for these options to be available. You can also embolden, underline and display your text in italics style from this window, although these options are, of course, also available on the Formatting toolbar.

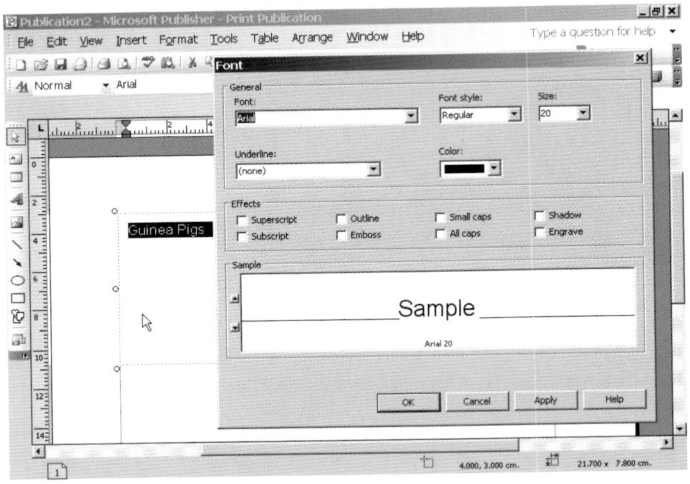

Figure 4.11 Font window

Alignment (Justification)

You can align (justify) your text using the icons on the Formatting toolbar. These allow you to align (justify) your text in four ways (Figure 4.12). These are:

Left	Right	Centred	Double
AAAAA	AAAAA	AAAAA	AAAAA
AAA	AAA	AAA	A A A
AAAA	AAAA	AAAA	A A A A
AA	AA	AA	A A
AAAA	AAAA	AAAA	A A A A

Figure 4.12 Alignment (Justification)

- left – the left text edge is parallel with the margin and the right is ragged
- right – the right text edge is parallel with the margin and the left is ragged
- centred – the text is aligned down the centre of the page with both edges ragged
- justified – both left and right text edges are parallel with the margins (it is sometimes called double justification).

Highlight the text and select the respective icons from the toolbar.

Inserting text and pictures

Although you can enter text into your publication from the keyboard, desktop publishing is primarily designed to allow you to manipulate objects to produce high-quality presentations of information. One such object is text, which is best prepared using a word processor. This can either be text copied from other Office applications and pasted into the publication or imported text files.

To insert text files you select the Insert menu and the Text File option with the text frame highlighted. This opens the Insert Text window which allows you to choose the file you want to insert. In a similar way you can insert pictures by copying them from other Microsoft® Office applications, inserting image files or choosing images from Clip Art collections. To insert a picture you need to select the Insert menu then highlight the Picture option to reveal a short

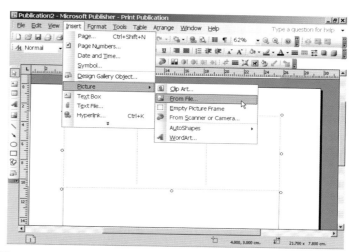

Figure 4.13 Picture options

menu of options. Figure 4.13 shows the Picture menu options. You can insert a Clip Art image, a picture saved in a folder, create an empty picture frame or import an image from a digital camera or scanner using these functions. When they appear in the publication they are often too large and need to be resized using the handles. The Objects toolbar offers an alternative way of creating an empty picture frame in the form of the Picture Frame Tool.

When you first select these options you may be presented with a message indicating that the functions need to be installed from the Microsoft® Office master disks. If this happens seek help unless you are confident that you can install the functions. They convert files to a format that Microsoft® Publisher can accept. Clip Art collections provided by Microsoft® Office are often not installed on the computer and need to have the CD-ROMs which hold them inserted in the correct drive so that they can be accessed.

Manipulate images

Microsoft® Publisher provides a variety of functions to help you manipulate images. These include:

- Flipping the image
- Resizing the image
- Cropping the image.

To flip or rotate an image you need to select it (i.e. click on the image to enclose it in a frame) and then choose the `Arrange` menu and highlight the `Rotate or Flip` option to reveal a submenu. This offers a range of functions including:

- `Free Rotate`
- `Rotate Left 90°`
- `Rotate Right 90°`
- `Flip Horizontal`
- `Flip Vertical`.

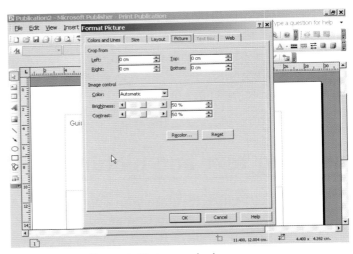

Figure 4.14 Format Picture window

To resize an image you need to select it and then choose the `Format` menu and the `Picture` option. This opens the Format Picture window (Figure 4.14) that allows you change the size of the image, crop and also rotate it. The options are provided under several tabs displayed across the top of the window.

Amend text

The functions to manipulate and amend text that are available in many Microsoft® Office applications are also offered in Microsoft® Publisher. You can therefore cut, copy, paste, insert, delete and find and replace text. The process is very similar to other applications; you need to highlight the text and then select the required function. Text is inserted by clicking the pointer in the location where you want to add to or amend it. The `find and replace` function operates in an identical way to other Microsoft® Office applications except that a task pane is opened rather than a window.

Lines and borders

All Microsoft® Publisher objects are enclosed in frames which are invisible when printed unless they are turned into borders. You are provided with the functions to enclose frames with lines of different thicknesses or more artistic surrounds. These are available by selecting the `Format` menu and `Text Box` to reveal the Format Text Box. If you select the `Colors and Lines` tab you will see

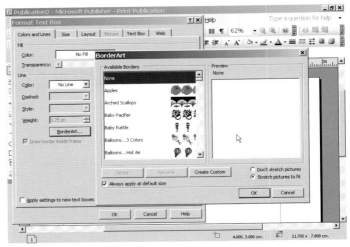

Figure 4.15 Format Text Box – Colors and Lines tab

the basic line and borders tools. Click on the BorderArt button to open the BorderArt window of options (Figure 4.15). These functions are only available if the frame you are enclosing is highlighted (i.e. handles showing).

In the Format Text Box and BorderArt window you can experiment with different choices of line styles. These appear in the Preview area.

On the Objects toolbar (i.e. down the left side of the Microsoft® Publisher working area) are several tools that allow you to add lines and simple shapes such as:

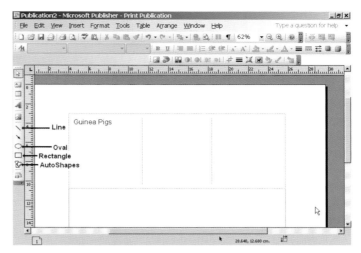

Figure 4.16 Objects toolbar tools

- Line tool
- Oval tool
- Rectangle tool
- AutoShapes tool.

Figure 4.16 shows examples of four tools.

Exercise 39

Importing text and pictures

1 Load Microsoft® Publisher by selecting the Start button, highlighting the All Programs option and clicking on the Microsoft Publisher item or by double-clicking on the Publisher icon on the desktop.

2 Microsoft® Publisher will appear (Figure 4.1).

3 If you have only recently completed the previous exercise (i.e. in this session) then in the Open section of the New Publication task pane, you will see the Landscape Columns file. This can be loaded by clicking on it.

   If you completed the exercise some time ago then you will need to load it from your floppy disk. Insert the disk into the drive and select the File menu then the Open option to reveal the Open Publication window. Select the floppy disk in the Look in: box by clicking on the down arrow button to reveal a list of options. This will reveal the files on your floppy disk. Double-click on the Landscape Column publication to load the file or single-click on it and then on the Open button.

4 The publication will appear in the working area. If you click within the text frame you will see the location of the flashing cursor. Move the cursor to one line below the heading (Guinea Pigs) by pressing the Enter key with the cursor at the end of the heading.

5 In the File Management and e-Document Production unit, you undertook an exercise and created some text about guinea pigs. We are now going to import this text file into the publication. Highlight the text frame, select the Insert menu and the Text File option to reveal the Insert Text window. Insert your floppy disk containing the Guinea Pigs file or, if you do not have the file, any other text file containing a short passage since this is a practice publication.

6 Select the floppy disk in the Look in: box by clicking on the down arrow button to reveal a list of options. This will reveal the files on your floppy disk. Double-click on the Guinea Pigs file to load it or single-click on it and then on the Open button.

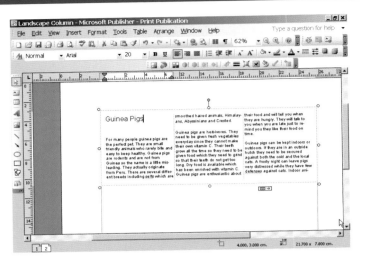

Figure 4.17 **Page one**

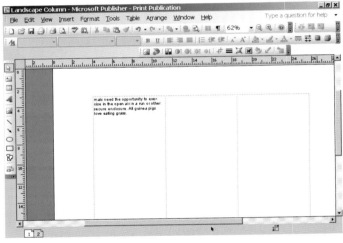

Figure 4.18 **Second page**

7 The text file will load into your publication starting at the cursor and flowing across the three columns. If it overflows the columns you will see a message appear asking if you want the automatic flow of text to be undertaken. Click on Yes to accept the automatic flow. Another message will appear asking if you want Microsoft® Publisher to create a new text box. Again click on Yes and a final message telling you a new page has been created will appear and that the display is showing the second or new page. Click on OK to remove it and look at your publication.

You should see a new page with three columns and below the working area you will see the numbers 1 and 2, with 2 highlighted indicating that it is the page you are considering. If you click on 1 then the first or original page will appear. Figures 4.17 and 4.18 show the two pages.

8 The next step is to insert a picture into your publication. Select the Insert menu, highlight the Picture option and click on Clip Art . This will reveal the Insert Clip Art

task pane on the left of the display. In the Search for: box enter animals and click on `Go`. A selection of animal related images will appear. Explore the pictures and choose one by positioning your pointer on it to reveal a down arrow button. Click on the down arrow button to open a menu. Choose the `Insert` option and the image will appear in your publication. Alternatively click on the image and it will be inserted into your publication.

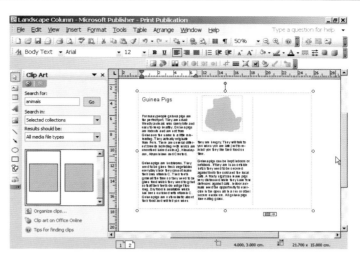

Figure 4.19 Amended publication

9 You can move the picture or resize it using the mouse pointer in the same way as with the text frame. Experiment with moving the image, including placing the picture inside the text frame. You will see the text move to make room for the image. This shows that you can stack frames on top of each other.

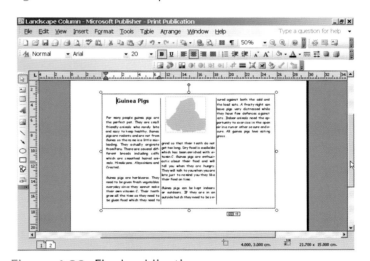

Figure 4.20 Final publication

10 With the image inside it, resize the text frame to occupy the whole page and observe what happens.

11 The publication should now look similar to Figure 4.19. Close the Clip Art task pane.

12 You can change the alignment (justification) of the text using the Formatting toolbar. Centre the heading text (Guinea Pigs) by highlighting the words and using the `Centre` icon on the toolbar. Embolden the title. Change the imported text to Comic Sans (or a font of your choice), character size 12 and double-justify by again highlighting the text and using functions on the toolbar.

13 Select the `Format` menu and `Text Box` option to reveal the Format Text Box. Explore the options to provide a border for your publication with a line dividing the columns. Your publication should look similar to Figure 4.20 if you have used the guinea pig text.

14 Save your publication by selecting the `File` menu and the `Save` option. The Save As

window will not appear since the system assumes you are updating your previously saved file Landscape Column. If you wanted to create a new saved file then you would need to select the `Save As` option. This would reveal the Save As window for you to enter a new filename.

15 Close the application by clicking on the `Close` button in the top right-hand corner of the window or by selecting `File` and then the `Exit` option.

Spacing

It is important that the appearance of the text serves the purpose you intend. Often you have only a limited amount of space in which to fit a range of information (i.e. text and pictures). This requires you to balance the content of your publication and is especially true when you have a publication divided into columns. Microsoft® Publisher provides functions with which you can adjust the spacing of your text.

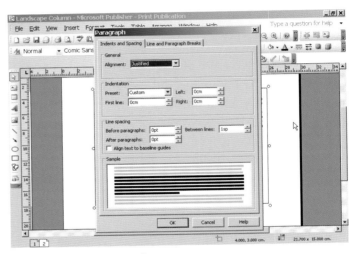

Figure 4.21 Paragraph

These are available in the `Format` menu within the `Character Spacing` and the `Paragraph` options when the text frame is highlighted.

The Character Spacing window allows you to shrink or stretch the characters. You need to highlight the text you want to work on and then increase or decrease the scaling using the up and down arrows. You can see the effects in the sample area at the bottom of the window.

The Paragraph window (Figure 4.21) provides the means of setting the space between lines of text, and before and after paragraphs, letting you finely adjust the presentation between columns or over a page. The changes can be seen in the sample area to help you judge the effects.

By using the Indentation section of the Paragraph window, you can indent the left and right edges of the text or the first line of your paragraph. The sample area allows you to see the effects of your changes. By setting an indent you will provide a standard look to your publication. It is normal to standardize publications (e.g. the first line of each paragraph is indented in the same way). To create a first line indent click on the down arrow box next to the Preset area. This will display a list of options including 1st Line Indent. Click on the option and you will see the effect in the sample area.

Having the ability to change the character size and font of the text with line spacing means you can carefully adjust the balance of each page. It requires some experimentation to gain the best results.

Printing

A key factor in desktop publishing is the printing of your publication. You can do this with your own local printer or you can save the publication as a file on a disk to take it to an external printer.

Before printing your publication it is important to check your work. A spellchecker is accessed by selecting the Tools menu, highlighting Spelling and clicking on Spelling . This will identify spelling mistakes. However, there are other possible errrors within a publication, such as the insertion of a blank frame. These can be identified using the Design Checker which is opened by selecting the Tools menu and the Design Checker option. This will open the Design Checker task pane. If you use the Design Checker with Landscape Column it will tell you that page 2 is blank. A final and probably the best check is simply to read and review the publication yourself.

To print your publication you select the File menu, then the Print option and click on the OK button. The printer will print your publication using the standard default settings.

More Practice

Activity 1

1 Load Microsoft® Publisher by selecting the Start button, highlighting the All Programs option and clicking on the Microsoft Publisher item or by double-clicking on the Publisher icon on the desktop.

2 Select the Blank Print Publication option in the New Publication task pane from the New section of the task pane.

3 The blank publication will occupy the centre of the working area

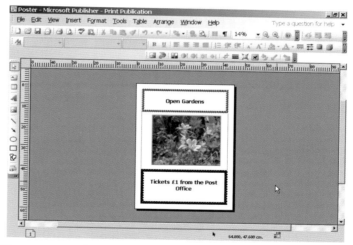

Figure 4.22 Poster

with the Publication Designs task pane on the left. Close the task pane.

4 Your task is to create a poster for an open garden event in a village.

5 Using Page Setup in the File menu, select the poster publication type with a portrait orientation and a paper size to be 45 x 60 cm.

6 Using the Layout Guides in the Arrange menu, set the margins to 2.5 cm.

7 Create a text frame to cover the top quarter of the poster and enter Open Gardens as a heading using a character size of 72 and a font called Tahoma (or a font of your choice). Centre and embolden the heading.

8 Using the Insert menu and Picture option, select and insert a relevant item of Clip Art or an image of your choice.

9 Finally, insert a second text frame at the bottom of the poster.

10 Enter the address where tickets can be obtained for the show using Tahoma (or a font of your choice) and a character size of 72 (e.g. Tickets are available at the Post Office). Present the text effectively.

11 Now enclose your three frames in suitable borders using the Format menu and the Text Box or Picture option. Remember that the border tool operates on a frame.

12 Adjust the text and picture positions to improve the impact of the poster. Figure 4.22 shows my effort.

13 Save your poster by selecting the File menu and the Save option.

14 Print your poster by selecting the File menu, the Print option and the OK button. If you are using an A4 printer then the poster will occupy several sheets.

15 Close the application by clicking on the Close button in the top right-hand corner of the window or by selecting File and then the Exit option.

Activity 2

1 Load Microsoft® Publisher by selecting the Start button, highlighting the All Programs option and clicking on the Microsoft Publisher item or by clicking on the Publisher icon on the desktop.

2 Select the Blank Print Publication option in the New section of the New Publication task pane.

3 The blank full page will occupy the centre of the working area with the Publication Designs task pane on the left of the display. Close the task pane.

4 Your task is to create a newsletter for a community group.

5 Using Page Setup in the File menu, set the layout to custom, size 20 x 30 cm and the orientation to portrait.

6 Using the Layout Guides in the Arrange menu, set the margins to 1.5 cm.

7 Create a text frame to cover the whole page. Using the Text Box option within the Format menu (remember the text frame must be highlighted), divide the page into three columns with a spacing of 0.4 cm and margins of 0.15 cm.

8 Create a second text frame across the top of the page (over the first text frame) in which to place your heading. Enter the heading Community Newsletter in Arial Black with a character size of 36. Centre the heading.

9 Select the Insert menu and Picture option and insert an appropriate Clip Art picture into the publication. Position the image in the centre of the newsletter below the heading and covering the three columns.

10 Create another text frame in the bottom right-hand corner of the page in the third (right-hand) column. This is going to give the Community group's address for correspondence. So enter the address below:

Community Group

Green Community Centre

New Walk

New Town

11 Use the Paragraph option on the Format menu to adjust the line spacing.

12 Save your newsletter by selecting the File menu and the Save option. You have

effectively created a master document for future editions. You can add the remaining text depending on the news when the newsletter is issued. Save the file as Newsletter.

13 Import a text file into the newsletter. You can choose any file but ideally it should be only a short piece of text. Use the Insert menu and the Text File option.

14 Observe how the text flows around your image frame and down the columns.

15 Using the Paragraph window, indent the paragraphs by 1 cm (remember to highlight all the text you want included) and then set the line spacing between lines to 1.5, and 1 before and after each paragraph.

16 Change the text font to Arial (or a font of your choice) and character size to 12 (or a size of your choice). Set the alignment (justification) to justify (double) (remember to highlight all the text you want included). Try to produce a balanced newsletter.

17 Surround the whole newsletter with an appropriate border. Enclose the address and heading frames in separate borders.

18 Save the newsletter under a new filename by selecting the File menu and the Save As option. Use the name New Newsletter.

19 Print your revised newsletter by selecting the File menu, Print option and OK button.

20 Close the application by clicking on the Close button in the top right-hand corner of the window or by selecting File and then the Exit option.

SUMMARY

1 **Load Microsoft® Publisher** Use either the Start button and the All Programs menu or double-click on the Publisher icon on the Windows® desktop.

2 **Close** Click on the File menu item and the Exit option or click on the Close button in the top right-hand corner of the application window.

3 **Save a file on to a floppy disk** Insert a floppy disk into drive A: and click on the File menu and Save . Select the floppy disk and enter the filename. Having saved a file once, you can update it by clicking on the File menu and Save without the Save As window appearing again. This simply overwrites the original file.

4 **Set page size and orientation** Select the File menu then the Page Setup option. This will reveal the Page Setup window.

5 **Set guides** Select the Arrange menu then Layout Guides to reveal the Layout Guides window.

6 **Insert a text frame** Select the Text Box tool on the Objects toolbar. The mouse pointer will change to cross hairs to allow you to position your text accurately. Position the top left-hand corner where you would like to locate the frame and then, holding the mouse button down, move the pointer down to form a rectangle.

7 **Move and resize a frame** Position the mouse pointer over a handle and the pointer will change shape (double arrow). By holding down the mouse button you can change the shape of the frame. Position your mouse pointer over the frame lines away from

the handles and the pointer will change shape (star). By holding down the mouse button you can move the frame.

8 **Change font and character size** Highlight the text. Select the small down arrow button to the right of the character size box to reveal a list of sizes. Click on the size of your choice. Select the small down arrow button to the right of the font box to reveal a list of fonts. Click on the font of your choice.

9 **Serif and sans serif fonts** The list of fonts includes those that are of the serif and sans serif types. A serif font has small flags on the ends of the characters (i.e. they are more fancy) while a sans serif does not (i.e. they are more plain).

10 **Alignment (Justification)** Highlight the text and select the respective icons from the Formatting toolbar.

11 **Inserting text and pictures** Select the Insert menu and the Text File option. This opens the Insert Text window which allows you to choose the file you want to insert. Select the Insert menu and highlight Picture to reveal the four options of Clip Art, From File, Empty Picture Frame and From Scanner or Camera. Alternatively text and pictures can be copied and pasted from other Microsoft® Office applications.

12 **Insert a picture frame** Select the Picture Frame tool on the Objects toolbar. The mouse pointer will change to cross hairs to allow you to position your frame accurately.
Position the top-left hand corner where you would like to locate the frame and then, holding the mouse button down, move the pointer down to form a rectangle. Alternatively select the Insert menu, highlight Picture to reveal the four options of Clip Art, From File, Empty Picture Frame and From Scanner or Camera. Select Empty Picture Frame and a frame will appear in the publication for you to position and size.

13 **Lines and borders** Select the Format menu and Text Box to reveal the Format Text Box window.

14 **Drawing and shape tools** Select the tools (e.g. Line, Oval, Rectangle and AutoShapes) from the Objects toolbar.

15 **Character and line spacing** Select the Format menu and either the Character Spacing or the Paragraph option with the text frame highlighted. This will reveal either the Character Spacing or Paragraph windows.

16 **Indent paragraphs** Select the Format menu and the Paragraph option with the text frame highlighted. This will reveal the Paragraph window.

17 **Checking** Select the Tools menu, highlight the Spelling option to reveal a short menu and click on Spelling. Select the Tools menu and the Design Checker option. This will open the Design Checker task pane.

18 **Printing** Select the File menu then the Print option and click on the OK button.

19 **Flip or rotate an image** Select the image (i.e. click on the image to enclose it in a frame) and then choose the `Arrange` menu and highlight the `Rotate or Flip` option to reveal a submenu. This offers a range of functions.

20 **Resize an image** Select the image then choose the `Format` menu and the `Picture` option to open the Format Picture window. Select the `Size` tab to resize the image using the scale function.

21 **First Line Indent** Select the `Format` menu and the `Paragraph` option.

Creating an e-Presentation

This chapter will help you to:

- identify and use presentation graphics software correctly
- set up a slide layout
- select fonts and enter text
- import and insert images correctly
- use the drawing tools
- format slides and presentation
- re-order slides and produce printed handouts
- manage and print presentation files.

Assessment

This unit does not assume any previous experience of using a computer. However, you may find it useful to have completed Unit 1 (File Management and e-Document Production). You will be assessed through a practical realistic assignment which is designed to allow you to demonstrate your knowledge and skills against each objective. Your tutor can provide you with more guidance.

Presentation applications

Microsoft PowerPoint® 2003 is a presentation application. It provides the resources to create presentations in the form of overhead projector slides, computer presentations and handouts. It is used extensively in both business and education. A sales manager may develop a presentation to persuade customers to buy a new product, a teacher may use it as a visual aid to make a subject more understandable and a manager may employ the application to explain changes in the organization.

This chapter is based on Microsoft PowerPoint® 2003 and Figure 5.1 shows the PowerPoint® interface. It is an application with many functions to assist in producing exciting and interesting presentations by providing a wide range of templates, graphic images and text tools.

When you load Microsoft PowerPoint® it starts with a display divided into four areas. These are:

- toolbars and menus (e.g. Standard, Formatting and Drawing toolbars are shown)
- a blank slide occupying the work area
- Getting Started task pane on the right of the display – this allows you to create new presentations using the Open section options
- Tabs pane on the left of the display which provides two different ways of gaining an overview of the presentation you are creating.

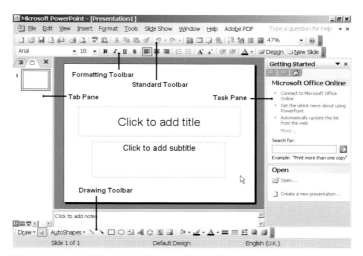

Figure 5.1   Microsoft PowerPoint®

Create a new presentation

We are going to create a new blank presentation so we need to click on the Create a new presentation option in the Getting Started task pane. The display will change replacing the Getting Started Task Pane with the New Presentation task pane (Figure 5.2). This provides a variety of ways of creating a presentation, from a blank one to using templates provided by Microsoft PowerPoint®. If you select the Blank presentation option in the New section of the task pane then the Slide Layout task pane appears.

This provides a variety of templates that you can use to design your slides. You can select a template either by clicking on the template so that it appears in the working area or by placing the mouse pointer over the template to reveal a down arrow box which, if clicked, opens a menu of options including Insert New Slide. When the pointer is placed on a template then a small label (e.g. Title Slide) will appear giving you the name of the template.

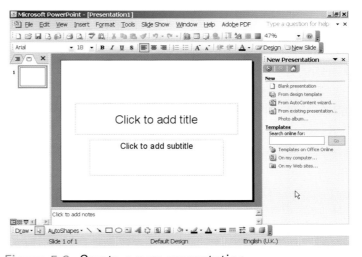

Figure 5.2   Create a new presentation

Figure 5.3 shows the title template which is used to begin a presentation. At the moment the slide is transparent. PowerPoint® provides you with a variety of tools to add background colours and an overall design to your slides. These are available in the Format menu and Slide Design option. When you select this option the Slide Layout task pane will be replaced with the Slide Design task pane (Figure 5.4).

The Slide Design task pane offers three different sets of designs:

- Design Templates – different layouts for the slides
- Color Schemes – different combinations of colours for the slides
- Animation Schemes – different animations for the slides.

When you select one of the options the section below changes to show the different choices. In Figure 5.4 the Design Template option has been chosen so the area is a scroll box with a variety of designs. To select a design you click on it and you will see it appear in the working area.

Once you have established the design of the slides you can then add the text that forms the message of your presentation. The title slide offers you two text boxes in which you can add text. These are the title and subtitle. After clicking in the boxes, you simply enter text from the keyboard.

A presentation consists of several slides. Once you have completed the title slide, you then need to add a new blank slide. This is done by selecting the Insert menu and then the New Slide option (Figure 5.5). This will insert a new slide into the working area, in this case, a Title and Text slide (Figure 5.6). However, you can change this slide by choosing a new layout from the Slide Layout task pane that also appears when a new slide is inserted. The design of the new slide (e.g. background colours) remains the same as the first slide. It is important in any presentation that the slides are consistent, as this helps the audience to understand the presentation. If

Figure 5.3 Blank presentation

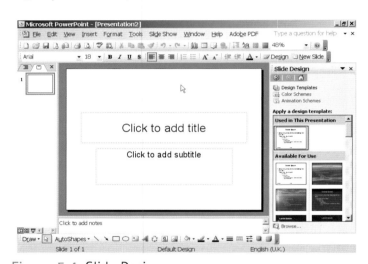

Figure 5.4 Slide Design

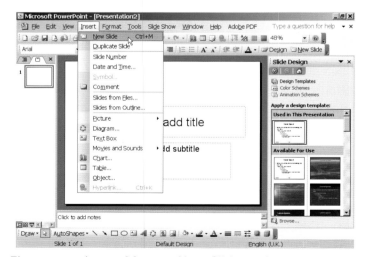

Figure 5.5 Insert Menu – New Slide option

each slide is different, with multiple designs and colours employed, there is the danger that the people listening to the presentation will be distracted from the message.

The new slide text layout is chosen in the same way as previously discussed (i.e. click on the selected template), allowing you to present information in several different ways and to include illustrations in the slide. Some options are:

■ Title and text in a single rectangle

■ Title and text presented in two parallel rectangles

■ Title and text in one rectangle with a chart or other image in another.

Figure 5.6 New slide

Each template shows the text or image areas enclosed in a rectangle. These are called placeholders and can either be transparent (i.e. no border) or enclosed in a border.

The rest of the presentation can be developed in this way by adding slides one by one. PowerPoint® lets you edit your slides so it is possible to develop a presentation rapidly by outlining each slide and then completing the presentation later.

Although New CLAiT does not require you to use its more advanced features, PowerPoint® does provide the means of animating slides so that your text can appear to fly on to the slide from almost any direction. The transition from one slide to the next can be made interesting by a variety of means. Some of these features are available in the Slide Show menu.

Organizations tend to develop standard house styles for all presentations carried out by their staff. They have often produced their own design templates including features such as company logos and colour schemes. It is useful to find out if your employer has a house style since you will be expected to follow it and also it may save you a lot of preparation time.

Exercise 40

Creating a presentation

1 Load Microsoft PowerPoint® using either the All programs menu or the PowerPoint icon on the desktop.

2 Select the Create a new presentation option from the Open section of the Getting Started task pane. This will open the New Presentation task pane. Select the Blank presentation option from the New section. This will open the Title Slide in the working area. Select the Format menu and the Slide Design option to open the Slide Design task pane. Explore the different design templates and select the Blends design template. When you place the mouse pointer over a design its name will appear. Enter CLAiT 2006 as the title.

3 Create a second new slide using the Insert menu and New Slide option. A title and text slide will appear. Enter the following bullet points:

– Level 1 Qualification

– Certificate – 3 Units

and the title – CLAiT 2006. You can insert new bullet points by pressing the `Enter` key at the end of the previous line (e.g. after entering Qualification).

If you make a mistake and identify it immediately you can delete the text by using the `Backspace` key. If you do not notice it until the slide is finished then click in the text where the error is. This will move the cursor to the location and you can now delete or insert text at this position.

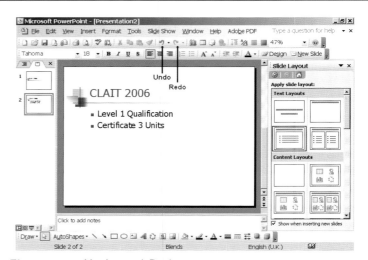

Figure 5.7 **Undo and Redo**

An alternative way of dealing with mistakes is to use the Undo function on the Standard toolbar (Figure 5.7). If you place the cursor over the `Undo` or `Redo` icons then a message will appear to help you identify them. Undo removes the last action you have carried out. You can use `Undo` repeatedly so that you can remove several actions. You can effectively undo the `Undo` action by using the function `Redo` on the Standard toolbar. Practise using `Undo` and `Redo`.

To move to another slide you can use the scroll bar on the right of the display or click on the slide list to the left-hand side of the display. Practise by returning to the first slide and then to the second one.

4 Create a third slide using the `Insert` menu and `New Slide` option, entering the following bullet points under the same title of CLAiT 2006:

– Mandatory unit
– Optional units

5 Create a fourth and final slide, entering the following bullet points under the same title of CLAiT 2006:

– Thank you
– Insert your name

Figure 5.8 shows the final slide within the PowerPoint®

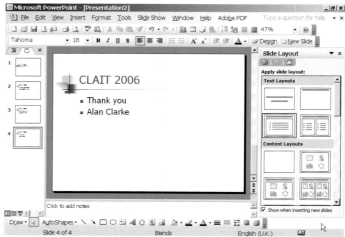

Figure 5.8 **Final Slide**

working area. Notice that on the left-hand side of the display an overview of the four-slide presentation you have created can be seen.

6 It is important to check your presentation for spelling mistakes to avoid embarrassing yourself when you show your slides. To check your slides select the Tools menu and the Spelling option. If you have entered the text correctly then a message 'The spelling check is complete' will appear. If the check reveals mistakes they will be shown within the Spelling window and alternative spellings will be offered for you to choose from.

7 Save the presentation you have created on to a floppy disk. This procedure is the same in all Windows® applications – you save a presentation, spreadsheet, database or graphic image in exactly the same way.

insert a floppy disk into drive A:

click on the File menu and a menu will open showing a list of options. Select Save As and the window will open.

8 Click in the File name: box and enter A:\CLAiT 2006. Click on the Save button on the right of the window. You have now saved your presentation as a file called CLAiT 2006. You may hear the drive A: working during this process.

9 To run the slide show you have created select the View menu and then click on the Slide Show option. The presentation will fill the screen and you can move between slides by clicking the left mouse button. When the presentation is over you will return to PowerPoint®. Alternatively select the Slide Show menu and the View Show option.

10 You can close Microsoft PowerPoint® now by clicking on the File menu and a menu will appear with a list of options. Click on the Exit option at the bottom of the list. An alternative way is to click on the Close button in the top right-hand corner of the application window.

Editing your presentation

As with other Microsoft® Office applications, you are able to add, delete and replace parts of your presentation using functions such as:

- Cut, copy and paste (Figure 5.9)
- Find and Replace (Figures 5.10 and 5.11).

Cut, copy and paste work by using the mouse pointer to highlight the text or object you want to edit.

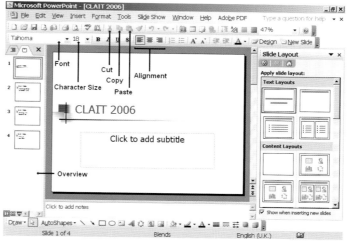

Figure 5.9 Standard toolbar – Cut and Copy

Highlighting is undertaken by clicking the mouse pointer at the chosen location and holding down the left mouse button while dragging it over the text or object. The text is shown to be highlighted by the background darkening. When the selected text is highlighted you can release the mouse button. To cut or copy the highlighted area you click on the Standard toolbar icon (Figure 5.9). These functions are also available on the Edit menu (Figure 5.10).

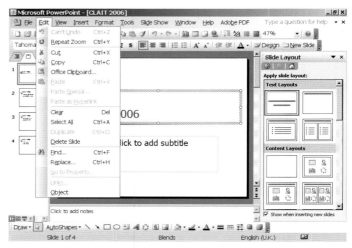

Figure 5.10 Edit Menu

The Cut function removes the highlighted area completely and you can then move it to a new location by using the mouse pointer. A new location is selected by positioning the pointer and clicking. The new position is identified by the cursor being moved (i.e. in the same way as the cursor is moved in Microsoft® Word). Now click on the Paste option or icon and the cut section is placed back into the presentation. The Copy function operates in the same way except that the original highlighted area is not removed.

Cut and copy are very useful functions since a key element in any presentation is consistency. These functions allow you to ensure quickly and effectively that identical elements are present on all slides (e.g. titles, company logos etc.).

Presentations often consist of many slides and if you need to change some text on every slide it can be a long and tedious process. PowerPoint® provides a way of finding a particular section of text of any length and replacing it with an amended phrase. This is not only fast but also free from errors such as spelling mistakes caused by having to enter replacement text from the keyboard.

Search and replace is available as an option on the Edit menu called Replace (Figure 5.11). By selecting Edit and then Replace, a window will appear (Figure 5.11) with two text boxes. Click in the top box and enter the words you wish to find then click in the lower box and enter the words you want to replace them with. There are also two options shown by the check boxes in the bottom left-hand corner of the window:

■ Match case
■ Find whole words only.

Match case means that the search will locate only these phrases that are identical in case (e.g. capitals) to the text entered in the window. Find whole words only restricts the search to matches that are entire words, otherwise the search finds words that are parts of longer words (e.g. a search for car will match with carton, care and careless). This option is important if you are searching for a single word.

Once you have completed the two text boxes you can start the search by clicking on the Find Next button. The search starts from the location of the cursor and proceeds through the presentation. Whenever a match is located you have the choice of replacing it by clicking on the Replace button, which changes that single entry. You then need to click on Find Next again to continue the search. An alternative is to click on Replace All , which will change all the matches to the new text. Use this option only if you are completely certain that you want to change them all.

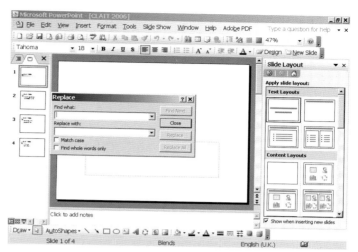

Figure 5.11 Replace

Slide order

An important function available in Microsoft PowerPoint® is the ability to the change the order of the slides. This is provided in the View menu within the Slide Sorter option. When this is selected the display changes to show all the slides (Figure 5.12). Slides can then be dragged and dropped into a new order using the mouse pointer. Clicking on the slide you wish to move and holding down the left mouse button allows you to move it to a new position.

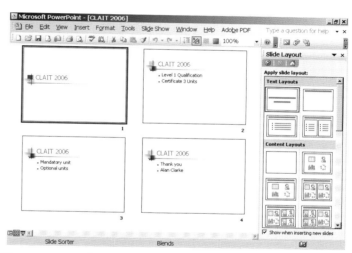

Figure 5.12 Changing the slide order

If you highlight a slide with a single click you can also cut, copy and paste slides using the functions on the Standard toolbar and within the Edit menu.

Exercise 41

Editing a Presentation

1   Load Microsoft PowerPoint® using either the All programs menu or the PowerPoint icon on the desktop.

2   In the Open section of the Getting Started task pane you may see a list of files including CLAiT 2006 . Double-click on the CLAiT 2006 file shown in the list. The CLAiT 2006 presentation will be loaded, but remember to have your floppy disk inserted in the A: drive. If the file is not in the list click on the More option to open the Open window. This will allow you to locate the file on your floppy disk.

3 Using the Replace function in the Edit menu, change the title text from CLAiT 2006 to CLAiT 2006 Qualification on all four slides.

4 Using the Cut function, move the text Level 1 Qualification from the second slide to the subtitle box on slide one and amend the text by deleting the word Qualification.

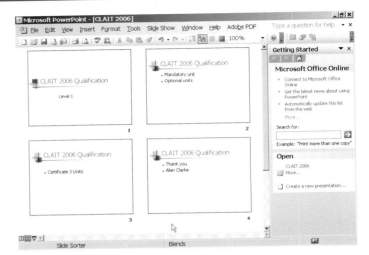

Figure 5.13 Revised presentation

5 Change the order of the slides by moving slide three to make it slide two.

6 Spellcheck the presentation. Figure 5.13 shows the revised presentation.

7 Save the presentation you have created on to a floppy disk. This procedure is the same in all Windows® applications – you save a presentation, spreadsheet, database or graphic image in exactly the same way:

insert a floppy disk into drive A:

click on the File menu and a menu will open showing a list of options. Select Save As and a window will open.

8 Click in the File name: box and enter A:\CLAiT 2006 revised. Click on the Save button on the right of the window. You have now saved your presentation as a file called CLAiT 2006 revised. You may hear drive A: working during this process.

9 To run the slide show you have created, select the View menu and then click on the Slide Show option. The presentation will fill the screen and you can move between slides by clicking the left mouse button. When the presentation is over you will return to PowerPoint®. Alternatively select the Slide Show menu and the View show option.

10 You can close Microsoft PowerPoint® now by clicking on the File menu item and a menu will appear with a list of options. Click on the Exit option at the bottom of the list. An alternative way is to click on the Close button in the top right-hand corner of the application window.

Enhancing your presentation

Microsoft PowerPoint® 2003 has a variety of functions that allow you enhance your presentation. Many of these functions are similar to those available in other Microsoft® Office applications (e.g. Microsoft® Word) and include:

- slide orientation
- background colour
- bold, italics and underline
- alignment (justification) (left, right and centre)
- bullet points
- change fonts and character size
- indent text (i.e. promote and demote text)
- insert graphics (i.e. pictures and charts).

Orientation

The orientation of the slides can be either landscape or portrait and is selected by using the Page Setup function in the File menu. This also allows you to choose the orientation for printing the handouts, overhead slides and any notes.

Background

In a similar way you can apply a background colour to your slides through the Format menu and the Background option to open the Background window. This windows lets you choose the colour of the background and apply it to all slides or to an individual one. Good practice is to have one consistent background throughout the presentation.

Formatting

The Formatting toolbar (Figure 5.14) provides access to the functions that enable you to embolden text, write in italics, underline, align (justify), change fonts and alter the size of characters. Microsoft® Office provides a wide range of fonts and character sizes. If you click on the small down arrow alongside the font and size boxes on the toolbar, a menu of options will drop down. Click on the selected option. You can do this before you enter text so that the words you enter will appear in the font and size of your choice or you can change the text you have already entered.

To change already entered text you must first highlight it and then make your choice from the drop-down menus. The font and size of your text is critical for an effective

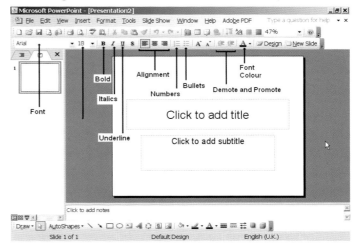

Figure 5.14 Formatting toolbar

presentation since you are seeking to capture your audience's attention. The font must be attractive and interesting to the audience but must not distract from the message you are presenting. The size of characters must be selected carefully to ensure that the slides are visible from the back row, and it is useful to test your slides in the room. It is also important to check the legibility of your slides since colour combinations that appear very effective on the screen can be poor when projected or printed on to an overhead projector slide.

Promote and demote text (Figure 5.14)

PowerPoint® provides tools to promote and demote text. This essentially means that you can structure your bullet points to enhance the main points and show the difference between main and subsidiary issues. By highlighting the text and selecting either the `promote` or `demote` icons on the Formatting toolbar you can add or remove an indent.

These options offer you a variety of ways to emphasize your message and draw the attention of your audience to the critical points. Fonts, character size, bold, italics and underlining all make text stand out.

Alignment (Justification)

Another useful function is alignment (justification). You can align your text so that it is left-, centre- or right-aligned. Left-aligned (justified) means that the text starts parallel to the left margin and is uneven on the right edge (i.e. the normal way text is presented). Right-aligned (justified) means that text is aligned parallel to the right margin and is uneven on the left. This is an unusual way to present text and is rarely used in a presentation. Centre-aligned (justified) means that the text is centred down the middle of the slide. In presentations, centred is frequently used to draw the audience's attention to the words. Left-aligned is also used since it is the most readable way of presenting text.

In a similar way to the use of bold, italics and underline, you can select the alignment (justification) before entering the text by clicking on the icon on the Formatting toolbar or you can choose to change the alignment (justification) later. Highlight the words you wish to align (justify) and click on the appropriate alignment (justification) icon. You can align (justify) a single word, a sentence, a paragraph, a slide or indeed the entire presentation or you can combine all three ways.

Bullet points

An important device in a presentation is the bullet point list. This is a simple list of items beginning with a symbol (e.g. numbers or geometric symbols) to differentiate it from the rest of the text. It is useful since during a presentation you will be using the slides to indicate the key points of the topic, which can be shown as individual bullet points.

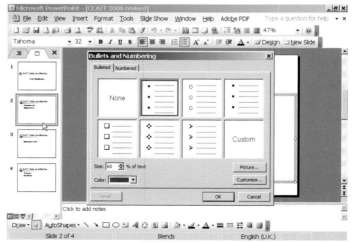

Figure 5.15 Bullets and Numbering

Microsoft PowerPoint® provides you with a selection of bullet points to choose from, accessed from the `Format` menu. By clicking on the `Format` menu, the drop-down menu is revealed and you can click on the `Bullets and Numbering` option to show the Bullets and Numbering window. Figure 5.15 shows some bullet symbol options and the `Picture` button provides access to a wider variety. The `Numbered` tab reveals styles of numbering that can be used as bullets. You need to explore the wide range of options.

The PowerPoint® templates assume you are using bullet points so will automatically provide lists. However, you can change the default setting by clicking on the `Format` menu, selecting `Bullets and Numbering` and choosing a bullet style. Your chosen style will then appear as you enter the text. You can alter the bullet at any time by highlighting the item and choosing a new style. You can change a single item or a whole list.

Illustrations

Pictures can make a presentation more interesting. To insert a picture into a slide you need to click on the `Insert` menu, highlight the `Picture` option and a second menu will appear to the right of `Insert`. This provides you with various choices. Clip Art images are provided with PowerPoint® to help you design presentations. `From File` allows you to select images you have created yourself or have bought. We will consider only the `Clip Art` option.

By clicking on `Clip Art` you open a library of pictures to select from (Figure 5.16). Figure 5.16 shows you the Clip Art task pane that is initially displayed. This allows you to search for the clip relevant to a particular topic.

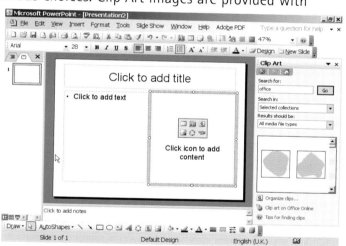

Figure 5.16 Clip Art

The pane display will change to show the results of your search (i.e. a series of images). To select a picture, you position the pointer on it to reveal a button with a down arrow. If you click on the button a short menu of options will appear. The top option (`Insert`) will place the image on your slide. However, at this point you may get an error message telling you the pictures are on another disk. This is the Microsoft® Office installation disk and if you have it you need to place this disk in the CD-ROM drive.

The image will either be placed at the cursor or, if your slide has no

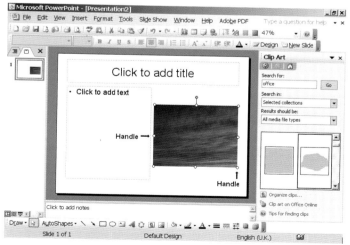

Figure 5.17 Position image

cursor showing, in the middle of the slide. A frame surrounds the image and, if you move the mouse pointer over the image, it changes to a star shape (Figure 5.17). By holding down the left mouse button when it is over the image you can drag it around the slide and position it. You fix the image by releasing the mouse button and clicking away from the graphic. However, if you click on the graphic image again, the frame will reappear and you can move it to a new position.

An alternative approach is to select a slide layout that includes pictures and to click on the Clip Art icon. The Select Picture window (Figure 5.18) will appear which allows you to search for a Clip Art image and insert it in the way described above.

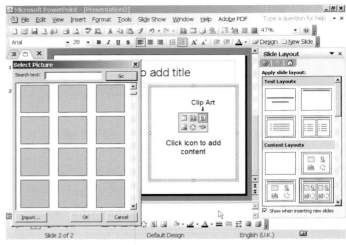

Figure 5.18 Select Picture

Lines and Drawings

Microsoft PowerPoint® offers functions that enable you to add lines and drawn shapes such as Rectangles, Ovals and AutoShapes (i.e. many different outlines). These are available on the

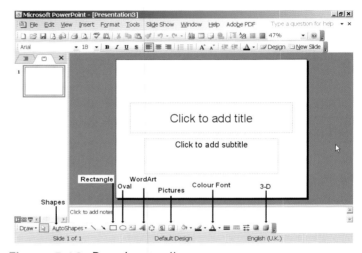

Figure 5.19 Drawing toolbar

Drawing toolbar. In addition you can shade objects or fill the shapes with colour using the Fill Color and Line Color functions. You can colour text, insert 3-dimensional shapes and add special effects to text (e.g. WordArt). Figure 5.19 illustrates the Drawing toolbar functions.

Exercise 42

Enhancing your presentation

1 Load Microsoft PowerPoint® using either the All programs menu or the PowerPoint icon on the desktop.

2 In the Open section of the Getting Started task pane there should be a list of files. Double-click on the CLAiT 2006 revised file shown in the list. If the file is not shown

then click on the $\boxed{\text{More}}$ option to reveal the Open window and locate the floppy disk. Click on the CLAiT 2006 revised file shown on the disk, but you must have inserted your floppy disk which contains the presentation file. The CLAiT 2006 revised presentation will be loaded.

3   During this exercise you are going to use the various PowerPoint® functions to enhance your presentation. The first step is to emphasize the titles on each slide and in particular on the opening one. On the initial slide, change the title font to Algerian (or another you feel has impact), the character size to 48 and embolden it. You need to highlight the title and then select the font, character size and the bold option. Once you have made your selections, simply click away from the highlighting to see the changes made. You may need to widen the text box to allow the title to appear on a single line.

4   Next, change each title on the other slides to Algerian but with character size 44.

5   The slide bullet points were produced using the default options so you need to change them to a bullet symbol of your choice. Systematically highlight each list of bullet points and select another bullet symbol (i.e. $\boxed{\text{Format}}$ menu and $\boxed{\text{Bullets and Numbering}}$ option). It is worth exploring the different options to identify one you like and feel is appropriate.

6   Now change all the other text to a font and character size different from the title (e.g. Arial). Explore the different options until you find a font that looks good. Remember to highlight the text and use the font and character options on the Formatting toolbar.

7   Centre your bullet points (e.g. using the alignment (justification) icons on the Formatting toolbar) and check to see if you feel this is an appropriate way of presenting the text. If you do not like the way it appears, change the alignment (justification) to left-justified.

8   Insert a graphic image on the opening slide to provide interest. Remember to move to this slide by using the scroll bar and then select the $\boxed{\text{Insert}}$ menu, highlight the $\boxed{\text{Picture}}$ option and click on $\boxed{\text{Clip Art}}$. Try to pick an image appropriate to the study of an information and communication qualification. The image will need to be moved around the slide until you place it in an appropriate spot.

9   While the image is enclosed within its frame, placing the mouse pointer over an edge will change its shape to a double-headed arrow. If you hold down the left mouse button you can change the shape of the picture. Try to alter the size of the image.

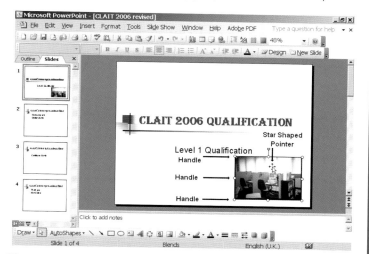

Figure 5.20 **Inserting a picture**

You will need to pull two sides or the corner to keep it symmetrical. You can move the whole image by placing your pointer over the picture until it changes shape into a star (Figure 5.20). You can now drag the image to a new location.

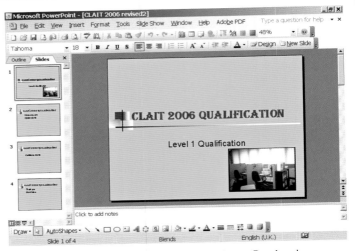

Figure 5.21 CLAiT 2006 Qualifications Revised

10 Change the background colour of all the slides (Format menu, Background option and Background window). Use the Preview option in the Background window to explore the different colours. Figure 5.21 shows the results of my changes.

11 Spellcheck your presentation (Tools menu and Spelling option).

12 Save the presentation you have created on to a floppy disk. This procedure is the same in all Windows® applications – you save a presentation, spreadsheet, database or graphic image in exactly the same way:
insert a floppy disk into drive A:
click on the File menu and a menu will open showing a list of options. Select Save As and a window will open.

13 Click in the File name: box and enter A:\CLAiT 2006 revised2. Click on the Save button on the right of the window. You have now saved your presentation as a file called CLAiT 2006 revised2. You may hear drive A: working during this process.

14 To run the slide show you have created, select the View menu and then click on the Slide show option. The presentation will fill the screen and you can move between slides by clicking the left mouse button. When the presentation is over you will return to PowerPoint®. Alternatively select the Slide Show menu and the View show option.

15 You can close Microsoft PowerPoint® now by clicking on the File menu and a menu will appear with a list of options. Click on the Exit option at the bottom of the list. An alternative way is to click on the Close button in the top right-hand corner of the application window.

Headers and Footers

With Microsoft PowerPoint® 2003 you can add headers and footers to your slides in a similar way to other Microsoft® Office applications. This is very useful in a presentation since you can automatically date and number your slides as well as add any standard comments. As part of the assessment you will be asked to identify your slides by inserting your name and study centre number in the footer. To add a header and footer, select the View menu and the Header and Footer option. This reveals a window (Figure 5.22) in which the Slide tab provides you with options to select the date and time, which are automatically updated, to number your slides and to add text as a footer. The other tab, Notes and Handouts , lets you add headers and other footers to your handouts and notes.

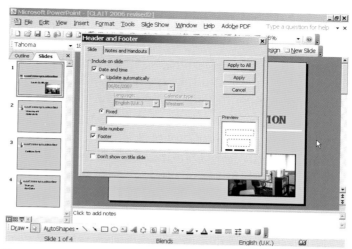

Figure 5.22 Header and Footer

Printing your presentation

So far, we have considered how to create a presentation which appears on the computer screen or which could be projected using a data or video projector. However, in many cases you will want to print your slides to provide a set of handouts or to be able to project them on an overhead projector (OHP), which involves printing them on transparencies. There are different types of transparencies depending on your printer (i.e. laser and inkjet). It is important to check that you are using the correct type since using

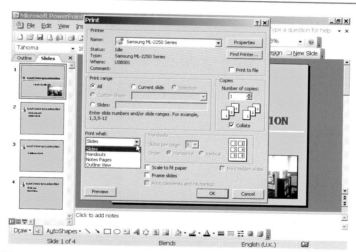

Figure 5.23 Print what

the wrong one may result in poor slides or even damage your printer.

To print your slides you need to click on the File menu and the Print option. This will reveal the Print window (Figure 5.23). The Print window is divided into areas. These are:

1 Printer – this shows you the name of the printer that will be used.
2 Print range – there are a variety of options which you select by clicking on the radio buttons (i.e. All , Current slide , Selection , Custom Show and Slides). The All option prints the whole presentation. Current slide prints only the slide being viewed at that moment. Selection prints the area of the slide which has been highlighted, and Slides allows you to select some of the slides by entering their numbers in the text box alongside.
3 Copies – this allows you to print more than one copy and to collate them.
4 Print what – by clicking on the small down arrow at the end of the box, a list of options is revealed allowing you to print slides (transparencies), handouts, notes pages and outline view. Figure 5.23 shows the different options which you select by clicking.

The different Print what options are:

- slides – prints the images on to transparencies and paper.
- handouts – prints the slides on to paper so that each person in your audience has a copy of your presentation to take away. If you select handouts you will also be able to choose how many slides to present on a page and in some cases you can leave space for notes.
- notes pages – you can add notes to your slides so that the audience gets a copy of the slides and your speaking notes.
- outline view – this is a list of all the text on the whole presentation. It is useful to help you check that you have not left out any important points.

Exercise 43

Printing

1 Load Microsoft PowerPoint® using either the All programs menu or the PowerPoint icon on the desktop.

2 In the Open section of the Getting Started task pane there may be a list of files with CLAiT 2006 Revised2 amongst them. Double-click on the CLAiT 2006 revised2 file shown in the list (Figure 5.24). If it is not listed then click on the More option to reveal the Open window. Locate the floppy disk files and open CLAiT 2006 revised2. You must have inserted your floppy disk into the drive. The presentation will be loaded.

3 You are going to print your slides and produce audience notes (i.e. a handout).

4 Print your slides on to paper initially to check how they look.

Transparency film is quite expensive so it is worth checking before you waste it. Transparencies are loaded into the printer in the same way as paper but make sure you are using the correct type of transparency for the printer (e.g. inkjet or laser transparencies). It can damage your printer if you use the wrong type. Read the instructions on the transparency box as you may need to insert them in a particular way.

5 All printers have default settings and you will be using these to print. PowerPoint® defaults to printing slides as landscape images but handouts, notes pages and outlines as portrait images. Defaults can be changed.

6 Print your slides (File menu, Print , change Print what to Slides (it may already be set to this option) and OK button). The printer defaults to printing all your

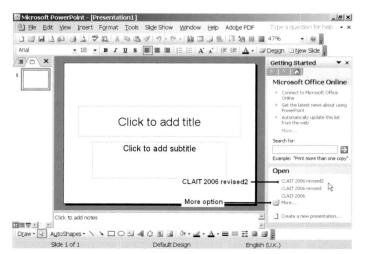

Figure 5.24 Open presentation

slides so you do not need to change the Print range settings. There is also a Preview button on the bottom left of the window which will show you how the slides will appear.

7 Print handouts (File menu, Print , change Print what to Handouts and OK button). The printer defaults to printing six thumbnail images on each page and, therefore, since your presentation comprises four slides, four thumbnail images of the slides will be printed. If you look to the right of the Print dialog box you will see how the thumbnails will appear. There is also a Preview button on the bottom left of the window which will show you how the handouts will appear.

8 Print the notes pages (File menu, Print , change Print what to Notes Pages and OK button). In this case your presentation is printed on four sheets with a copy of the slide at the top and a space below for any notes you may have added.

9 Print outline view (File menu, Print , change Print what to Outline View and OK button). The outline is printed on a single sheet.

10 Take a moment to consider the different printer outputs. You can close Microsoft PowerPoint® now by clicking on the File menu and a menu will appear with a list of options. Click on the Exit option at the bottom of the list. An alternative way is to click on the Close button in the top right-hand corner of the application window.

Master slides

There is a special type of slide called a master slide which allows you to define the fonts, character sizes, colour and layout that will be used throughout your presentation. This is very helpful in ensuring that you provide a consistent appearance for your slides. Anything you place on the master slide will appear on all the slides.

When you start a new presentation you create a master slide by selecting the View menu, highlighting the Master option and clicking on Slide Master . The master slide appears (Figure 5.25). In some cases a small window called Slide Master View will also appear – drag it towards the toolbars and you will see it form a new toolbar. To define fonts, click on the area and then change the font, character sizes and other features (e.g. insert picture). These features will be reproduced throughout the presentation.

Once you have defined your master, go ahead with designing each slide and you will see the standard features appear on each of them. If you want to make a change, then by altering the master slide you can change all the slides.

Exercise 44

Master slide

1 Load Microsoft PowerPoint® using either the `All programs` menu or the `PowerPoint` icon on the desktop.

2 Select `Create a new presentation` from the Open section of the Getting Started task pane. This will open the New Presentation task pane. Click on the `Blank presentation` option in the New section of the task pane. A title slide will appear in the working area and the Slide Layout task pane will appear.

3 Select the `File` menu and the `Page Setup` option to set the slide orientation to landscape.

4 Select the `View` menu and highlight the `Master` option to reveal an additional menu. Select the `Slide Master` option to reveal the outline of the master slide (Figure 5.25). A small window called Slide Master View may appear. Drag the window towards the toolbars and it will form a new one.

5 In order to change or add borders to the top text box you need to right-click in the placeholder and select the `Format Placeholder` option. This opens the Format AutoShape window (Figure 5.26). Change the line colour to black by clicking on the down arrow at the end of the C̲olor: box and on the `OK` button. You will see that the title placeholder will be enclosed in a black rectangle.

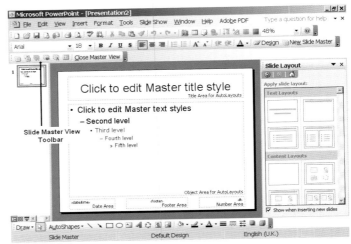

Figure 5.25 Master slide

6 You can amend the master layout by left-clicking within the text placeholders. Change the text of the title area to Arial, character size 36 and bold. The title should be centred.

7 The first-level bullet should be Arial, character size 24 and left-aligned.

8 The second-level bullet

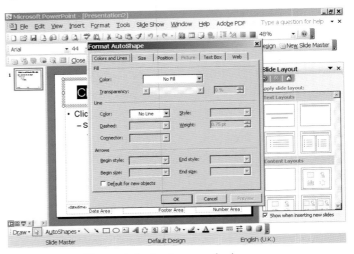

Figure 5.26 Format Autoshape window

should be Arial, character size 20, left-aligned and indented from the first-level bullet. The bullets should be separated by one character space. Delete the other bullet levels.

9 Create a footer showing your name, automatic date and time. The slide number should be displayed on the bottom right of the slide (i.e. View menu and Header and Footer option).

10 Change the background colour to one you like (e.g. cyan) by selecting the Format menu and the Background option to reveal the Background window. Click on the down arrow to reveal colours, select your one then click on the Apply to All button. You will see the background colour change.

11 Save the presentation you have created on to a floppy disk. This procedure is the same in all Windows® applications – you save a presentation, spreadsheet, database or graphic image in exactly the same way:

insert a floppy disk into drive A:

click on the File menu and a menu will open showing a list of options. Select Save As and a window will open.

12 Click in the File name: box and enter A:\Master. Click on the Save button on the right of the window. You have now saved your presentation as a file called Master. You may hear drive A: working during this process.

More Practice

Activity 1

Sell a product

1 Load Microsoft PowerPoint® using either the All programs menu or the PowerPoint icon on the desktop.

2 You are going to develop a presentation to sell the Wireless Laser Printer (WLP). PowerPoint® is often used for sales presentations.

3 Create a master slide by selecting the View menu, highlight the Master option and choose the Slide Master option.

4 Select the landscape orientation using the File menu and Page Setup option.

5 Select the font Tahoma, character size 40 and bold for the title placeholder at the top of the slide. Centre the title.

6 Select the font Times New Roman, character size 36 and italics for the first-level bullet point. The bullets are left-aligned. Delete the other bullet levels – this presentation only employs level 1 bullets. Choose a bullet character.

7 Enter your name, automatic date and time in the footer (View menu and

Header and Footer option). The slide number should be shown on the bottom right-hand side of the slide.

8 The background colour should be white (select the Format menu and Background option).

9 Save the presentation using the filename Sales.

10 Create slide 1 by selecting the View menu and choosing the Normal option. This will open the title template in the working area. Insert the title Wireless Laser Printer and select a Clip Art image below the title placeholder (i.e. Insert menu, highlight Pictures and the Clip Art option).

11 Insert a new slide (Insert, New slide and select a template with title and text areas).

12 Insert Wireless Laser Printer on the title bar and then add the following bullets:
   1   No Cables
   2   Radio Communication
   3   Under £200

13 Insert a new slide Insert, New slide and select a template with title and text areas).

14 Insert Wireless Laser Printer as the title and the following bullets in italics:
   1   20 pages a minute
   2   600 dots per inch
   3   Quiet Operation
   4   Design Life 100,000 pages
   5   3 year warranty

15 Insert a new slide (Insert, New slide and select a template with title and text areas).

16 Insert Wireless Laser Printer as the title and the following bullets in italics:
   1   Acme Printer Company
   2   234 New Way, Birmingham
   3   info@acmestar.co.uk
   4   Your name, Sales Representative.

17 SpellCheck your presentation.

18 Save the presentation you have created on to a floppy disk with the filename Sales (File menu and Save option).

19 Print your slides and a handout with all the slides on one page (File , Print option and OK button).

20 To run the slide show you have created, select the View menu and then click on the Slide Show option. The presentation will fill the screen and you can move between slides by clicking the left mouse button.

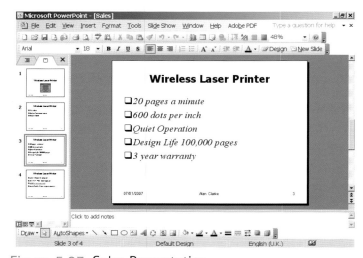

Figure 5.27 Sales Presentation

When the presentation is over you will return to PowerPoint®. Alternatively select the Slide Show menu and the View show option. Figure 5.27 shows slide 3.

21 You can close Microsoft PowerPoint® now by clicking on the File menu and a menu will appear with a list of options. Click on the Exit option at the bottom of the list. An alternative way is to click on the Close button in the top right-hand corner of the application window.

Activity 2

Amend a presentation

1 Load Microsoft PowerPoint® using either the All programs menu or the PowerPoint icon on the desktop.

2 In the Open section of the Getting Started task pane there should be a list of files. Double-click on the Sales file shown in the list. The Sales presentation will be loaded, but you must have inserted your floppy disk which contains the presentation file.

3 Change the orientation of the presentation from landscape to portrait (File menu and Page Setup option).

4 Change the text on slide 3 from 20 pages a minute to 25 pages a minute.

5 Add a line below the bullet point text on slides 2, 3 and 4 (Line icon on Drawing toolbar).

6 Save the presentation with the new filename Sales Revised (File menu and Save As).

7 Print the four slides as handouts with four slides on a page (File menu, Print option, Print what section and OK button).

8 Change the order of the slides so that slide 3 becomes slide 2 (View menu and Slide Sorter option). Figure 5.28 illustrates the process. Compare the appearance of the slides in portrait orientation with your earlier presentations in landscape.

9 Print the outline view of the presentation with your name as a footer for this printout (i.e. View menu, Header and Footer option and Notes and Handouts tab).

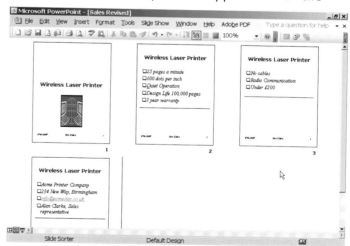

10 Save the amended presentation as the file Sales Revised2 (File menu and Save As).

11 To run the slide show you have created, select the View menu and then click on the Slide Show

Figure 5.28 Order of slides

option. The presentation will fill the screen and you can move between slides by clicking the left mouse button. When the presentation is over you will return to PowerPoint®. Alternatively select the Slide Show menu and the View show option.

12 You can close Microsoft PowerPoint® now by clicking on the File menu and a menu will appear with a list of options. Click on the Exit option at the bottom of the list. An

alternative way is to click on the Close button in the top right-hand corner of the application window.

Activity 3

Explain a hobby

1 Load Microsoft PowerPoint® using either the All programs menu or the PowerPoint icon on the desktop.

2 You are going to develop a presentation to explain why collecting postcards is interesting and fun. PowerPoint® is often used to explain a subject to an audience.

3 Create a master slide by selecting the View menu, highlight the Master option and choose the Slide Master option.

4 Select the landscape orientation using the File menu and Page Setup option.

5 Select the font Times New Roman, character size 44 and bold for the title placeholder at the top of the slide. Centre the title.

6 Select the font Arial, character size 36 and italics for the first level bullet point. The bullets are left aligned. Choose a bullet character. Delete the other bullet levels.

7 Enter your name, an automatic date and time in the footer (View menu and Header and Footer option). The slide number should be shown on the bottom right-hand side of the slide.

8 The background colour should be yellow (select the Format menu and Background option).

9 Save the presentation using the filename Collecting.

10 Create slide 1 by selecting the View menu and choosing the Normal option. This will open the title template in the working area. Change the title template by selecting the template that shows a title placeholder at the top of the slide and text placeholder below from the Slide Layout task pane on the right of the display (Format menu and Slide Layout option). Insert the title Postcard Collecting and then add the following bullets to the text placeholder:

1 Postcards are over 100 years old
2 1896 in Great Britain
3 Thousands of collectors
4 All ages and backgrounds
5 Many different themes e.g. local history

11 Insert a new slide (Insert , New slide) and select a template with title and text areas. Insert Postcard Collecting in bold as the title and the following bullets:

1 Wide price range
2 From 10p to many pounds
3 Photographic to artist-drawn cards
4 Local history
5 Many books to explain the hobby

12 Insert a new slide (Insert , New slide) and select a template with title and text areas. Insert Postcard Collecting in bold as the title and the following bullets:

1 Many collectors' fairs
2 Postcard clubs
3 Monthly magazine
4 Dealers
5 Websites

13 Insert a new slide (Insert , New slide) and select a template with title and text areas. Insert Postcard Collecting in bold as the title and the following bullets:

  1 Visit the postcard display
  2 Ask any questions

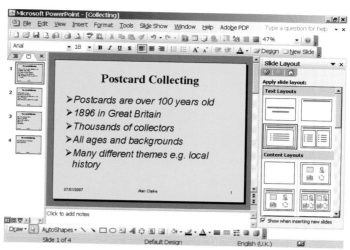

Figure 5.29 Collecting Presentation

14 Spellcheck your presentation.
Figure 5.29 shows the first slide of the collecting presentation.

16 Save the presentation you have created on to a floppy disk:

insert a floppy disk into drive A:

click on the File menu and a menu will open showing a list of options. Select Save and the Save As window will open.

16 Click in the File name: box and enter A:\Collecting. Click on the Save button on the right of the window. You have now saved your presentation as a file called Collecting. You may hear the drive A: working during this process.

17 Print your slides and a handout (File , Print option and OK button).

18 To run the slide show you have created select the View menu and then click on the Slide Show option. The presentation will fill the screen and you can move between slides by clicking the left mouse button. When the presentation is over you will return to PowerPoint®. Alternatively select the Slide Show menu and the View show option.

19 You can close Microsoft PowerPoint® now by clicking on the File menu and a menu will appear with a list of options. Click on the Exit option at the bottom of the list. An alternative way is to click on the Close button in the top right-hand corner of the application window.

SUMMARY

1 **Load Microsoft PowerPoint®** Use either the `Start` button and the `All Programs` menu or double-click on the `PowerPoint` icon on Windows® desktop.

2 **Close** Click on the `File` menu item and the `Exit` option or click on the `Close` button in the top right-hand corner of the application window.

3 **Save a file on a floppy disk** Insert a floppy disk into drive A: and click on the `File` menu and `Save`. Select the drive (Floppy disk A:) and enter the filename. Having saved a file once, you can update it by clicking on the `File` menu and `Save`, without the Save As window appearing again. This simply overwrites the original file.

4 **Start a new presentation** Select `Create a new presentation` from the Getting Started task pane on the right of the display to reveal the New Presentation task pane. Select `Blank Presentation` in the New section.

5 **Select new layout** Select a layout by positioning your pointer on the desired template in the Slide Layout task pane to reveal a button with a down arrow. Click on the button to reveal a menu. Select `Insert New Slide`.

6 **Delete text** You have two keys (i.e. `backspace` and `delete`) which both work from the position of your cursor. `Backspace` key – this removes text, character by character, to the left of the cursor position. `Delete` key – this removes text, character by character, to the right of the cursor position.

   There is also `Undo` and `Redo`. `Undo` removes the last action you have undertaken, while `Redo` carries out the actions removed by `Undo`. `Undo` can be used to remove text that has just been typed.

7 **Select design template** Select the `Format` menu and the `Slide Design` option to open the Slide Design task pane on the right of the display. Choose a design.

8 **Spellcheck** Select the `Tools` menu and the `Spelling` option.

9 **Change slide order** Select the `View` menu and the `Slide Sorter` option.

10 **Insert graphics** If you have used a graphics template then you need to click on the `Insert Clip Art` icon on the slide to reveal the Select Pictures window. Search for a suitable image.
   Select the `Insert` menu, highlight the `Picture` option to reveal another menu of options. Select the `Clip Art` item to open the Clip Art pane. You may see an error message telling you the pictures are on another disk. This is the Microsoft® Office installation disk and you need to place this disk, if you have it, in the CD-ROM drive.

11 **Move the image** Place the mouse pointer over the image and the pointer will change (i.e. to a star) to indicate that the picture can be dragged by holding down the left mouse button.

12 **Change the font, character size and text characteristics (bold, italics and underline)** Highlight the text you want to change. Change the font and/or character size by

selecting the item in the drop-down list on the Formatting toolbar. Change the text characteristics (i.e. bold, italics and underline) by selecting the icon on the Formatting toolbar.

13 **Change the text alignment (justification)** Highlight the text you want to change. Select the alignment (justification) option by clicking on the icon on the Formatting toolbar.

14 **Replace text** Select the `Edit` menu and the `Replace` option. The Replace window appears. Enter the text you want to replace in the Find what: box and the replacement text in the Replace with: box.

15 **Bullets** Select the `Format` menu and the `Bullets and Numbering` option. The Bullets and Numbering window gives you a range of styles to choose from.

16 **Orientation** Select the `File` menu and the `Page Setup` option.

17 **Background** Select the `Format` menu and the `Background` option to open the Background window.

18 **Header and Footer** Select the `View` menu and the `Header and Footer` option.

19 **Printing** Select the `File` menu and the `Print` option.

20 **Masters** Select the `View` menu, highlight the `Master` option and click on `Slide Master`, `Handout Master` or `Notes Master`.

Chapter 6

Unit 6

e-Image Creation

This chapter will help you to use a drawing package to:

- identify and use appropriate software correctly in accordance with laws and guidelines
- use basic file-handling techniques for the software
- download digital pictures from a digital camera
- import, crop and resize images
- enter, amend and resize text
- manipulate and format page items
- manage and print artwork.

Assessment

This unit does not assume any previous experience of using a computer. However, you may find it useful to have completed Unit 1 (File Management and e-Document Production). You will be assessed through a practical realistic assignment which is designed to allow you to demonstrate your knowledge and skills against each objective. Your tutor can provide you with more guidance.

Drawing applications

There are many computer applications concerned with the production and manipulation of images. You can capture them using digital cameras and scanners, purchase collections known as Clip Art or simply create your own from scratch. Almost anyone can create pictures using a computer drawing package. Computer pictures are called graphics. Windows® has a drawing application built into it called Paint (Figure 6.1) which provides you with tools to draw lines, curves, circles and rectangles as well as to add colour to your images and change the orientation of the image. Microsoft® Word has built-in drawing tools (select the View menu, highlight the Toolbars option and click on Drawing).

There are two types of graphic images:

- bitmaps
- vectors.

A bitmap image is composed of dots called pixels. The more pixels in a given amount of space (e.g. a square inch) the clearer the image or the higher the resolution of the picture. Each pixel is associated with the number of colours that can be displayed. An 8-bit image can use 256 colours while a 24-bit image can use 16.7 million colours.

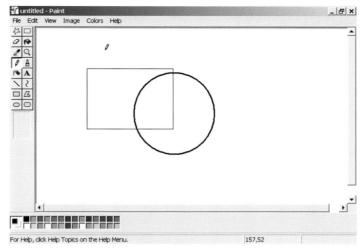

Figure 6.1 Microsoft® Paint

Vector images are defined by mathematical formulae rather than pixels. This defines the start and finish of the line and allows it to be easily changed. Vector images can be resized and still stay in perfect proportion. Although you can change a bitmap image, it will often distort if the change is too radical. However, bitmaps can probably show more detail than vector images since every pixel of the image is employed.

This chapter is based on CorelDRAW® 10, a professional vector drawing package with numerous useful tools for working with bitmaps and vectors.

File formats

Graphics created by a painting or drawing package are stored on the computer as files. There is a variety of file formats that are used to represent graphics. The main ones are:

- JPEG – Joint Photographic Expert Group is a bitmap format which is used extensively on the World Wide Web. Files which are in JPEG format are shown with an extension .jpeg or .jpg
- GIF – Graphics Interchange Format is a bitmap format which is also used extensively on the World Wide Web. Files in GIF format are shown by the extension .gif
- TIFF – Tagged Image File Format is a bitmap format widely used in the graphics industry. Files in this format are shown by the extension .tif
- Windows® bitmap – this is the standard format for graphics in the Windows operating system. Files in this format are shown by the extension .bmp
- Windows® Metafile – this is the Windows vector graphics standard format. Files in this format are shown by the extension .wmf
- Encapsulated Postscript – this is a vector file format which is shown by the extension .eps.

There are many other graphic file formats which have been designed for specific tasks. It is possible to convert from one to another but in some cases this will affect the quality of the image.

CorelDRAW

Figure 6.2 shows the CorelDRAW application. When it is loaded, a window overlays the application offering you a variety of choices in the form of six icons. These are:

- New Graphic – to start a new image
- Open Last Edited – to allow you to continue working on the last image
- Open Graphic – to open an existing image
- Template – to open a standard template
- CorelTUTOR – to access a tutorial on how to use CorelDRAW
- What's New? – provides you with an overview of CorelDRAW.

You should select the
New Graphic icon (Figure 6.2) and the overlay window will close, revealing the main application display (Figure 6.3). The centre of the display shows the document area in which you can create a new graphic image. On the left is the toolbox containing a variety of the drawing tools, on the right is the colour palette which allows you to select

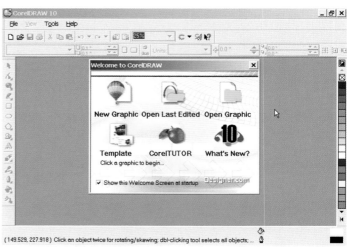

Figure 6.2 CorelDRAW

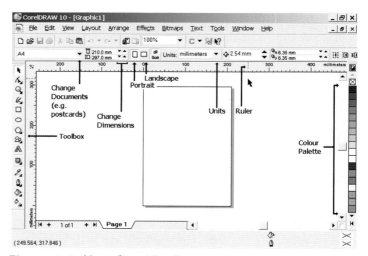

Figure 6.3 New Graphic display

drawing and painting colours and on the top are the menu and toolbars. The nearest toolbar to the working area shows the size of the document that you are creating. In Figure 6.3 it shows an A4 page. The toolbars in CorelDRAW change according to the action you are undertaking, which can be confusing initially.

Exercise 45

Explore CorelDRAW

1 CorelDRAW is opened either by selecting the `Start` button, highlighting the `ALL Programs` option and clicking on the `CorelDRAW` item or by double-clicking on the `CorelDRAW` icon on the Windows® desktop.

2 Select the `New Graphics` icon.

3 Explore the different menus and toolbars.

4 Explore the use of the drawing tools. Change the size of the drawing document using the down arrow on the toolbar near to the A4 box (left-hand side of the toolbar).

5 Select the `File` menu and locate the `Import`, `Print` and `Save` options.

6 Move your mouse pointer across the document and observe the rulers. You should see that the pointer's position is shown on each ruler. This is intended to help you position items on the page.

7 Locate the colour palette on the right-hand side of window.

8 Continue to explore until you are comfortable with finding your way around the application

9 Close the application either by selecting the `File` menu and the `Exit` option or by clicking on the `Close` button in the top right-hand corner of the window.

New image

When you select the `New Graphic` icon, the default document is an A4 page. This can be changed by using the arrow keys on the toolbar (Figure 6.3). You can select from a wide range of different documents (e.g. different page sizes, envelopes and postcards), change the actual size of the page, choose either landscape or portrait orientation and even alter the units of measurement of the page size (e.g. millimetres or inches).

Importing images

Pictures can be provided by:

- scanning images
- taking pictures using a digital camera
- selecting from collections of Clip Art
- drawing and painting your own graphics.

CorelDRAW can work with images from any source. Clip Art collections of many thousands of images can be bought and used. If you have access to a scanner or digital camera, you can use these resources to produce pictures. CorelDRAW can take these images in order to enhance and extend them. It is possible for the application to add captions to a digital picture explaining the different parts of the image.

CorelDRAW provides a straightforward way of importing images that allows you to:

- crop images (i.e. cut away parts of the picture you do not need)
- resize images
- precisely position imported images on your artwork.

To import an image you need to select the File menu and the Import option. This reveals the Import window (Figure 6.4). The first step to importing an image is to locate the folder in which it is stored on your computer. Do this by clicking on the down arrow at the end of the Look in: box which will reveal a list of drives on which the folder could be stored.

If you select C: (the computer's internal hard disk), the working area will be filled with all the folders stored on that disk. To see what is in each folder, you need to click on it and it will open to show you its contents. This could be more folders and again you need to click on them to reveal their contents.

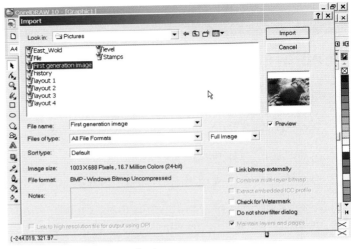

Figure 6.4 Import window

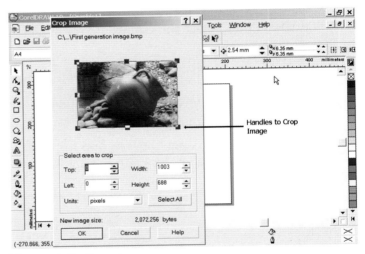

Figure 6.5 Crop image

If you click on A:, the working area will show you the contents of the floppy disk. By clicking on D: you access the CD-ROM drive and if a CD-ROM is inserted you will be able to see its contents. Clip Art is often distributed on CD-ROMs since they can hold hundreds and in some cases thousands of images.

Figure 6.4 shows a folder called Pictures which is stored on the hard disk (i.e. C:). These images are the result of taking digital photographs, using screen capture software and drawing applications. It is good practice to set the Files of type to All File Formats using the down arrow button near the box. This will show you all the files available whereas other options will only reveal files of the type selected. This can sometimes confuse because it can seem that the image you want has disappeared.

To identify the image the window has a preview feature. If you click in the Preview radio button (a tick will appear), you can see each file that you highlight. Figure 6.4 shows an image of a garden water feature. You can review the images until you find the one you want. When you have identified the correct picture, you click on the Import button.

In the middle of the Import window is a small box which in Figure 6.4 has the words Full Image in it. The down arrow next to the box, if clicked on, will reveal all the options. These are:

- Full Image – this is the most straightforward option since the chosen image is imported unchanged.

- Crop – this opens a further dialog box (window) to allow you to identify what parts of the image you want to import (Figure 6.5). It provides you with a preview of the image.

- Resample – this lets you change the resolution of an image and reduce its size (Figure 6.6).

The Crop and Resample windows enable you to manipulate the image after you have chosen to import it and, when this has been done, the image is inserted into the document by clicking on the OK button.

When importing the image into the main application area, you need to choose where to place it. This is done using a changed mouse pointer which allows you to position the top left-hand corner of the image precisely. Figure 6.7 shows the positioning of an image. The positioning pointer is placed at the desired point and the mouse button clicked. The image will now appear enclosed in a frame with a number of black squares (called handles). If the mouse pointer is placed on the handles it changes to a double-headed arrow. If the mouse button is held down after the pointer has changed shape, you can drag the shape of the image around. The enclosure is removed by clicking away from the image and can be replaced by clicking on the image.

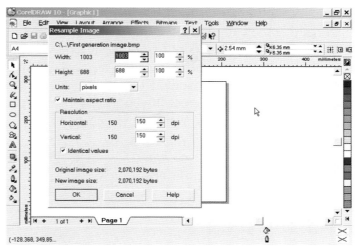

Figure 6.6 Resample image

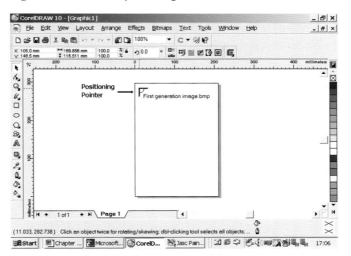

Figure 6.7 Positioning imported image

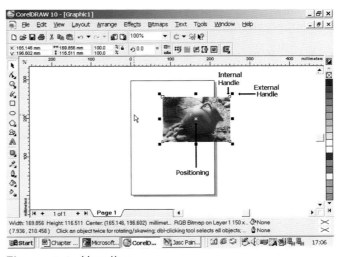

Figure 6.8 Handles

Figure 6.8 shows external and internal handles. Internal handles are located at each corner of the image and let you skew the image using the mouse pointer which changes shape to that of a large arrowhead. Further out from the internal handles is a larger rectangle which has external handles with which you can change the size of the image. At the centre of the image is a cross. If you place your mouse pointer over this cross it turns into a star. By holding down the mouse pointer, you can move the image to new positions.

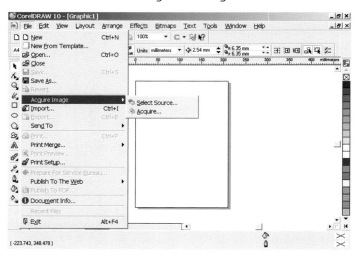

Digital camera

Digital cameras are very useful for capturing images. Pictures taken with a digital camera can be imported directly into CorelDRAW by using the `File` menu and highlighting the `Acquire Image` option to reveal a short menu. Select `Select Source` to open the Select Source window in order to pick the digital camera and then `Acquire` to choose the image from the camera (Figure 6.10). The camera must be linked to the computer and this is normally achieved using a cable supplied with the camera which plugs into the USB port on the computer.

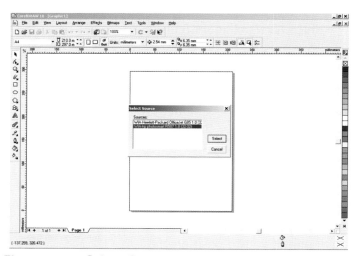

Figure 6.10 Select Source

Digital cameras are usually provided with software so that pictures can be transferred into a folder on a computer. Images can then be imported from this folder into CorelDRAW as an alternative to directly selecting the pictures from the camera.

Figure 6.11 shows the Get Pictures window which opens when the `Acquire` option is selected. It allows you to highlight images to import into CorelDRAW. They are imported when you click on the `Get Pictures` button in the CorelDRAW working area.

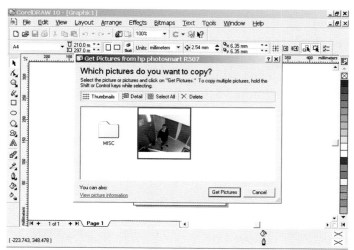

Figure 6.11 Imported digital image

Exercise 46

Importing an image

1 CorelDRAW is opened either by selecting the Start button, highlighting All Programs and clicking on the CorelDRAW item or by double-clicking on the CorelDRAW icon on the Windows® desktop.

2 Select the New Graphics icon.

3 Select the File menu and Import option to reveal the Import window. Identify the folder in which the images are stored and use the preview facility to review the images. Select the Crop option and double-click on the picture's filename. The image will appear in the Crop window (Figure 6.5).

Before  **After**

Figure 6.12 **Cropping**

4 Use the enclosure handles to crop the chosen image. Figure 6.12 shows before and after cropping. You can use the handles for large crops and then Select area to crop for precise detail.

5 When you are ready, click on the OK button and the positioning pointer will appear on the document for you to position the image precisely. Locate the picture in the centre but in the top

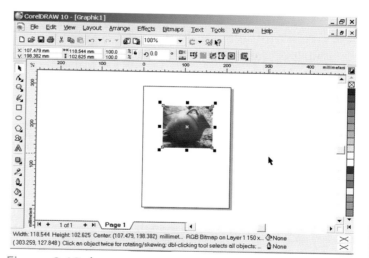

Figure 6.13 **Image**

half of the page and click. The image of the water feature or your own picture will be placed on the document. In some cases the image will be larger than the page and you will need to use the handles to resize the picture to fit the page.

6 Figure 6.13 shows the image on the document.

7 By clicking on the centre cross you will see the handles change shape. If you place your mouse pointer on these handles it too will change shape (i.e. a partial circle with arrows on each end or parallel arrows facing opposite directions). The partial circle will allow you to rotate the image while the parallel arrows enable you to skew the image.

Experiment with the two pointers by holding down the mouse button to move the image.

8 Skew the image. Turn it upside down and at right angles (Figure 6.14).

9 When the image is enclosed in its handles it is possible to copy or cut it using the functions on the Edit menu and the options Cut, Copy and Paste. These are also available on the Standard toolbar.

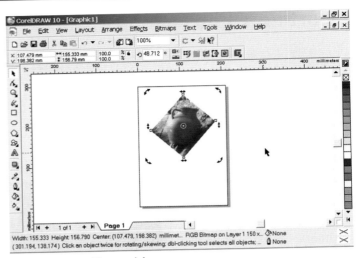

Figure 6.14 Skewed image

10 Select the Edit menu and the Copy option and then Paste. If you observe carefully you will see the image flicker. You now have two images of the garden water feature, one placed precisely on top of the other, so drag the top image down the page by clicking on the image and holding down the mouse button. You can paste as many copies of the image as you want.

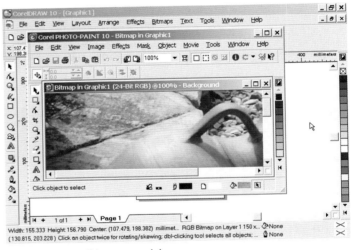

Figure 6.15 Bitmapped Image

11 Delete the first image – you do this by clicking on it to enclose it and then either select the Edit menu and the Delete option or you can press the keyboard's Delete key.

12 An alternative approach to manipulation is to use the Arrange menu and the Transformations option. This provides access to the Transformation window which is positioned alongside the graphic image. Explore the options (e.g. mirror to produce an Edit Bitmap Image mirror image). To remove the window click on the cross in the top right-hand corner of the window.

13 Bitmapped images can also be edited. Click on the right mouse button to reveal a menu and select the Edit Bitmap option (Figure 6.15). This enables you to undertake detailed changes to the image.

14 Experiment with changing the image.

15 Save the image by selecting the File menu and the Save option. This will reveal the Save Drawing window. You need to decide where you will save your image. This is done by clicking on the down arrow near the Save In: box to reveal a list of options (Figure 6.16). Select floppy disk and insert a disk into the drive. Click in the File name: box and enter Imported Image. Click on the

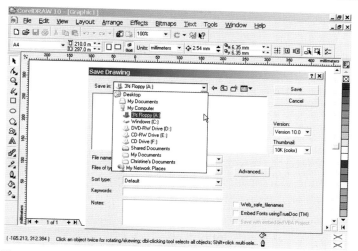

Figure 6.16 Save In

Save button. Your image is now saved as the file Imported Image.

16 Close the application either by selecting the File menu and the Exit option or by clicking on the Close button in the top right-hand corner of the window.

Exercise 47

Change resolution

1 CorelDRAW is opened either by selecting the Start button, highlighting All Programs and clicking on the CorelDRAW item or by double-clicking on the CorelDRAW icon on the Windows® desktop.

2 Select the New Graphics icon (Figure 6.17).

3 Select the File menu and Import option to reveal the Import window. Identify the folder in which the images are

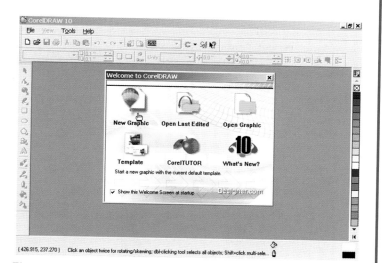

Figure 6.17 New Graphics icon

stored and use the preview facility to review the images. Select the Resample option and double-click on the picture's filename. Click on the Import button. The image will appear in the Resample window (Figure 6.6). Change the resolution to 30 pixels/inch and click on the OK button.

continued

4 The positioning pointer will appear on the document for you to position the image precisely. Locate the picture in the centre but in the top half of the page and click. In my case the image of a ship with tugboats will be placed on the document. In some cases the image will be larger than the page and you will need to use the handles to resize the picture to fit the page (Figure 6.18).

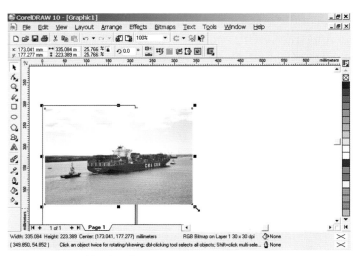

Figure 6.18 **Resize image**

5 Experiment with changing the image.

6 Save the image by selecting the File menu and the Save option. This will reveal the Save Drawing window. You need to decide where you will save your image. This is done by clicking on the down arrow near the Save in: box. This will reveal a list of options. Select floppy disk and insert a disk into the drive. Click in the File name: box and enter Resampled Image. Click on the Save button. Your image is now saved as the file Resampled Image.

7 Close the application either by selecting the File menu and the Exit option or by clicking on the Close button in the top right-hand corner of the window.

Exercise 48

Digital camera

1 CorelDRAW is opened either by selecting the Start button, highlighting All Programs and clicking on the CorelDRAW item or by double-clicking on the CorelDRAW icon on the Windows® desktop.

2 Select the New Graphics icon.

3 Connect your camera to the computer using the cables supplied with it.

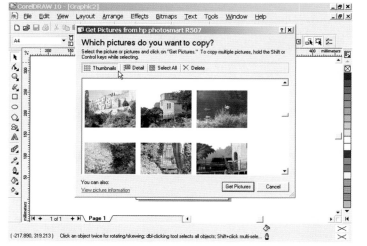

Figure 6.19 **Thumbnails**

4   Select the File menu, highlighting Acquire Image option to reveal a short menu. Select the Select Source to open the Select Source window in order to pick the digital camera and then Acquire to choose the image from the camera.

5   A window will open showing you the images stored on your camera. They may be shown as a series of small images (thumbnails), as a list of files or other variations depending on your camera. It is probably best to select the thumbnails option (Figure 6.19) if it is offered so you can browse the images and pick the ones you need.

6   To select an image, highlight it by clicking on the picture and then on the appropriate button. In my case it is a button called Get Picture but it may simply be an OK button or something similar.

7   The image will appear on your page in CorelDRAW.

8   Experiment with manipulating the image.

9   Save the image by selecting the File menu and the Save option. This will reveal the Save Drawing window. You need to decide where you will save your image. This is done by clicking on the down arrow near the Save in: box. This will reveal a list of options. Select floppy disk and insert a disk into the drive. Click in the File name: box and enter Digital Image. Click on the Save button. Your image is now saved as the file Digital Image.

10 Close the application either by selecting the File menu and the Exit option or by clicking on the Close button in the top right-hand corner of the window.

Create a graphic image

To create a graphic image you need to employ the tools available from the CorelDRAW toolbox which are available on the left edge of the application window (Figure 6.3 shows the different tools). You can draw squares, circles, rectangles, ellipses, triangles, straight and curved lines as well as freehand drawings. Tools used to manipulate an imported image are also available for images drawn by yourself. To help you identify the tools a label appears when you position the pointer over them.

Interactive Fill

You can fill a shape you have created by selecting the Interactive Fill Tool by clicking on it to reveal a series of options and then a colour from the palette (right-hand side of the application). This can be done after or before creating the shape but if you have created the shape you must select it to indicate the one that you want the colour to act on. If you select the Interactive Fill Tool and colour before selecting a shape then a window (Uniform Fill) will warn you.

Freehand Tool

The Freehand Tool is used to draw lines. If you click on the small arrow in the botton corner of the icon then a series of versions of the tool appear. They include:

- Freehand Tool – to draw freehand rather like a pencil
- Interactive Connector Tool – allows you to connect points and so draw straight lines

Exercise 49

Creating an image

1 CorelDRAW is opened either by selecting the Start button, highlighting All Programs and clicking on the CorelDRAW item or by double-clicking on the CorelDRAW icon on the Windows® desktop.

2 Select the New Graphics icon.

3 Click on the Freehand Tool and try to draw a diagonal line across the page (top left to bottom right). The pointer takes the form of cross hairs to help position the start and finish of the line. You start by clicking where you want to begin and drag the line to the opposite corner then click the button again when you want to finish. If you place the mouse pointer over Tool icons then a label will appear to identify them.

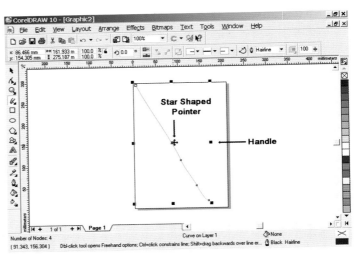

Figure 6.20 Pointer changing

4 The line will be surrounded by an enclosure of handles and a central cross. If you place the pointer over the centre you will see it change into a star (Figure 6.20). If you hold down the mouse button you can drag the line around. Try to move the line.

5 If you place the pointer over a handle it changes shape to a double-headed arrow and if you hold down the mouse

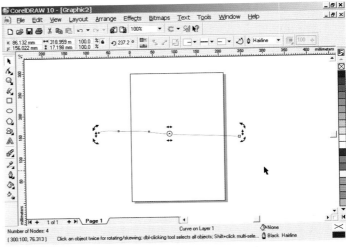

Figure 6.21 Handles change into curved arrows

button, you can reshape the line. Experiment with the different handles. You can use the Undo and Redo icons on the Standard toolbar to retrace your steps.

6   If you click again on the centre you will see the handles turn into curved arrows (Figure 6.21). These curved handles are used to rotate or skew the line using the mouse pointer. The mouse pointer turns into a partial circle and, if you hold down the button, you can rotate the line; or the pointer turns into two parallel lines which you can use to skew the image. Experiment with rotating and skewing the line.

7   Draw a curved freehand line by clicking where you want to start and releasing the button where you want to stop. Notice that along the curve are small squares or handles. If you place your pointer on one of these it will change shape into a large arrow. If you hold down your mouse pointer you can manipulate the shape of the line. Experiment with reshaping the line.

8   Click on the Pick Tool and then on the shapes you have created. They will be enclosed and if you press the Delete key, the shape will disappear. Clear all the shapes you have created.

9   Click on the Interactive Fill Tool and the colour palette (select red). A window will appear called Uniform Fill. You should choose the Graphic option and the OK button.

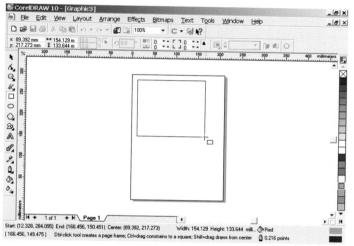

Figure 6.22   Rectangle

10   Click on the Rectangle Tool. The pointer will once more change to cross hairs and you again start by clicking and holding down the tool. If you move diagonally you will see a rectangle appear. Draw a square using the rulers as a guide (Figure 6.22). The square will be enclosed and filled with red. You can change the shape by moving the handles or move the square by using the central cross. You can even drag the image off the page into the

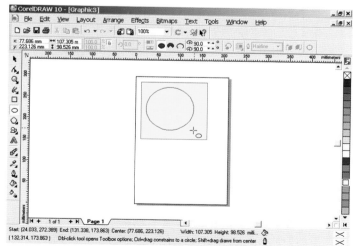

Figure 6.23   Draw an ellipse

surrounding area. This is a useful place to store objects until you are ready to use them. Again, if you click on the centre cross or double-click with the Pick Tool you access the rotational handles. Experiment with rotating the square.

11 Click on the Interactive Fill Tool and the colour palette (yellow).

12 Click on the Ellipse Tool and attempt to draw an ellipse within the square which will fill with the colour yellow. You will need to drag the ellipse handles to achieve the outcome (Figure 6.23).

13 Click on the Interactive Fill Tool and the colour palette (blue).

14 Click on the Freehand Tool and draw a triangle within the square. Your picture should resemble something similar to Figure 6.24.

15 Continue to experiment with the different tools until you are confident that you can use them. If you find that the enclosure disappears and you cannot get it to reappear then you are probably clicking with the ordinary mouse pointer when you need to use the Pick Tool.

16 Save the image by selecting the File menu and the Save option. This will reveal the Save Drawing window. You need to select the location where you will save your image. This is done by clicking on the down arrow near the Save in: box to reveal a list of options. Select the floppy disk and insert a disk into the drive. Click in the File name: box and enter Graphical Shapes. Click on the Save button. Your image is now saved as a file entitled Graphical Shapes.

17 Close the application either by selecting the File menu and the Exit option or by clicking on the Close button in the top right-hand corner of the window.

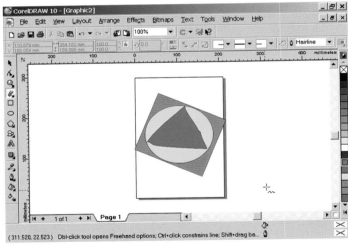

Figure 6.24 Graphic image

Line thickness

In the exercise we used quite thin lines but CorelDRAW allows you to vary line thickness using a toolbar option shown in Figure 6.25. You change the thickness of the lines by selecting the `Freehand` Tool, clicking on the down arrow next to the line thickness box to choose from the list of options and then drawing your line. The thickness will be transferred to the other tools (e.g. rectangles will have the new line thickness). When you select the thickness, you may reveal a message which may not make a lot of sense to you at this point in time. Simply click on the `OK` button.

You can adjust the thickness of a line that was drawn earlier by selecting it (i.e. enclosing it in handles) using the `Pick` Tool and then choosing the line thickness. This is the general way to edit a shape using the various tools provided by CorelDRAW.

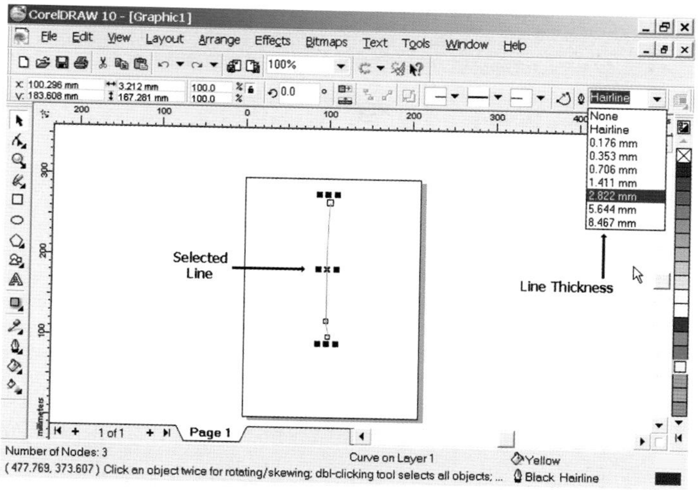

Using text

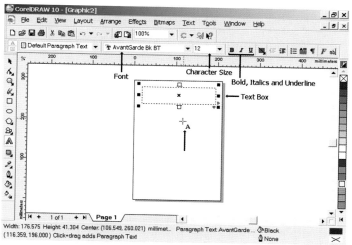

Figure 6.25 Line thickness

Figure 6.26 Text

Located in the Toolbox is a `Text` Tool which you use to draw a rectangular area in which you can enter text from the keyboard. When you select the `Text` Tool, a new toolbar is opened in the application (Figure 6.26) which allows you to select fonts, character sizes, embolden, write in italics and underline text. This is done by clicking on either the icons or on the down arrows to reveal lists of options. Notice the pointer changes shape to cross hairs with the letter A outside of the text rectangular area and to a bar inside the box.

Exercise 50

Using text

1 CorelDRAW is opened either by selecting the `Start` button, highlighting `All Programs` and clicking on the `CorelDRAW` item or by double-clicking on the `CorelDRAW` icon on the Windows® desktop.

2 Select the `New Graphics` icon.

3 Select the `Text` Tool and create a text rectangle on the document. Then select Arial Black font and character size 48. The cursor flashes in the text rectangle to show you where the text is going to be inserted (Figure 6.27). Enter:

This is text.

4 You can edit your work by using the `Backspace` key to delete text or insert the cursor by clicking in the required place using the mouse pointer. Insert 'a' between 'is' and 'text' (i.e. This is a text) and then the word rectangle after the word 'text'. It should finally read:

This is a text rectangle.

If you have not made your text box large enough you may not see the word 'rectangle'. You need to resize the box and it will then appear.

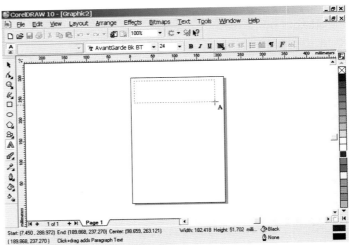

Figure 6.27 Text rectangle

5 The text rectangle is enclosed in a similar way to the graphic images and if you place the mouse pointer over the handles you can resize it. The text remains unchanged. To change its size requires it to be highlighted using the mouse and a new character size chosen from the toolbar.

6 Change the text size to 36.

7 The text rectangle can be moved using the centre handle and the mouse pointer which changes into a star when placed over the

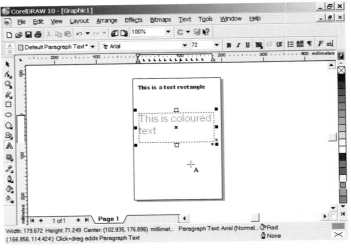

Figure 6.28 Text

centre handle. By holding down the mouse button you can drag the rectangle to a new position.

8   If you select the `Pick` Tool and double-click with it on the text rectangle you will see the rotational and skew handles appear. These allow you to rotate or skew the text. Explore the options.

9   You can enter coloured text by selecting the `Text` Tool and then clicking on your

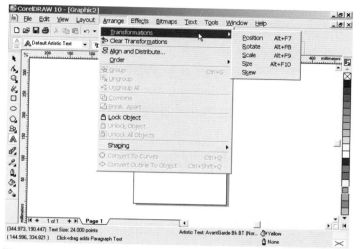

Figure 6.29 Transformation options

choice of colour in the palette on the right-hand side of the application window. Enter:

This is coloured text

using an Arial Font, size 72 in red. Figure 6.28 shows the results of entering the two pieces of text.

10   An alternative approach is to select the `Arrange` menu and the `Transformation` option (Figure 6.29). Explore the options.

11   When the text rectangle is enclosed you can cut, copy and paste its contents or delete the whole rectangle. Experiment with making copies and deleting them. The options are available on the `Edit` menu.

12   When you are confident you can enter, amend and manipulate text then close the application by either selecting the `File` menu and the `Exit` option or clicking on the `Close` button in the top right-hand corner of the window.

Print

The quality of an image depends on its resolution but there are considerable differences between viewing an image on the screen and printing the graphic on to paper. The quality of monitors and printers varies considerably. A typical monitor may have a resolution of 72 dots per inch while a printer will often print using 300, 600 or 1200 dots per inch. To print a screen image using a high resolution may produce a larger or smaller print image compared with the display. It is not a matter of what you see is what you get (WYSIWYG) since the translation between screen and paper often means a change in size. However, CorelDRAW helps by presenting your image on a distinct size of page so that you can see how it will look when printed.

CorelDRAW shows you the size of the document on which you are creating your images and enables you to change its size using the toolbar. If you change the document size after creating an image you will see the page changes size but the image stays the same. This indicates that you need to resize the picture. When the image is enclosed by handles (highlighted) you can see the exact size of the graphic on the toolbar. If you move the handles to resize the image the figures on the toolbar will change accordingly.

CorelDRAW provides you with tools to specify how your images are going to be presented. To print an image select the File menu and the Print option to reveal the Print window. At the bottom of the Print window is a Print Preview button so you can see how the image will appear when printed. When you are satisfied, return to the Print window by clicking on the Close button and then on the OK button to print.

More Practice

Activity 1

Design the artwork for a postcard

1 CorelDRAW is opened either by selecting the Start button, highlighting All Programs and clicking on the CorelDRAW item or by double-clicking on the CorelDRAW icon on the Windows® desktop.

2 Select the New Graphics icon.

3 Select Japanese Postcard from the toolbar list (Figure 6.30) and give the postcard a landscape orientation.

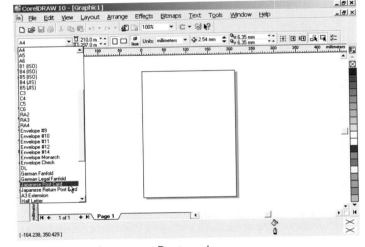

Figure 6.30 Japanese Postcard

4 Click on the Freehand Tool and draw a straight line down the centre of the card using the rulers as a guide (Interactive Connector Tool may be helpful). Click on the Rectangle Tool and draw a rectangle to show where the stamp should be placed. Click again on the Freehand Tool to draw the four lines for the name and address to be written. If you draw one you can use copy and paste to produce the others.

5 Click on the Text Tool and insert the word 'To' aligned with the bottom of the stamp. Use Arial font and size 18 characters.

6 Click on the Freehand Tool and change the line thickness to 0.706. If a message appears simply click on the OK button. Click on the Rectangle Tool and draw a border around the other side of the postcard.

7 With the rectangle you have just created enclosed within its handles, select the File menu and the Import option. Crop the image so that it will fit the space available.
Import an image into the rectangle and, using its handles, resize and position the image to fill the rectangle. In my case I have used a picture of a street scene taken with a digital camera (Figure 6.31). You can use anything that is available.

New CLAiT 2006 for Office 2003

8 If you want to make the image unusual you can flip it using the Mirror buttons. You will see them on the toolbar when the image is enclosed (if you place your mouse pointer over options on the toolbar, labels will appear to help you identify them – the Mirror buttons are near the centre of the toolbar). Try it and see what happens (Figure 6.32). You can retrace your steps using the Undo icon or option on the Edit menu. This toolbar also shows you the exact dimensions of your image.

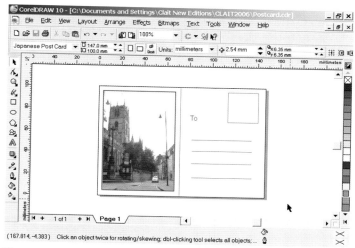

Figure 6.31 Street scene

9 Save the image by selecting the File menu and the Save option. This will reveal the Save Drawing window. You need to select the location where you will save your image. This is done by clicking on the down arrow near the Save in: box to reveal a list of options. Select the floppy disk and insert a disk into the drive. Click in the File name: box and enter Postcard. Click on the Save button. Your image is now saved as the file Postcard.

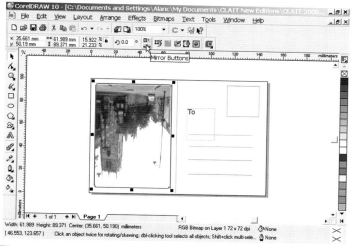

Figure 6.32 Mirror buttons flipping image

10 Select the File menu and the Print option to reveal the Print window. Click on the Print Preview button and check your postcard. If you are happy, click on the Close button to return to the Print window and then on the OK button.

11 Close the application by either selecting the File menu and the Exit option or clicking on the Close button in the top right-hand corner of the window.

Activity 2

Design artwork for a compact disc

1 CorelDRAW is opened either by selecting the Start button, highlighting All Programs and clicking on the CorelDRAW item or by double-clicking on the CorelDRAW icon on the Windows® desktop.

2 Select the New Graphics icon.

3 Insert a size of 430 mm by 430 mm by clicking in the size boxes on the toolbar and entering the new size (Figure 6.33). You are going to create the artwork for a music CD.

4 Select the Freehand Tool and change the size of line to 0.706. Select the Rectangle Tool and click on the red colour in the palette. Draw a rectangle inside the document leaving a small margin around the outside. You should see a red rectangle form.

5 Select the Ellipse Tool and draw a small circle outside the document area. It will be filled with red. However, while it is still enclosed, click on the yellow colour in the palette and you will see the circle change colour. Now copy the circle using the Copy and Paste functions on the Edit menu or the toolbar icons. Remember that the pasted circle will appear on top of the original shape so will need to be dragged away. When you have three circles, move them to form a diagonal across the red rectangle.

6 Select the Text Tool and draw a text rectangle away from the document area and enter:
Rock Music
using a font and character size of your choice.

7 Rotate the text until it is at a 45 degree angle. Copy the text twice more and drag it so that it rests diagonally across each circle. Your CD cover should look something like Figure 6.34.

8 Experiment with the design to improve its appearance (e.g. rotate the text so that it is at different angles).

9 Save the image by selecting the File menu and the Save option. This will reveal the Save Drawing window. You need to select the location where you will save your image. This is done by clicking on the down arrow near the Save in: box. This will reveal a list of options. Select the floppy disk and

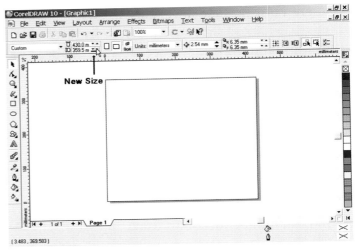

Figure 6.33 New size

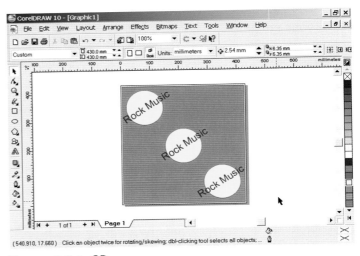

Figure 6.34 CD cover

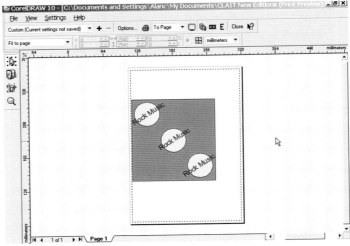

Figure 6.35 Print Preview

insert a disk into the drive. Click in the File <u>n</u>ame: box and enter CD Cover. Click on the `Save` button. Your image is now saved as the file CD Cover.

10 Select the `File` menu and the `Print` option to reveal the Print window. Click on the `Print Preview` button and check your cover (Figure 6.35). If you are happy, click on the `Close` button to return to the Print window and then on the `OK` button.

11 Close the application either by selecting the `File` menu and the `Exit` option or clicking on the `Close` button in the top right-hand corner of the window.

Activity 3

On the Hodder and Stoughton website (www. hodderclait. co.uk) associated with this book you will find the following images:

1 Canal in Winter

2 Countryside in Winter

3 Winter Walk.

Using them or your own graphics create the design outlined in Figure 6.36 ensuring that the images maintain their original proportions and are not distorted. However, you can resize them.

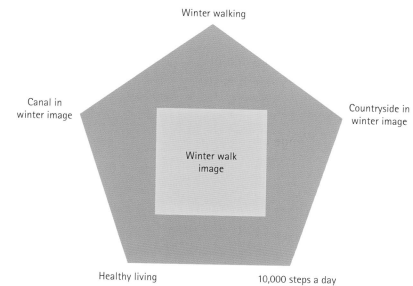

Figure 6.36 Walking design

1 Create a design that is A1 size and landscape orientated.

2 Change the background colour to green (`Interactive Fill` Tool, `Palette` and `Rectangle` Tool).

3 Create a polygon (five-sided) shape covering the middle of the rectangle (`Polygon` Tool). Fill this area with white.

4 Import the image Winter Walk and insert it inside the polygon (`File` menu and `Import` function). You will need to resize the image to ensure it fits.

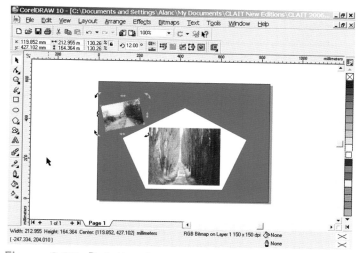

Figure 6.37 Rotating image

5 Save your design with the filename Walking.

6 Import the image Canal in Winter and insert it in the left-hand corner of the design outside the polygon. You will need to resize the image to ensure it fits.

7 Rotate the image until its base is parallel to one side of the polygon (Figure 6.37).

8 Import the image Countryside in Winter and insert it in the right-hand corner of the design outside the polygon. You will need to resize the image to ensure it fits.

9 Rotate the image until its base is parallel to one side of the polygon.

10 Save your design with the filename Walking.

11 Enter the text Winter Walking in blue above the polygon in the centre of the design using Arial Black Font and a character size of 100.

12 Enter the text Healthy Living in yellow and rotate this message by 90 degrees anticlockwise. Use Times New Roman font and a character size of 100 and embolden the text.

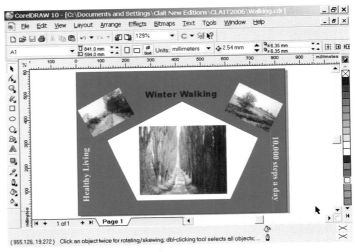

Figure 6.38 Walking

13 Insert Healthy Living on the left-hand side of the design.

14 Enter the text 10,000 steps a day in yellow and rotate this message by 90 degrees clockwise. Use Times New Roman font and a character size of 100 and embolden the text.

15 Insert 10,000 steps a day on the right-hand side of the design.

16 Save your design with the filename Walking. Figure 6.38 illustrates our efforts.

17 Print your design in colour and then compare your work with the outline (Figure 6.36) for accuracy.

18 Close the application.

SUMMARY

1 **Open CorelDRAW** Select the `Start` button, highlight the `All Programs` option and click on the `CorelDRAW` item or double-click on the `CorelDRAW` icon on the Windows desktop. Select the `New Graphics` icon.

2 **Close CorelDRAW** Select the `File` menu and the `Exit` option or click on the `Close` button in the top right-hand corner of the application window.

3 **New image** Use the arrow buttons on the toolbar to select from options to choose page sizes or different types of documents, change the actual size of page, have either landscape or portrait orientation and alter the units of measurement of page size (e.g. millimetres or inches).

4 **Import** images Select the `File` menu and the `Import` option to reveal the Import window.

5 **Crop or resample image** Select from Full Image, Crop and Resample by clicking on the down arrow to the right of box on the Import window. This will reveal the Crop and Resample windows which allow you to manipulate the image. Click on the `OK` button when ready.

6 **Edit bitmaps** Right-click on the image and select `Edit Bitmap` .

7 **Manipulate images** By clicking on the image you enclose it with handles. Using the mouse pointer you can resize and move images.

Click again on the centre or double-click using the `Pick` Tool and the handles will turn into curved arrows. The curved handles allow you to rotate or skew the line using the mouse pointer. When the mouse pointer turns into a partial circle, you hold down the button and then you can rotate the line. When the pointer turns into two parallel lines, you can use them to skew the image. Alternatively select the `Arrange` menu and the `Transformation` option.

8 **Digital camera images** Select the `File` menu, highlighting the `Acquire Image` option to reveal a short menu. Select `Select Source` to open the `Select Source` window in order to pick the digital camera and then `Acquire` to choose the image from the camera.

9 **Line thickness** Select the `Freehand` Tool, click on the down arrow next to the line thickness box on the toolbar to choose from the list of options and draw line. Adjust the thickness of a line by selecting it (i.e. enclosing it in handles) using the `Pick` Tool and then choosing the line thickness.

10 **Draw a graphic image** Click on the various tools in the toolbox on the left edge of the application window. These allow you to draw squares, circles, rectangles, ellipses, triangles, straight or curved lines and freehand drawings.

11 **Print** Select the `File` menu and the `Print` option to reveal the Print window. Click on the `Print Preview` button to see how the image will appear when printed. Click on the `Close` button and then on the `Print` button.

Web Page Creation

This chapter will help you to create a web page by:

- identifying and using appropriate software correctly
- importing, formatting and placing text and image files
- inserting relative, external and e-mail hyperlinks
- managing and printing web pages.

Assessment

This unit does not assume any previous experience of using a computer. You may find it useful to have completed Unit 1 (File Management and e-Document Production). You will be assessed through a practical realistic assignment which is designed to allow you to demonstrate your knowledge and skills against each objective. Your tutor can provide you with more guidance.

What is a web page?

When surfing the World Wide Web, you read and interact with many different documents. These are known as web pages which, when linked together, are called websites. A web page is created using a special language called the Hypertext Markup Language or HTML. This allows you to design the presentation of the page's information (i.e. text and images) so that anyone viewing the page using an application called a web browser can see the information. The HTML supplies the browser with the instructions to create a web page from different elements such as text, pictures, sounds and videos. The HTML code is simply a text document with special commands (i.e. HTML commands) embedded in the text. HTML commands are sometimes known as tags. They tell the browser to, for example, show an image, underline text or enclose an area in a border. The images, text and sounds are not HTML but rather separate files which the code locates and presents in the browser. HTML is a language that organizes information into an attractive, interesting and readable form.

A web page can be as long as you want it to be. It can contain a vast amount of information or only a single item. The designer decides on the contents and the length of the page. Many web pages need their users to scroll down them to access their contents. It is good practice to limit the length of a page to no more than four A4 sheets. This minimizes the possibility of users getting lost and confused within the page. This possibility is increased when web pages are linked to others using hypertext links. These are places on the page which, when clicked on with a mouse pointer, cause the browser to jump to a new page. Links can be single words or phrases, pictures, icons and almost anything else you decide to make a link. There are a number of common conventions in designing links and possibly the most well known is the underlined word which signals that it is a link to another page.

HTML applications

Originally, to design a web page you had to understand the HTML language in depth. However, several HTML editors using a WYSIWYG (What You See Is What You Get) approach are now available. You can visually create a page so that you can see how it appears as you design it. This is obviously easier than writing lines of code and having to visualize mentally the resulting page. This normally leads to the final appearance being different to that which you intended so you are forced to amend the code.

Word processors (e.g. Microsoft® Word) and desktop publishing applications can convert their documents into HTML automatically. This is a useful productivity tool when you want to place a document you have created on to a web page quickly. However, the precise presentation of the information is often different in a browser to that created in the word processor. You are converting between two different formats and there is often a need for a degree of compromise between them. If you rely on using a word processor to develop all the content for a web page it will rapidly come to look like an office noticeboard while a professional HTML editor will add quality and impact to the raw information.

This chapter is based on Microsoft FrontPage® 2003, an editor capable of developing complex websites with many different web pages. We will only be considering a limited range of its capabilities but it will provide you with the foundation to develop your knowledge and skills later.

Microsoft FrontPage® 2003

FrontPage® is loaded either by clicking on the Start button, highlighting All Programs and then selecting the Microsoft FrontPage 2003 item or by double-clicking on the FrontPage icon on the Windows® desktop. Figure 7.1 shows the FrontPage® application. This consists of:

- menu and toolbars – these provide the various functions available to you and are similar to those in other Microsoft® Office applications

- Page work space – this is the area in which you create, view and edit your page

- Getting Started task pane – this provides access to many of the functions required when creating a new page

- Views – these four tabs give you access to the different views of the FrontPage® operation:

1   Design – to edit the page in WYSIWYG mode
2   Split – splits the screen to show you the page and also the HTML code

3 Code – to edit the HTML code directly

4 Preview – to see what the page may look like in a browser.

Microsoft FrontPage® 2003 is shown with its default settings, which is indicated in the bottom right of the display (Figure 7.1). To change the settings you need to double-click on it to reveal the Page Options window.

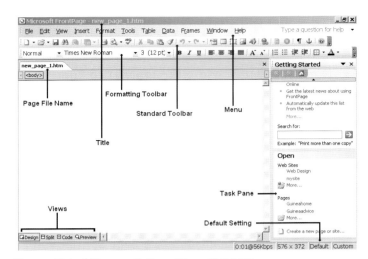

Figure 7.1 Microsoft FrontPage® 2003

Exercise 51

Exploring FrontPage®

1 Load Microsoft FrontPage® either by clicking on the Start button, highlighting All Programs and then selecting the Microsoft FrontPage 2003 item or by double-clicking on the FrontPage icon on the Windows® desktop.

2 Maximize the application window to fill the display using the maximize button in the top right-hand corner if the application is displayed in a window.

3 The display should be similar to that shown in Figure 7.1. Click on the Design View tab if another view is shown

4 The top of the working area should show new_page_1.htm indicating that you are working on the first page – .htm is the extension for the HTML files.

5 The cursor will be flashing on the top line of the area. Enter:

This is a new page.

6 If you click on the Code tab you will see the HTML code to present this simple text. Figure 7.2 shows this.

7 We can also see some of the HTML tags such as:

<html> marks the start of the HTML commands
</html> marks the end of the HTML commands

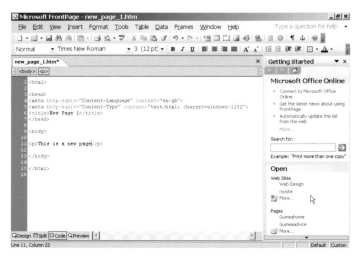

Figure 7.2 HTML Code

<head> marks the beginning of an HTML document
<body> shows the start of the main body of a document
</body> shows the end of the main body of a document
<p> indicates the start of a paragraph.

Other tags are:

<b> </b> bold
<a href> </a> hypertext links.

If you are interested in creating a simple page using HTML then try the optional exercise at the end of the chapter.

8. Explore the Split (Figure 7.3) and Preview views. Click on the Design View tab.

9 Explore the different options comparing menus and toolbar layouts with other Microsoft® Office applications. Try to locate:

the Insert menu and the File and Picture options

the File menu and the Open, Save, Print and Exit options

the Format menu and the Background option.

10 Continue to explore the application until you are confident that you can find your way around the interface.

11 Close the application by selecting the File menu and Exit option or by clicking on the Close button in top right-hand corner of the window. You may be asked if you want to save your work; on this occasion, click on the No button.

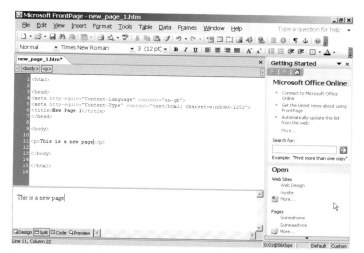

Figure 7.3 Split View

Designing a web page

Before you begin to design a page it is useful to consider what you intend to achieve and who will be reading its contents. FrontPage® provides a variety of options and the main error new designers make is to use too many of them. You could display a page with dozens of different fonts, a wide range of character sizes, lots of colour, several pictures and lots of emphasis. In practice, the overuse of the different design elements will result in a poor page which is difficult to read and understand. It is good practice to keep your designs simple.

For example:

1 Colour can add interest so a background colour is a useful device to enhance your web pages.
2 Varying character sizes helps draw the reader's attention to the content of the page but it should not be overused.
3 Pictures add interest to a page but are best used when they relate to the text on the page or the subject of the website.
4 The use of bold and italics to emphasize particular pieces of text is effective so long as it is not used too often.

Entering and emphasizing text

Microsoft FrontPage® provides you with two ways of picking fonts and character sizes. Firstly, you can select the down arrow button to the right of the font or character size box to reveal a list of options from which you can choose by clicking on the item. When you then enter text it is in the font and size you have chosen. Alternatively you can highlight the text and then select the font and size.

The size of characters is shown in two different ways within FrontPage® – the normal points way that is used in all the Microsoft® Office applications (e.g. character size 10) and also in HTML sizes. The two sizes are both shown on the Formatting toolbar (Figure 7.4).

For example:

HTML	Points
1	8
2	10
3	12
4	14

You can enter text which is bold, in italics or underlined by either selecting the option initially and then entering the text or by highlighting and changing them later.

You can align (justify) text and pictures on your page by using the alignment (justification) options on the toolbar. Again, this can be done prior to inserting the text or picture or afterwards by highlighting the object and then making the selection. Figure 7.4 shows the different options available on the Formatting toolbar.

You can align (justify) a whole page or vary the alignment (justification) down the page. This means, for example, you can have a heading and a picture centred, while the main body of words is left-aligned (justified). This is often an effective way of indicating the relationship of different elements on the page (e.g. headings).

A web page needs to present an engaging image to visitors so that they will read the content and return for more on another occasion. When you are designing the display you need to control the flow of text around the page. In a sense you are guiding the user around your material. You can do this through combining the different elements of the page together to control the flow of text (e.g. tables of information, text, pictures and using alignment). It is useful to plan your page and a few moments spent sketching out how you think it should look are often repaid in an attractive page.

Some simple design considerations are:

- Keep it simple and concise
- Make it easy to find information
- Be consistent
- Show relationships between the different parts of the content.

You can use the different elements to define areas of the page which can serve different purposes. For example, news can always be centred and appear beneath the title. By left- or right-aligning an image you allow yourself to present text alongside it

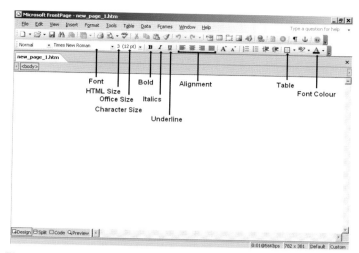

Figure 7.4 Formatting toolbar

thus giving the visual message that the text relates to the image. A blank space can separate different topics. You need to consider what you are trying to achieve and plan your page to achieve it.

Checking text

A website potentially may be viewed by thousands of people so it is very important that you check the spelling, grammar, layout and number of words displayed. FrontPage® provides you with a spellchecker (Tools menu) and if you prepare your text in Microsoft® Word and import it then you can use its Spelling and Grammar checker and Word Count tool. Users of websites rarely read every word. They browse or scan the material for interesting content. It is therefore useful to minimize the amount of text displayed. The Word Count tool in Microsoft® Word is therefore useful to check how much text you intend to show.

Exercise 52

Creating a web page

1 Load Microsoft FrontPage® either by clicking on the Start button, highlighting All Programs and then selecting the Microsoft FrontPage 2003 item or by double-clicking on the FrontPage icon on the Windows® desktop.

2 Maximize the application window to fill the display using the maximize button in the top right-hand corner if the application is displayed in a window.

3 The display should be similar to that shown in Figure 7.1. Click on the Design View tab if another view is shown. The first step is to create a folder in which to store all the files and other resources that you use to create the web page and eventually the website. This is known as the disk-based website. It ensures that you have everything for your website in one location.

4 Select the File menu and the New option. This will reveal the New task pane. Select the More Web Site Templates option from the New Web Site section. This will open the Web Site Templates window (Figure 7.5). The default location of the Web Site folder is c:\Documents and Settings\Alan Clarke\My Documents\My Websites. In your case your name will appear instead of Alan Clarke, or whoever is the computer's user. You can also use the Browse button to select another location.

5 Now select the Empty Web Site template by double-clicking. A new tab will appear in the working area called Web Site (Figure 7.6). This shows the folder in which all your files for this site will be stored.

6 We are going to create a simple web page for a company called First Generation. Click on the new_page_ 1.htm tab to reveal the blank web page. Change the view to Design if necessary.

7 Select Arial font and a character size of 36 (using the Formatting toolbar) and enter the main heading as First Generation Company. Centre this heading by highlighting the text and clicking on the centre alignment (justification) icon.

8 Press Enter twice to move the cursor down the page.

9 The next step is to insert a suitable picture to gain the attention of the users. Do this by selecting the Insert menu, highlighting the Picture option and clicking on the Clip Art item. This will reveal the Clip Art task pane which allows you to search for pictures related to a particular theme. The results of the search are shown as thumbnail images from which you can select an image by placing your pointer on it. A button

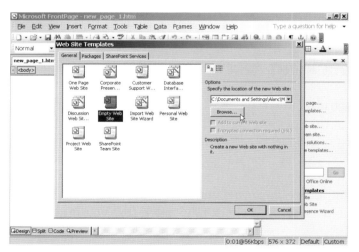

Figure 7.5 Web Site Templates

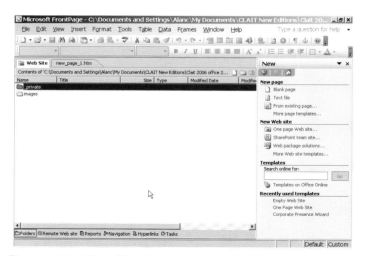

Figure 7.6 Web Site folder

appears that will open a menu when you click on it. The option Insert will add the Clip Art image to your page.

You may get a message telling you that the Clip Art requires you to insert the Microcost® Office master CD-ROM into the appropriate drive since the Clip Art is stored on this disk. You can also insert your own pictures by selecting From File instead of the Clip Art option and then direct FrontPage® to the folder containing your images.

10 Since you last chose centre alignment (justification), your image will be placed in the centre of the page. The cursor will be flashing alongside the image so that if you select left, centre or right alignment (justification) the image will move to relate to that alignment (justification). Explore the different alignments (justifications) and position the image where you feel is best.

11 If you click on the picture you will see the image enclosed within square dots (i.e. handles). If you place your pointer on these dots the pointer will change shape and if you hold down the mouse button you can change the shape of the image. Experiment with this to resize your picture. Figure 7.7 shows the picture handles and the changing shape of the cursor.

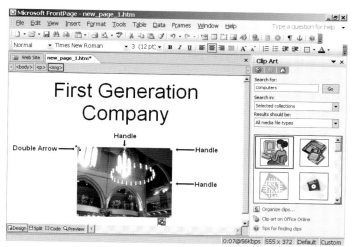

Figure 7.7 Image changes

12 Press Enter to move the cursor down the page. We will next enter the links to the rest of the site.

13 Enter:

Contacts   Products   Prices   News –   leaving five spaces between each word.

Centre the words.

14 You have created a simple page. Preview the page and look at the HTML code for this page by selecting the Code View tab. Check the layout and proofread the text to make sure it is correct.

15 To save your web page select the File menu then the Save option to reveal the Save As window. This will show the folder that you created to save your pages. Now click in the File name: box and enter from the keyboard the name First_ Generation_ Company.htm (it may appear automatically) and click on the Save button. You will hear the drive working and the publication will be saved as a file called First_Generation_Company.htm.

continued

16 You may be presented with a second window asking if you want to save the embedded files. In this case it means the Clip Art image. Click on the OK button and the window will clear. The embedded file will be saved to the folder. If you now click on the Web Site tab you will see the files that you have saved. Return to the web page by clicking on the page tab.

17 Now print the page by selecting the File menu and the Print option to reveal the Print window. Click on the OK button to print the page using the printer default settings.

18 Change the View tab to Code and print the code using the same procedure. You will now have printouts of the code and the visual presentation of the page.

19 Close the application by selecting the File menu and Exit option or by clicking on the Close button in the top right-hand corner of the window.

Standard toolbar

The Standard toolbar provides a range of tools (Figure 7.8) which include alternative ways of inserting pictures, printing and saving using the toolbar icons. In addition, the Undo and Redo icons allow you to recover from making a mistake. You can reverse what you have done by clicking on Undo. If you make an error in using Undo, then you can reverse this with Redo.

As with other Microsoft® Office applications you can cut, copy and paste text and pictures around a web page or between Microsoft® Office applications and FrontPage®. These functions operate by highlighting the text or picture and then selecting the Cut or Copy icon. The cut function removes the highlighted area and you can paste it (relocate) into a new position by placing the cursor at the desired location and clicking on the Paste icon. The copy function works in the same way but does not remove the original text or picture.

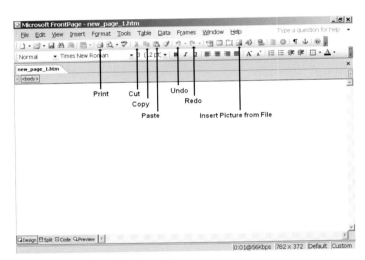

Figure 7.8 Standard toolbar

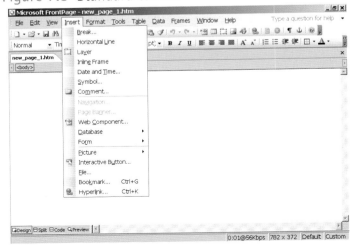

Figure 7.9 Insert menu

Inserting text files

Although you can enter text from the keyboard, it is also possible to import text as files or paste it from other Microsoft® Office applications into your web page. To import a text file, position the cursor at the location on the page where you want the text to be inserted. Using the Insert menu (Figure 7.9) and the File option you can import text into the page. Once the File option is selected, the Select File window is opened which allows you to choose the file to be inserted.

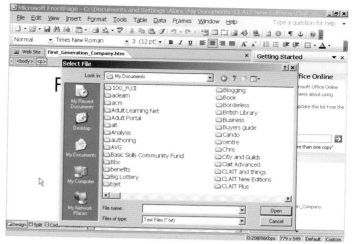

Figure 7.10 Select File

In order to select a file you need to know where it is located within your computer or on your floppy disk. To find the location, click on the down arrow button to the right of the Look in: box. A list of drives will appear such as 3½ Floppy (A:) and C:. C: is normally the designation for the computer's internal hard disk in which most files are stored within folders. In Figure 7.10 you will see that in the folder My Documents are many other folders.

To discover what each folder contains, double-click on it and its contents will appear in the working area. When you locate the text file you want to include, you can either double-click on it or single-click to insert its name in the File name: box and then on the Open button. The text file will then be opened on the web page.

Exercise 53

Inserting a text file

1 Load Microsoft FrontPage® either by clicking on the Start button, highlighting All Programs and then selecting the Microsoft FrontPage 2003 item or by double-clicking on the FrontPage icon on the Windows® desktop.

2 Maximize the application window to fill the display using the maximize button in the top right-hand corner if the application is displayed in a window.

3 The display should show the Web Site tab with the files that you created in the previous exercise. Across the botton of the working area you should see that the View tabs have changed to show different ones – Folders, Remote Web Site, Reports, Navigation, Hyperlinks and Tasks.

4 Click on Create a new page or site in the Open section of the Getting Started task pane. The task pane will change to New. Select the Blank page option in the New page section of the task pane. The working area will now display a blank page with a tab called new_page_1.htm.

continued

5 We are going to insert a text file into a simple web page. It is important to check the text file for spelling and grammar errors and to undertake a word count to ensure the correct number of words is displayed. This can be done in Microsoft® Word before the file is imported into FrontPage®.

6 If you have undertaken the word-processing unit you will have created some text files that you will have saved

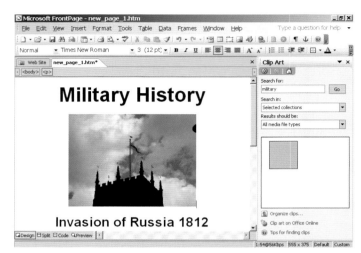

Figure 7.11 Military History Page

to a floppy disk. This exercise is based on inserting one of them although you can use any text file you like.

7 Insert the floppy disk containing the file into the drive. Position your cursor three lines down the new page by using the Enter key. Select the Insert menu and the File option to reveal the Select File window. Choose the floppy disk option in the Look in: box and double-click on the text file of your choice. We are going to select the Invasion of Russia (created earlier in word-processing exercises). If your disk appears blank this may be because the Files of type box contains a type not present on the disk. You will need to change it by clicking on the down arrow button at the end of the box and selecting All Files (*.*) which will look for files of all types. It is good practice always to set the box to this option.

8 Observe what happens. You may briefly see a message saying that the file is being converted into HTML code and then the file will appear (you may miss it if you blink) on the page. You are now free to enhance its appearance but before we attempt that look at the file in the Code View. See if you can identify the paragraph breaks from the HTML code (<p>).

9 Highlight the title Invasion of Russia – 1812 and change its font to Arial, size 24 and centre it. Delete the hyphen.

10 Highlight the rest of the passage and change the font to Times New Roman and size 12.

11 Above the title Invasion of Russia insert the page heading Military History using Arial but in size 36. Centre the text and embolden it.

12 Insert an appropriate Clip Art or other image between the page heading and the passage title. Left-align (left-justify) the picture. Experiment with resizing the image to get the best effect.

13 You have created another simple page (Figure 7.11). In Figure 7.11 notice that you need to scroll the page in order to see the whole content. Preview the page and consider its

HTML code. It is also important to check the spelling and grammar of your web page. A web page will potentially be seen by thousands of people so it is important that it is perfect.

14 To save your web page, select the File menu then the Save option to reveal the Save As window. The location should be the Web Site folder that you have already created. Click in the File name: box and enter from the keyboard the name Military_History.htm and click on the Save button. You will hear the drive working and the publication will be saved in the folder as a file called Military_History.htm.

15 You may be presented with a second window asking if you want to save the embedded files. In this case this means the Clip Art or other image. Click on the OK button and the window will clear. Click on the Web Site tab to see the files. It should now contain the files for First Generation Company and Military History, probably two files each if the embedded files have also been saved.

16 Now print the page by selecting the File menu and the Print option to reveal the Print window. Click on the OK button to print the page using the printer default settings.

17 Change the View tab to Code and print the code using the same procedure. You will now have printouts of the code and the visual presentation of the page.

18 Close the application by selecting the File menu and Exit option or by clicking on the Close button in the top right-hand corner of the window.

Background colours and images

Colour can create attractive and interesting designs. Microsoft FrontPage® provides the tools to change the background colour of your page or to use a picture as the background. Your text is thus presented on top of the picture or colour. When selecting a colour ensure that it provides a contrast to the text colour (or foreground colour) and thus makes the text legible.

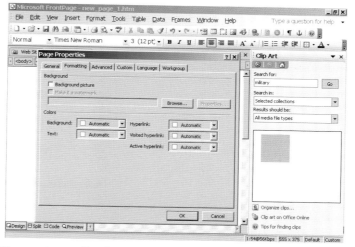

Figure 7.12 Background colour

The background colour or picture is set using the Format menu and the Background option. This will reveal the Page Properties window (Figure 7.12). The background settings can be seen on the Formatting tab display.

At the top of the display is an item called Background picture. This is activated by clicking in the small blank square in front of the item. A small tick will appear in the square and the box alongside the <u>B</u>rowse button becomes white. You can insert the source of the picture in the box (e.g. A:\Picture.gif) which will become the background image. If you cannot remember the exact location of the image you can browse the hard disk or floppy disk to locate it by clicking on the `Browse` button. This opens the Select Background Picture window from which the image can be selected.

Below the Background picture area of the Page Properties window is the section dealing with colour. There are five options to choose from:

- `Background` – the norm is white
- `Text` – the norm is black
- `Hyperlink` – this shows the colour of the underlining of a text link, with the norm as blue
- `Visited hyperlink` – this shows the colour of the underlining when a link has been used in the past, with the norm as purple
- `Active hyperlink` – this shows the colour of the underlining when a link is currently active, with the norm as red.

The link colours are fairly standard and should not be changed. The normal text colour is black and should also not often need to be changed, unlike background colours. If the down arrow to the right of the Background Automatic box is clicked then a palette of colours is revealed. To select a new background colour click on it and it will then appear in the box.

Exercise 54

Changing background colours

1 Load Microsoft FrontPage® either by clicking on the `Start` button, highlighting `All Programs` and then selecting the `Microsoft FrontPage 2003` item or by double-clicking on the FrontPage icon on the Windows® desktop.

2 Maximise the application window to fill the display using the maximize button in the top right-hand corner if the application is displayed in a window.

3 Open the file First_ Generation_ Company.htm by double-clicking on its name (Figure 7.13). The First Generation Company page should now appear in FrontPage®.

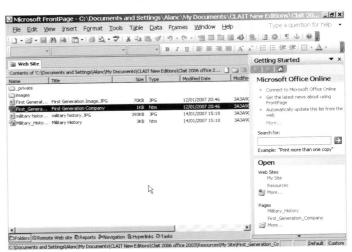

Figure 7.13 First Generation Company file

Alternatively in the Getting Started task pane to the right of the display in the section Open you may see First_Generation_Company.htm listed. If you click on the name the web page will open.

4 Explore the different background colours, checking the effects the colour has on the image and text. In particular make sure the text is legible. Figure 7.14 shows my efforts to use colour.

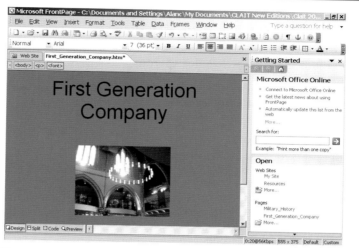

Figure 7.14 First Generation

5 When you are confident, save the revised page and close Microsoft FrontPage®.

Graphics file formats

If you add pictures or other graphic elements (e.g. borders, lines and shapes) to your web page then its size will increase. This can be important if your space for storing the website is limited or you anticipate many users who will not have access to a high-speed (broadband) link. In general it is good practice to minimize the size of your images by physically resizing them and also by saving them in file formats suitable for the web. The main formats used for web page images are:

- JPEG
- GIF
- PNG.

You can convert images to these formats by right-clicking on the picture and selecting the Picture Properties option. This opens the Picture Properties window that lets you convert the image to one of the above formats (i.e. General tab).

Hyperlinks

An important feature of web pages is their ability to be connected or hyperlinked both to other pages within the same site and to other sites. The word hyperlink is often shortened to link. There are four main types of link available to you when you are designing a web page. These are:

- A simple link between two pages you have created. This will allow you to design a route through the site you are building.

- A link to a file stored on your computer so that you have access to extra material on your page. You could load a PowerPoint® presentation to explain an idea or subject to your users.

- A link to a web page which is part of another site on the World Wide Web. This is a widely used link and most sites have many of this type.

- A link to an e-mail editor to allow you to send an e-mail to a chosen location. You could use

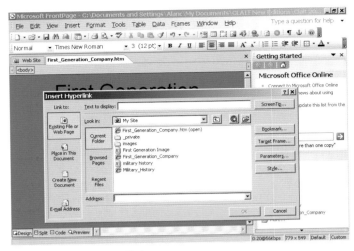

Figure 7.15 Hyperlinks

this link to let your users comment on the design of the page or to order products advertised on the page or for any other communication need.

Links are activated by clicking on them and usually take one of two main forms: an underlined word or phrase, or a picture. The picture can be an icon, a large image or even the whole screen.

Microsoft FrontPage® gives you access to the hyperlinks through selecting the Insert menu and the option Microsoft Hyperlink to reveal the Insert Hyperlink window (Figure 7.15). Across the working area of the screen you will see the location and name of the web page you are working on. In this example it is the First Generation Company.

The window provides you with the means of creating four types of link. These are shown as four icons displayed below the Link to. From top to bottom the icons enable you to:

- establish a link to an existing file or web page
- link within the current document
- link to a new document
- link to an e-mail location.

Exercise 55

Creating and testing hyperlinks

1 Load Microsoft FrontPage® either by clicking on the Start button, highlighting All Programs and then selecting the Microsoft FrontPage 2003 item or by double-clicking on the FrontPage icon on the Windows® desktop.

2 Maximize the application window to fill the display using the maximize button in the top right-hand corner if the application is displayed in a window.

3 Open the file First_Generation_Company.htm by double-clicking on its name (Figure 7.13). The First Generation Company page should now appear in FrontPage®.

Alternatively in the Getting Started task pane to the right of the display in the section Open you may see First_Generation_Company listed. If you click on the name the web page will open.

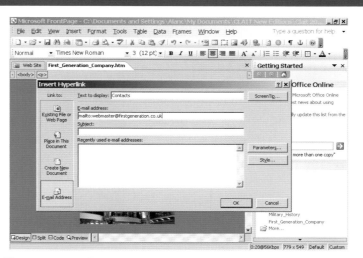

Figure 7.16 E-mail hyperlink

4 When we designed this page we provided four potential links at the bottom of the page. These are:

1 Contacts
2 Products
3 Prices
4 News

5 We will create links from each of these.

6 The contacts link is intended to allow users of the page to e-mail the company to ask for information, ask questions or comment on the page.

7 Highlight the word Contacts to identify it as the link you are going to create. Select the Insert menu and the Hyperlink option to open the Insert Hyperlink window.

8 In the Text to display box at the top of the window you should see Contacts displayed. In the working area in the centre of the window you should see First_Generation_ Company.htm (open) displayed (Figure 7.15). Click on the icon to create an e-mail link – this is the fourth down from Link to. It will open a new window (Figure 7.16).

9 Enter webmaster@firstgeneration.co.uk in the E-mail address box (Figure 7.16) and click on the OK button. The window will close, returning you to the web page.

10 Observe the Contacts link and you will see that it has changed colour to blue and is underlined which indicates that it is a link. Change the View tab to Preview and we will test the link.

11 Click on the Contacts link in the Preview View. You should see the e-mail page for the system that is set up on the computer you are using appear. In my case, this is Microsoft Outlook®. The e-mail address will be included in the blank e-mail page. It is important to test each link to ensure it does what you intend.

12 Return to the Design View by clicking on the Design tab. Highlight Products and again access the Insert Hyperlinks window. You are going to link the page to an existing web page on the World Wide Web. Select the Existing File or Web Page icon. Click on the World Wide Web icon which is the second icon to the right of the Look in: box (Figure 7.17). This opens your browser so you can locate your chosen page. Find the page you want to link to and then press the Alt and Tab keys to return to Insert Hyperlink window. You should see the page's address in the address box at the bottom of the window. Click on the OK button.

If you make a mistake you can remove the link by clicking on the button Remove Link in the Insert Hyperlink window once you have highlighted the link on your web page.

13 You have created a link from the First Generation Company page to the web page of your choice. When you select the OK button you will return to the First Generation Company page.

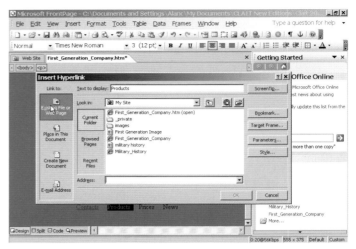

Figure 7.17 **Link to a file**

14 You should see the word Products has changed colour to blue, indicating a link has been established.

15 Test the link by changing to the Preview view and clicking on the Products link and you will see your page appear if the link has been correctly established. Click on the Design tab to return to the First Generation Company page.

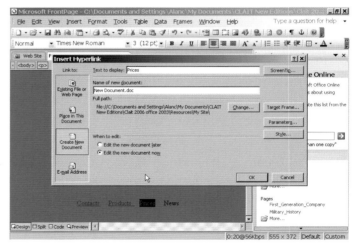

Figure 7.18 **New Document link**

16 Highlight Prices and again access the Insert Hyperlink window. You are going to create a link to a New Document. Click on Create New Document and the display will change (Figure 7.18) asking you to enter the path to the new document. I chose to make the link to a stored document I called New Document. Click on the OK button to return to the First Generation Company page.

17 You should see the word Prices has changed colour to blue, indicating a link has been established.

18 The last link is between News and another part of the page. The first step is to create a bookmark on the page to link to. Highlight the word Generation in the title and select the Insert menu and the Bookmark option to reveal the Bookmark window. This will display Generation and you need to confirm the bookmark by clicking on the OK button. Highlight News and access the Insert Hyperlink window. Click on the button called Place in This Document . The display will change to show a heading Bookmark

and a link to Generation (Figure 7.19). Highlight Generation and click on the OK button and you will return to the First Generation Company page.

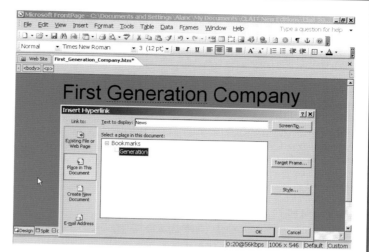

Figure 7.19 Link in page

19 You should see the word News has changed colour to blue, indicating a link has been established.

20 Test the link by changing to the Preview and clicking on the News link and you will see your view of the page change to focus on the word generation. The link has moved you within the page. Click on the Design tab to return to the First Generation Company page.

21 To save your First_Generation_Company web page, select the File menu then the Save As option to reveal the Save As window. The location should be shown as My Site, the folder you created earlier in this chapter with the filename of First_Generation_Company.htm. Save the file.

22 You may be presented with a second window asking if you want to save the embedded files. In this case this means the Clip Art image. Click on the OK button and the window will clear.

24 We are going to explore the effects of editing the HTML code. Click on the Code tab which will reveal the code. Experiment with changing the code and use the Preview tab to see the effects of the change.

Try removing align='center'> from the line <font face='Arial' size='7'>First <a name='Generation'>Generation</a> Company</font> by highlighting and pressing the Delete key.

In the Preview you will see that the title is now left-aligned (left-justified).

If you are interested in creating a simple page using HTML then try the optional exercise at the end of the chapter.

25 When you are finished close the page by selecting the File menu and Close. You will be asked if you want to save the changes. Click on No since you do not want to save the changes to the code.

26 When you edit code it sometimes will not take effect since FrontPage® is still working from the original code. It is therefore necessary to reload pages after saving the changes, to refresh the code in FrontPage®.

Web Page Creation

209

continued

27 Now Print the page by selecting the `File` menu and the `Print` option to reveal the Print window. Click on the `OK` button to print the page using the printer default settings.

28 Change the View tab to `Code` and print the code using the same procedure. You will now have printouts of the code and the visual presentation of the page.

29 Close the application by selecting the `File` menu and `Exit` option or by clicking on the `Close` button in the top right-hand corner of the window.

Link resources

When creating links, you have to remember that the resources you are linking to must be available when the web page is part of the website. There is no point linking to a file which, when the page is on the World Wide Web, is not available.

All the linked resources must therefore be retained and it is good practice to save everything to the same folder. In our exercises you have been asked to save everything to the Web Site folder. When you were saving your pages you were prompted to save the embedded files. This is a function of Microsoft FrontPage® that tries to help you retain all the data required for the web page. If you need to practise or develop your file management skills then consider Unit 1.

More Practice

Text files and images are available on the Hodder website (http://www.hodderclait.co.uk/).

Activity 1

1 Load Microsoft FrontPage® either by clicking on the `Start` button, highlighting `All Programs` and then selecting the `Microsoft FrontPage` item or by double-clicking on the FrontPage icon on the Windows® desktop.

2 Maximise the application window to fill the display using the maximize button in the top right-hand corner if the application is displayed in a window.

3 The display should show the Web Site tab with the files that you created in the previous exercises. Across the bottom of the working area you should see that the View tabs have changed to show different ones – Folders, Remote Web Site, Reports, Navigation, Hyperlinks and Tasks.

4 Click on `Create a new page or site` in the Open section of the Getting Started task pane. The task pane will change to New. Select the `Blank Page` option in the New page section of the task pane. The working area will now display a blank page with a tab called new_page_1.htm.

5 We are going to create a simple web page about the hobby of collecting stamps.

6 Enter the heading Stamp Collecting in a font of your own choice in size 36.

7 Centre and embolden the heading and insert a Clip Art image suitable for the subject,

centred on the page. Resize the image as appropriate. Alternatively insert the image Stamps available from the Hodder website (http://www.hodderclait.co.uk).

8 Below the picture enter, in a font of your choice and in size 12, the following text. Or insert the text file Stamp Collecting. In both cases the text should be left-aligned (left-justified). Remember to check the text file for spelling and grammar mistakes and to count the number of words.

Stamp Collecting is the largest collecting hobby in the world. It attracts people of all ages and backgrounds. This site aims to help people discover more about stamp collecting. The links below provide access to more information about the hobby. You can e-mail me by clicking on E-mail link. To link to the introduction page click on Introduction. If you click on the picture you will be linked to other sites about stamp collecting.

9 Leave two blank lines and enter:

Last updated by (your own name) on (the date)

10 Establish links from the word e-mail to an e-mail address, from the word Introduction to a new page and from the picture to a website of your choice. In all cases, highlight the text or picture and select the Insert menu and the Hyperlink option to reveal the Insert Hyperlink window. The link text should be size 14. The new page should be called introductionstamps2.htm.

11 Test your links using the Preview tab.

12 Select a suitable background colour.

13 Check your web page to ensure you have followed all the instructions. Proofread the page to check spelling, grammar and layout.

14 Figure 7.20 shows our attempts at this page in the Preview View. Notice that the cursor has changed shape when over a link (i.e. the image).

15 To save your Stamp Collecting web page, select the File menu then the Save option to reveal the Save As window. The location should be shown as My Site, the folder you created earlier in this chapter. Save the page as the file named Stamp+Collecting.htm.

16 You may be presented with a second window asking if you want to save the embedded files. In this case this means the Clip Art or Stamp image. Click on the OK button and the window will clear.

17 Now print the page by selecting the File menu and the Print option to reveal the Print window. Click on the OK button to print the page using the printer default settings.

18 Change the View tab to Code and print the code using the same procedure. You will now have printouts of the code and the visual presentation of the page.

19 Close the application by selecting the File menu and Exit option or by clicking on the Close button in the top right-hand corner of the window.

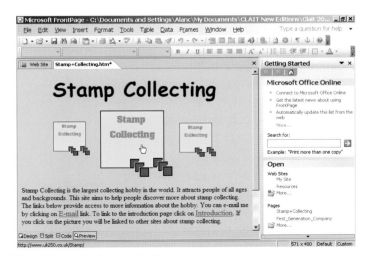

Figure 7.20 Stamp Collecting

Activity 2

1 Load Microsoft FrontPage® either by clicking on the Start button, highlighting All Programs and then selecting the Microsoft FrontPage 2003 item or by double-clicking on the FrontPage icon on the Windows desktop.

2 Maximize the application window to fill the display using the maximize button in the top right-hand corner if the application is displayed in a window.

3 The display should show the Web Site tab with the files that you created in the previous exercises. Across the bottom of the working area you should see that the View tabs have changed to show different ones – Folders, Remote Web Site, Reports, Navigation, Hyperlinks and Tasks.

4 Click on Create a new page or site in the Open section of the Getting Started task pane. The task pane will change to New. Select the Blank Page option in the New Page section of the task pane. The working area will now display a blank page with a tab called new_page_1.htm.

5 We are going to create a simple web page about a community group.

6 Enter the heading East Wolds Community Group in a font of your own choosing in size 36. Centre the heading. Leave one blank line and then enter the text below in a font of your choice but in size 14. Or insert the text file East Wolds. Remember to check for spelling and grammatical errors and to count the number of words displayed.

The East Wolds Community Group was founded in 1996 with the aim of supporting the development of the environment within East Wolds village and the people who live in the parish. The group have several main programmes of work underway including:

1   Preserving the local wild life
2   Ensuring access to the countryside
3   Maintaining footpaths

7 Fully align (justify) this text.

8 Leave two blank lines and enter:
Last updated by (your own name) on (the date)
The text should be size 14. Centre this text.

9 Change the background colour to green.

10 Insert a suitable Clip Art or saved image (e.g. East Wolds) appropriate to the subject centred on the page between the bottom line of text (i.e. 3 Maintaining footpaths) and Last updated.... Resize the image as appropriate.

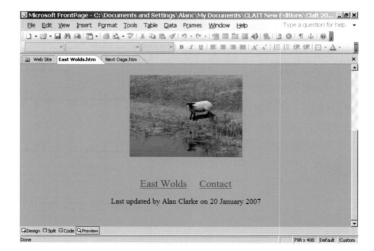

11 Leave two blank lines below the image and insert the text below to act as links using a font of your choice and a character size of 18. Centre them.

East Wolds   Contact

12 Establish links from the words

Figure 7.21 East Wolds

East Wolds to a new page and from the word Contact to an e-mail address. In both cases, highlight the text and select the Insert menu and the Hyperlink option to reveal the Insert Hyperlink window.

13 Test the links using the Preview . Spellcheck your page.

14 Figure 7.21 shows our attempts at this web page.

15 To save your East Wolds Community web page, select the File menu then the Save option to reveal the Save As window. The location should be shown as My Site, the folder you created earlier in this chapter. Save the page as the file named East Wolds.htm.

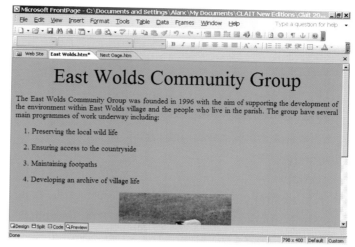

Figure 7.22 Amended Page

16 You may be presented with a second window asking if you want to save the embedded files. In this case this means the Clip Art or other image. Click on the OK button and the window will clear.

17 Now change the alignment of the three bullet points to left-aligned (left-justified) and indent them.

18 Add a fourth bullet point:

   4   Developing an archive of village life

19 Change Last updated by to Edited by. Reduce character size to 10.

20 Check your web page to ensure you have followed all the instructions. Proofread the page to check spelling, grammar and layout.

21 Save your amended page. Figure 7.22 shows the new page.

22 Now print the page by selecting the File menu and the Print option to reveal the Print window. Click on the OK button to print the page using the printer default settings.

23 Change the View tab to Code and print the code using the same procedure. You will now have printouts of the code and the visual presentation of the page.

24 Close the application by selecting the File menu and Exit option or by clicking on the Close button in the top right-hand corner of the window.

Activity 3 Optional exercise
Writing HTML

1 HTML files are simply plain text files and they can be created by many text editors including Notepad which is supplied as part of Microsoft Windows®.

2 To load Notepad, select the Start button, highlight All Programs , Accessories and click on Notepad .

3 Enter the text below:

```
<html>
<head>
```

```
<TITLE>A Basic Page</TITLE>
</head>
<body>
<H1>This is the first heading of the Page</H1>
<P>This starts the first paragraph</P>
<P>A new paragraph</P>
<P>Yet another paragraph</P>
</body>
</html>
```

4 This uses only a few tags. These were:

<html> marks the start of the HTML commands

</html> marks the end of the HTML commands

<head> marks the beginning of the HTML document

</head> marks the end of the main heading

<body> shows the start of the main body of a document

</body> shows the end of the main body of a document

<H1> marks the start of the first heading

</H1> marks the end of the first heading

<P> marks the start of a paragraph

</P> marks the end of a paragraph

5 Insert a floppy disk in to the computer's drive. To save your web page select the File menu then the Save As option to reveal the Save As window. Choose the location in which to store your page by clicking on the down arrow at the end of the Save in: box. This will reveal a list. Click on the floppy disk option. You will then see this appear in the box. Now click the File name: box and enter from the keyboard the name HTMLexample.htm and click on the Save button. You will need to add the extension .htm; this is vital or your browser will not recognize the code. You will hear the drive working and the file will be saved on the floppy disk as a file called HTMLexample.htm.

6 Close the application by selecting the File menu and Exit option or by clicking on the Close button in the top right-hand corner of the window.

7 Without connecting to the Internet open Internet Explorer or another browser either by clicking on the Start button, highlighting All Programs and then selecting the Internet Explorer item or by double-clicking on the Internet Explorer icon on the Windows® desktop.

8 Click on the address box and enter A:\HTMLexample.htm and press enter. Your page will be displayed.

9 Close the application by selecting the File menu and Close option or by clicking on the Close button in the top right-hand corner of the window.

SUMMARY

1 **Load Microsoft FrontPage® 2003** Click on the Start button, highlight All Programs and then select the Microsoft FrontPage 2003 item or double-click on the FrontPage icon on the Windows® desktop.

2 **Close Microsoft FrontPage®** Select the File menu and the Exit option or click the Close button in the top right-hand corner of the window.

3 **Create a website folder (disk-based website)** Click on the Design View tab if another view is showing. Select the File menu and the New option. This will reveal the New task pane. Select the More Web Site Templates option from the New Web Site section. This will open the Web Site Templates window . The default location of the folder is c:\Documents and Settings\Alan Clarke\My Documents\My Websites. In your case your name will appear instead of Alan Clarke or whoever is the computer's user. You can also use the browse button to select another location.
Now select the Empty Web Site template by double-clicking. A new tab will appear in the working area called Web Site. This shows the folder in which all your files for this site will be stored.

4 **Alignment (Justification)** Highlight the text and select the respective icons (i.e. left, right, centre or justify) from the Formatting toolbar.

5 **Select fonts and character size** Highlight the text. Select the small down arrow button to the right of the character size box to reveal a list of sizes. Click on the size of your choice. Select the small down arrow button to the right of the font box to reveal a list of fonts. Click on the font of your choice.

6 **Bold, italics and underline** Highlight the text and select the respective icons (i.e. bold, italics or underline) from the Formatting toolbar.

7 **Insert Clip Art images** Select the Insert menu, highlight the Picture option and click on the Clip Art item. This will reveal the Clip Art task pane which allows you to search for pictures related to a particular theme. The results of the search are shown as thumbnail images. Place your pointer on the image and a button with a down arrow will appear. If you click on the button a menu of choices will appear including the Insert option. This will insert the picture into the page.

8 **Insert files** Select the Insert menu and the File option to reveal the Select File window.

9 **Background colours and images** Select the Format menu and the Background option. This will reveal the Page Properties window.

10 **Creating hyperlinks** Highlight the word or image which will form the link. Select the Insert menu and the option hyperlink to reveal the Insert Hyperlink window.

11 **Print page** Change the View tab to Design . Select the File menu and the Print option to reveal the Print window. Click on the OK button to print the page using the printer's default settings.

12 **Print code** Change the View tab to `Code` . Select the `File` menu and the `Print` option to reveal the Print window. Click on the `OK` button to print the code using the printer's default settings.

13 **Convert image formats** Right-click on the picture and select the `Picture Properties` option (only available from the Design View) to reveal the Picture Properties window. Select the `General` tab.

14 **Size of characters** Character size is shown in two different ways in Microsoft Frontpage®. These are the normal points way used in all the Microsoft® Office applications and also in HTML sizes (e.g. HTML 3 is equivalent to 12 points).

Chapter

8

Unit 8

Online Communication

This chapter will help you use electronic communication to:

■ identify and use e-mail and browsing software

■ navigate the World Wide Web and use search techniques to locate data on the web

■ transmit and receive e-mail messages and attachments.

Assessment

This unit does not assume any previous experience of using a computer. However, you may find it useful to have completed Unit 1 (File Management and e-Document Production). You will be assessed through a practical realistic assignment which is designed to allow you to demonstrate your knowledge and skills against each objective. Your tutor can provide you with more guidance.

What is the World Wide Web?

The Internet is essentially a worldwide network linking millions of computers. It was initially developed to allow communication between research organizations and provides users with a range of services including:

■ E-mail (electronic mail)

■ World Wide Web (WWW).

It is possible to send e-mail messages anywhere in the world to anyone having an e-mail account. It is like being able to send a postcard almost instantaneously. It is fast and efficient and many people regard e-mail as one of the major benefits of the Internet.

The World Wide Web comprises an extremely large number of locations called websites which provide information about a subject or organization using text, sound, video and graphics. These sites are located on computers scattered all over the world, linked by telecommunication networks (e.g. telephone lines and optical cables). For many people the World Wide Web *is* the Internet in that there are now millions of websites offering information on almost every topic. Visiting them is known as surfing the web and browsing websites.

To explore the World Wide Web you need to use a browser, which is an application designed to allow you to view websites. There is a range of browsers including:

- Internet Explorer 7.0 (Figure 8.1)
- Netscape Navigator
- Mozilla Firefox.

There are others, including ones developed to help visually impaired users browse websites by reading the site contents aloud. Internet Explorer is currently the most widely used browser.

To send and receive e-mails requires access to an e-mail application. Internet Explorer is linked to e-mail software called Microsoft Outlook® 2003 (Figure 8.2) which provides the functions that allow you to send and receive e-mail. There are also a number of other e-mail systems including those that operate from websites.

Accessing the World Wide Web

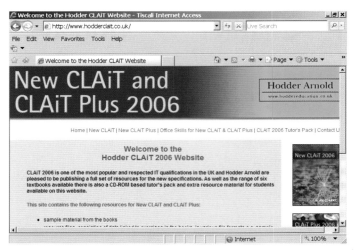

Figure 8.1 Internet Explorer 7.0

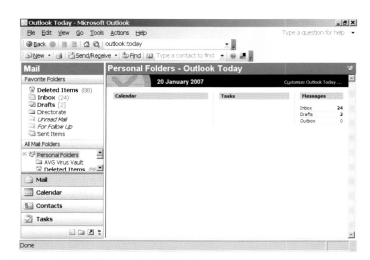

Figure 8.2 Microsoft Outlook

The process of accessing the World Wide Web depends on where you are trying to communicate from. If you are at a college or at work then it is probably very straightforward, involving simply loading the e-mail application or browser. The college or work networks are often linked to the Internet automatically. However, at home you will probably need to carry out the additional action of connecting to the Internet through an Internet Service Provider to which you have subscribed. Once you have made your connection, you can then load the browser or e-mail application. If you have broadband (e.g. ADSL – Asymmetric Digital Subscriber Line) at home then the process will be similar to college or work since many broadband systems offer a continuous link to the Internet although, since there is a range of ways of configuring systems, there may be differences depending on how the computer and broadband are set up.

Some hotels and other organizations offer wireless connections, meaning that if you have a laptop that is wireless-enabled you can access the Internet and send e-mails through your account simply by being within their buildings. This is becoming increasingly common but arrangements vary and in some cases there are charges or you need to register to use the service. At least one railway company now offers wireless connection to the Internet.

Surfing the World Wide Web

To locate a particular website you need to know its address or URL (Uniform or Universal Resource Locator). When this is entered into the Address bar and the Enter key is pressed, the browser searches for the website which is then shown in the browser window. In Figure 8.1 the address is http://www.hodderclait.co.uk and the browser shows the CLAiT website provided by Hodder Arnold to support the CLAiT series.

Website addresses are unique and are structured in a similar way to a postal or street address. The address or URL for the BBC is http://www.bbc.co.uk. This comprises:

- http – Hypertext Transfer Protocol; this tells the browser how to transfer the web page across the Internet so you can view it
- www – World Wide Web
- bbc – host of the website
- co – company
- uk – United Kingdom.

The general form is thus http://www.host.typeoforganization.country. However, websites in the USA do not use a country suffix. Other codes for some organizations and countries are:

- ac - university/academic
- .com – company
- .co – company
- .edu – educational institution
- .org – charity or not-for-profit organization
- .gov – government
- .mil – military
- .net – network
- .be – Belgium
- .ca – Canada
- .dk – Denmark
- .nl – Netherlands
- .ch – Switzerland

Structure of a website

A website consists of a variety of pages each displaying content in the form of text and graphics. Some will also provide sound and video. The pages can vary in length and you often need to scroll down them. Each page is linked to the others by hypertext links which, when clicked on, allow you to jump around the site. A website can be designed so that almost anything can be linked to something else. Links exist to connect items of information within pages as well as between different pages. This can sometimes be confusing since you may feel you have jumped to a new page whereas you have only moved to a new part of the same page. Websites vary in size and can be very large and complex. Figure 8.3 illustrates links between web pages. There can be links such as:

- from an image to a text passage
- from a word to the top of a page
- from an image to another picture
- from the bottom of one page to the top of another
- between pages and within pages.

Links may take the form of underlined words, of areas of the screen that change the shape of the mouse pointer when it passes over them or of buttons.

The standard address of a website (e.g. http://www.host. type.country) usually links you to what is called the home page of the site which is rather like the contents page of a book. It normally has links to the main parts of the site but it is also possible to link to individual pages within a website by extending the address (e.g. htttp://www.host.type. country/nextpage/other pages). This is useful when you want to direct people to a particular page but it can be confusing since by following a link you may suddenly find yourself in the middle of a new website. Links can be:

- between pages in a single site
- between pages in different sites
- within a single page.

Figure 8.4 illustrates a simplified structure of a website. This is presented as a series of layers but websites are often more complex than this with direct links from the home page to major parts of the site ensuring that you do not need to move through each layer. Although this is efficient, it is easy to get lost in a more complex website.

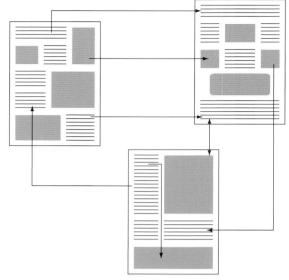

Figure 8.3 Links between web pages

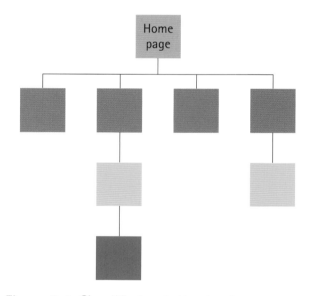

Figure 8.4 Simplified website structure

Exercise 56

Using the browser (Internet Explorer 7.0)

Establish a connection to the Internet – this will depend on your location (e.g. home, work or college).

1 Using the All Programs menu or by clicking on the Internet Explorer icon on the desktop, load the browser. The browser may appear either filling the entire screen or in a window. If you want to expand the window to fill the whole screen, use the Maximize button in the top right-hand corner of the window.

2 Enter http://www.bl.uk (this is the website of the British Library) in the Address bar and press Enter . It is vital to be 100% accurate when entering URLs since any mistake will result in your browser giving you an error message suggesting there is no website at that address. When the page appears in your browser, scroll down and view the content. This is the home page so you should be able to locate a menu of the contents of the site.

3 Try to locate the links to other pages. These will take the form of either underlined words, words in a different colour, areas that are highlighted when you move the pointer over them, pictures or the mouse pointer changing shape to become a hand.

4 Click on a link that looks interesting and watch what happens. You should see the page disappear and a new one take its place. Often the outline of the page will appear quickly but illustrations will take longer, although a frame showing their location may be revealed almost at once. It takes time for the contents of a page to load. The length of time changes depending on the size of the page (e.g. pages containing many illustrations are slow to load), how many people are visiting the site at the same time (i.e. the site gives equal priority to all visitors so if thousands of people are using the site at the same time it will be slow) and the number of people using the World Wide Web (i.e. the more people, the slower the access).

5 Explore the new page and again jump from this to another and so on. Investigate the site and see what you can find.

6 After a few jumps to new pages it may be difficult to remember the route you have taken. However, you can retrace your steps using the Back button on the toolbar which will move you back to the page you jumped from. You can return using the Forward button. The Back and Forward buttons are shown as arrows enclosed in a circle. When your pointer is over them a message will appear explaining where it will take you if you click on the button (e.g. Back to …).

7 Use Back and Forward and observe what happens. You may notice that pages are faster to load in some cases since your computer has stored the contents of the page and can therefore quickly access it.

8 Explore the site until you are confident that you can recognize links, move between pages and use the Back and Forward buttons.

9 You can jump from one website to another from anywhere, so delete the British Library URL and enter http://www.thebritishmuseum.ac.uk in the Address bar and press Enter .

continued

10 Observe the new website appear. This is the home page of the British Museum website. Explore this site practising linking to new pages, locating links and retracing your path.

11 When you are confident about navigating sites, close the browser by selecting the `File` menu and the `Exit` option or click on the window `Close` button in the top right-hand corner of the browser. You can exit the browser from any page within a site.

Searching a website

Unless the site is small or has limited links locating precise content is quite difficult if you simply follow the links. A large, complex site can be difficult to use, so many have a facility to search for chosen topics. Figure 8.5 shows an example of a site search facility or search engine. There are many different website search facilities that will help you to find information. They work by matching the words you enter into them with the topic you are seeking. Often there is a straightforward search facility which appears on

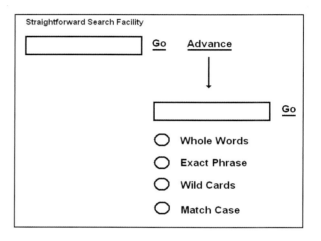

Figure 8.5 Example of site search engine

most pages in which you simply enter your search terms and click on a button and a more advanced engine that provides you with a range of options.

The search engine in Figure 8.5 works in a similar way to many others: you enter a word or words and it seeks to match them to content. In this case you are allowed to refine the nature of the match:

■ Whole Words – any of the words you have entered match any whole word in the content

■ Exact Phrase – the search phrase is matched exactly in the content

■ Wild Cards – this matches the structure of the search terms used, such as *ard that will match with yard, card and any other four-letter word ending with ard. The wild card can be any letter.

■ Match Case – the search must match the case (i.e. lower- or upper-case) of the search words.

The advanced search facility will sometimes present the results as a list in order of the closeness of the match. It is usually effective to start with a very wide search and then to refine it so that you do not get too many to review. The straightforward facility will often be effective and you should always try it first before using the advanced facility.

Specialist sites will often provide a search facility that links closely to the nature of the information they contain. For example a site dedicated to books will often allow you to search by author, book title, publisher and ISBN number as well as by general search terms.

Exercise 57

Search a single site

1   Establish a connection to the Internet – this will depend on your location (e.g. home, work or college).

2   Load the browser using the `All Programs` menu or by clicking on the `Internet Explorer` icon on the desktop. The browser may appear filling the entire screen or in a window. If you want to expand the window to fill the whole screen, use the `maximize` button in the top right-hand corner of the window.

3   Enter http://www.number10.gov.uk in the Address bar and press Enter – this is the website of 10 Downing Street, the home of the Prime Minister. This URL will jump you into the home page on which there is a straightforward search facility.

4   Enter a search term such as, voting into the search box and click on the `Go` button. A search page will appear showing the results of the search in the form of a list of items and also the advanced search facility.

5   The advanced search facility allows you to specify matching any words, all words, exact phrase and in title. There is also a link to more advanced facilities.

6   Investigate the site search facilities and explore the results of a number of different searches.

7   Enter the word tours with the option Find in the title only (click into the radio button alongside the option) and click on the `Go` button. A list of matches appears with a brief summary describing them to help you identify if it is the correct one.

8   In my cases there are ten matches all relating to the virtual tours of 10 Downing Street available from the website.

9   Search again for tours with the option Any Words and click on the `Go` button. In this case the search reports 159 matches and displays them ten at a time with what are judged the most relevant first. Your number will be different because the site will have changed since I searched it.

10 Try searching for other information using the different options.

11 You should notice that the more restrictive your search options, the smaller the number of matches.

12 Keep exploring the search facilities using different combinations of options until you are confident you understand how it works.

13 You can jump to the content matched by clicking on the link which is shown underlined when the pointer is placed on it. You will have to do this frequently to check if it is what you are searching for. To return, use the `Back` button.

14 When you are confident about searching, close the browser by selecting the `File` menu then the `Exit` option or click on the window `Close` button in the top right-hand corner of the browser.

Other opportunities to practise

There is a variety of ways that search facilities work on a website. If you would like to practise your search skills, try using the site search engines on:

- www.thebritishmuseum.ac.uk – British Museum
- www.bl.uk – British Library
- www.tate.org.uk – Tate Modern Gallery
- www.movinghere.org.uk – Moving Here site – The National Archive
- www.abebooks.com – a world wide book seller.

All five sites have powerful search facilities to help you locate information.

Searching the World Wide Web

There are millions of websites covering almost every subject. Many organizations provide search engines to help you locate content on the World Wide Web. They have indexed web pages so that you can search them by using key words. This is similar to searching a single website. However, while it is relatively easy to find the content on a single site using a site search engine, it is far more difficult on the World Wide Web because of the number of sites. World Wide Web search engines search for individual web pages rather than entire sites.

Search engines are essentially large databases of web pages that have been amassed automatically by the engine. This is carried out by using tools called spiders or robots which follow links between pages and index the pages they find. The index is directly related to the words presented on the web pages. When you enter your keywords for the information, you are searching the database and not the World Wide Web itself.

There are many search engines and, although they all work in broadly similar ways, there are differences between them. They differ:

- in the range of search options they provide
- in how they present or rank the results of a search.

There are two different types of search engine:

- individual
- meta.

Individual search engines are essentially what we have been describing. A meta engine does not develop its own database but rather searches the databases of several other individual search engines. They are therefore very useful in finding more elusive content.

Another way of finding content on the World Wide Web is by using devices called directories. Directories are very different from search engines. While you search an engine using keywords that you select as being related to what you are seeking, a directory provides you with categories to choose from. The contents of directories are chosen for you. The staff pick sites that they believe you will be interested in so they are in a sense making recommendations, whereas a search engine leaves the whole choice to you. Directories are very quick to use while a search engine can take time to identify suitable pages. However, the categories available to you in a directory are limited to what have been identified as popular items (e.g. computers, shopping and holidays), but a search engine places no limits on categories you can search for. In many cases you will be offered the choice of a search engine and a directory.

There are many different search engines and directories, of which several have United Kingdom versions. The list below shows a range of examples:

Alltheweb	http://www.alltheweb.com
AltaVista	http://www.uk.AltaVista.com
Bigbook	http://www.bigbook.com
Chubba	http://www.chubba.com
Excite	http://www.excite.com
Google	http://www.google.com
	http://www.google.co.uk
HotBot	http://www.hotbot.com
Looksmart	http://www.looksmart.com
Lycos	http://www-uk.lycos.com
Webcrawler	http://www.webcrawler.com
Yahoo	http://www.yahoo.com
	http://www.uk.yahoo.com

Search engines can also be used to find individual e-mail addresses. There are several that specialize in locating e-mail addresses:

Bigfoot	http://www.bigfoot.com
InfoSpace	http://www.infospace.com
Whowhere	http://www.whowhere.com
Yahoo People	http://people.yahoo.com

Meta search engines include:

Dogpile	http://www.dogpile.com
Metacrawler	http://www.metacrawler.com
Monster Crawler	http://www.monstercrawler.com
Lxquick	http://www.lxquick.com
Ask Jeeves	http://www.ask.com

Searching is easy to do but can be difficult to do well. Most search engines offer help in a variety of ways and it is useful to investigate these options. Different search engines operate in different ways so that undertaking an identical search using several will produce varying results. The next two exercises are based on comparing the same search using two different search engines (AltaVista and Google).

Exercise 58

Searching the World Wide Web – AltaVista

1 Establish a connection to the Internet – this will depend on your location (e.g. home, work or college).

2 Load the browser by using the All Programs menu or by double-clicking on the Internet Explorer icon on the desktop.

3 Enter http://www.uk.altavista.com in the Address bar and press Enter – this is the website of AltaVista. If you would like to compare this search engine with a directory then visit http://www.bigbook.com. Study the AltaVista search engine and notice that there are options to search for images, audio, video and news.

4 Return to the AltaVista search engine. We will try to locate a hotel in Edinburgh. So enter the word hotels into the box of the search engine and select the option which restricts the search to the United Kingdom (click on the radio button – a small circle which when you click on it inserts a dot in its centre to show it is active). Click on the Search button.

The results of my search were 350,000,000 pages matching the word hotels and also offering a number of sponsored matches about hotels. Your results will be different since the World Wide Web is continuously changing.

5 This is not very useful as there are too many matches. Let's refine the search by adding the word Edinburgh. You should enter hotels Edinburgh then select the UK option and click on the Search button.

6 In my case the results of this search were: 7,360,000 pages that match the words hotels Edinburgh, and also some sponsored matches relating to hotels in Edinburgh.

7 The number of matches is significantly reduced.

8 Refine the search by joining the words with a plus sign, i.e. hotels+Edinburgh. The engine will now search for pages containing both words. In this case AltaVista located 7,390,000 web pages which matched.

9 A final search involves enclosing the words in double inverted commas. This normally makes the engine search for pages in which the phrase hotels Edinburgh appears. AltaVista located 268,000 pages. Finally try to reverse the order of the words so enter "Edinburgh hotels". This produced 722,000 matches.

10 Change the search terms to make them more precise and observe the changes this causes with using the plus sign and inverted commas.

11 You can jump to any matching web page by clicking on the link (underlined and coloured words) to check if it is what you are looking for. To return to the search engine, use the Back button. Explore the search engine by carrying out a search to find web pages that interest you (e.g. look for pages about a hobby, football team, government or places of interest).

12 The matches are presented in the order that the search engine judges to be closest to

your search terms. If you explore the top 10 or 20 results you will often find what you are looking for. The sponsored links are often closely related to your search so that in our example they are hotel booking agents.

13 When you are confident about searching, close the browser by selecting the `File` menu and the `Exit` option or click on the window `Close` button in the top right-hand corner of the browser.

Exercise 59

Searching the World Wide Web – Google (Figure 8.6)

1 Establish a connection to the Internet – this will depend on your location (e.g. home, work or college).

2 Load the browser by using the `All Programs` menu or by clicking on the `Internet Explorer` icon on the desktop.

3 Enter http://www.google.com in the Address bar and press `Enter` – this is the website of the Google search engine.

4 Notice that this search engine offers options to search for images, groups, news, Froogle and more. Explore the other options and see what extra options are provided by `More`. You can also restrict searches to UK pages.

5 We will try again to locate a hotel in Edinburgh, so enter the word hotels into the search box. Limit the search to UK pages and click the Google `Search` button.

Figure 8.6 Google search engine

6 The result of the search were that Google located 22,900,000 pages with matches to the word hotels. There were also some sponsored matches. Your results will be different since the World Wide Web is continuously changing.

However, these results are far from useful in finding a hotel in Edinburgh since there are far too many matches. Let's refine the search by adding the word Edinburgh. You should enter hotels Edinburgh and click on the Google `Search` button. This search located 1,530,000 pages that match the words hotels Edinburgh.

continued

7 A third possible step is to modify the search by joining the words with a plus sign. The engine will search for pages containing both words. Google located 1,830,000 pages showing that it treated hotels Edinburgh the same as hotels+Edinburgh.

8 A fourth search is to enclose the words in inverted commas. This normally makes the engine search for pages that include the phrase hotels Edinburgh. Google located 99,000 web pages.

9 A final way is to reverse the search words and enter "Edinburgh hotels". Google located 628,000 pages.

10 Change the search terms to make them more precise and observe the changes this causes when using the plus sign and inverted commas.

11 Compare the results of the two searches and consider the effectiveness of different search approaches and search engines. It is useful to compare which pages each search engine identified in their top ten. In my case the last search "Edinburgh hotels" produced only one match that was common between the two search engines.

12 Explore the Google search engine by carrying out a search to find web pages that interest you (e.g. look for pages about a hobby, football team, government or places of interest).

13 When you are confident about searching, close the browser by selecting the `File` menu and the `Exit` option or click on the window `Close` button in the top right-hand corner of the browser.

Exercise 60

More comparisons and things

Try other comparisons. I also searched for hotels in Edinburgh using Yahoo UK (http://uk.yahoo.com) and that produced the following results:

1 hotels   - 55,100,000 matches

2 hotels Edinburgh   - 4,110,000 matches

3 hotels+Edinburgh   - 4,050,000 matches

4 "hotels Edinburgh"   - 161,000 matches

5 "Edinburgh hotels"   - 477,000 matches

Search engines often provide other services. When I searched using the Yahoo UK site it was a Saturday and I was able to access live information about all the Premiership football matches. Try finding out what news and other services the different search engines offer.

Saving information

Browsers provide functions allowing you to save the contents of web pages to save images and to save the URL so you can return to the page and print the page. All these functions require the browser to be accessing the chosen web page.

To print the page, select the File menu then the Print option, which will open the Print dialog box. Press the OK button in the Print dialog box and the web page will now be printed using the printer default settings. Web pages are quite often

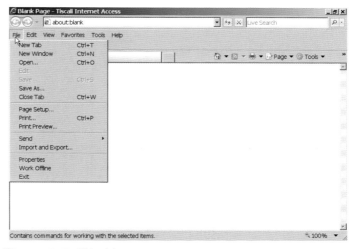

Figure 8.7 File Menu

long, so printing a web page can produce several A4 sheets. Figure 8.7 shows the File menu.

In a similar way, the contents of the web page can be saved by selecting the File menu and the Save or Save As options. This opens the Save dialog box. To save a web page as a file, you need to identify a folder in which to save it. This is done by clicking on the down arrow at the end of the Save in: box to open a list of the drives and folders. To select one, single-click on it. Once you have selected a folder you can name your file by clicking in the File name: box and entering the name using the keyboard. The file can now be saved by clicking the Save button. The latest browsers allow you to save both the text and images unlike the earlier ones which only allowed you to save the text and left gaps where the pictures should be.

You can also save images by positioning the mouse pointer over the picture and right-clicking. This will open a menu of options including Save Picture As . If you select this option then a window called Save Picture will open that offers you the opportunity to select the filename (i.e. the box at the bottom of the window called File name:) and the file type (i.e. the box at the bottom of the window called Save as type:). Usually this will be completed by the system

identifying the file. It is often JPEG or GIF since these are widely used on websites. The window also allows you to choose where to save the file to by using the Save in: box at the top of the window.

Once you have found a useful website it is important to be able to find it again. Internet Explorer lets you save the URLs in a special area called Favorites. To store a URL you need to be accessing the chosen website. You then select the Favorites menu and the

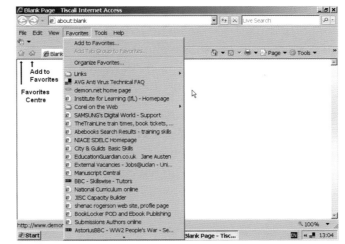

Figure 8.8 Favorites

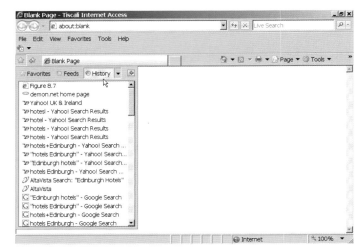

Add to Favorites option. There are also icons on the toolbar that provide access to the Favorites Center and Add to Favorites function. Figure 8.8 shows a list of favorites. To return to a favorite website you simply click on it. You can organize your favourites into folders, grouping related sites together.

The Favorites Center provides a list of favorites and also access to the history function (Figure 8.9). The Add to Favorites icon allows you to select a new favorite site and also to

Figure 8.9 History

organize favorites into folders. The functions duplicate those found in the Favorites menu.

Another way of returning to a useful website is to use the browser's history records. Internet Explorer keeps records of sites visited. However, this record system is often set to keep the list of sites visited for just a short time so its main task is to allow you to return to a particular site after a session visiting many different websites. Figure 8.9 shows the History record open. It is accessed by clicking on the History button in the Favorites Center.

Microsoft Outlook® 2003 (Figure 8.2)

When you first start to use e-mail it has a magical quality. You connect to the Internet, open your e-mail application (e.g. Microsoft Outlook®) and your e-mails arrive. What happens is that an e-mail is addressed in the same way as a letter or postcard. This address directs the e-mail to a location on the Internet where it is stored on a computer until you collect it, normally that of the Internet Service Provider who supplies your access to the Internet. In some cases that may be your employer or college. Often, as soon as you connect to the Internet and open your e-mail application, the mail automatically arrives. However, in others you will need to request that e-mails be sent to you (often called downloading) or even establish a link to the Internet before accessing your messages. It depends on your situation.

An important issue to remember is that computer viruses are often distributed by e-mail. You should always protect your computer system with up-to-date virus protection software. Most virus protection applications will allow you to set them so that all incoming and outgoing e-mail is checked. This is critical to protect yourself.

Microsoft Outlook® is an e-mail system that also offers many additional features to manage your activities (e.g. diary). You can access it from the All Programs menu or by clicking on the Microsoft Outlook icon on the Windows® desktop. This means you can use it independently from Internet Explorer. You do not need to be connected to the Internet in order to use Microsoft Outlook® to read old e-mail, to write a new e-mail or reply to one that you have received.

However, to send or receive new e-mails does require a connection to the Internet. Once you are connected then the e-mails you have created can be sent. This is like writing a letter at home and having to walk to the postbox to post it. This process of writing or reading e-mails while not being connected is called working off-line.

Figure 8.2 shows you the major Mail features of Microsoft Outlook® 2003. These are:

Figure 8.10 Inbox

- Inbox – this is the folder in which your e-mail is stored when it is received; it is sometimes called the mailbox.
- Outbox – this is the folder in which your e-mails are stored until they are sent (i.e. after you connect to the Internet).
- Sent Items – this is the folder in which all your e-mails that have been sent are stored.
- Deleted Items – this is the folder in which e-mails that have been deleted are stored. This is very useful to prevent mistakes from being made.
- Drafts – this is the folder in which e-mails that are only partially written are stored.
- Address Book (option available in the Tools menu) – this provides access to an electronic address book where e-mail addresses can be stored.

Many of these functions are shown on the left-hand side of the application in the task pane, with the exception of Address Book which is in the Tools menu. Outlook® provides you with these features to ensure that e-mails are safeguarded and organized. However, you can also use standard Windows® file-saving methods to save e-mails as files in other folders. This is useful if the e-mail relates to a particular topic and you have already created a folder for other files so that you can keep everything together.

Microsoft Outlook® 2003 also provides a range of functions to help you organize and manage your time. These are shown in the bottom of the task pane and are called Mail, Calendar, Contacts and Tasks. Mail is the e-mail system for helping you to send, receive and manage your messages. Calendar is essentially your electronic diary. Contacts allows you to record and maintain your contacts while Tasks is basically a means of planning your work through creating To Do lists.

We are going to focus on the Mail system. Incoming mail is displayed in the Inbox which you access by clicking on the Inbox function in the Folders list or in the main working area (i.e. right-hand side of the opening display). Figure 8.10 shows the Inbox. If you select an e-mail by single-clicking to highlight it you will see that the message appears in the window to the right. Outlook® offers a range of ways of showing messages and these are available in the View menu. To open the message so that it is displayed in a separate window you need to double-click on it.

To save an e-mail to an external folder, highlight the message and select the File menu and the Save As option. This will open the Save Message As window. This is identical to other Microsoft® Office applications. You need to:

- Select the drive (e.g. floppy disk) using the Save in: box down arrow

■ Select a filename using the File name: box. Windows® provides you with a name based on the contents of the document but it is always best to name your own files to ensure you can remember them.

If you have opened the message the process for saving to an external folder is the same.

You can also save your messages to a folder within the Inbox folder. In order to save your e-mails to an internal folder you must first create it. The first step is to highlight the Inbox folder within the folders list on the left of the display and then select the down arrow on the New button on the toolbar. This will open a menu of options from which you should choose Folder to reveal the Create New Folder window (Figure 8.11). You enter the name of the folder you want to create and then click on the OK button. Your new folder is created within the Inbox folder. You could create it within any of the folders.

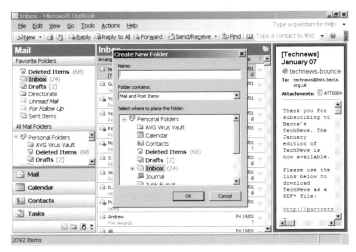

Figure 8.11 Create New Folder

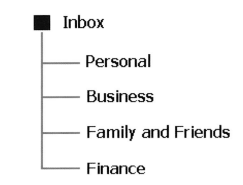

Figure 8.12 E-mail folders

Once you have started to use e-mail you will rapidly have too many messages to remember them all. It is therefore critical to organize them in folders so you can find them later. I used the Create New Folder window to place four folders within the Inbox. These are personal, business, family and friends and finance. Figure 8.12 shows the final folder structure which enables me to organize the management of my messages. Once you have saved a message it is important to remove it from the Inbox or you will quickly have a very long list of messages displayed. To delete an e-mail simply highlight it and press the Delete key on the keyboard or select the Delete option in the Edit menu.

When you want to read a saved e-mail you simply highlight the folder and you will see the saved messages appear in the Outlook's message area. You are then able to select the message you want to read and it will open so you can view it. When you send e-mails they are automatically saved in the Sent Items folder.

Sending messages

To send a new e-mail, click on the New button on the toolbar of Microsoft Outlook®. This will open the e-mail window (Figure 8.13). The layout of the message window guides you through how to write your message. You click into the area where you want to enter text. You need to enter an e-mail address, a subject and the contents of your message. You can also send copies of your message to other people. When you have completed your message, send it by clicking on the Send button. This is in the top left-hand corner of the e-mail window. If you are connected to the Internet, the e-mail will be sent immediately. If you are working off-line (i.e. you are not connected to the Internet) then the e-mail is

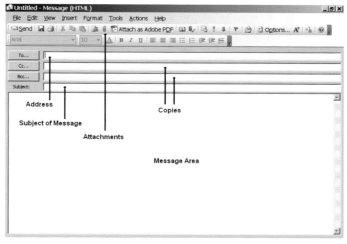

Figure 8.13 E-mail

stored in the Outbox and the number stored will be shown in brackets next to the title Outbox. You should see the number increase by one when you click on the Send button. The e-mail will be dispatched as soon as you next connect to the Internet.

E-mails are normally short messages but other computer files such as spreadsheet, word-processor or presentation files can be attached. This allows far more detailed information to be communicated. Sales staff, for example, can send their expense claims as spreadsheet files or managers their reports as word-processor files. These files, called attachments, are very useful and are easily added to the e-mail using the Insert File button (shown by a paperclip).

E-mail is very useful in business in that mail carries the sender's details. It automatically gets assigned a date and time of creation so that messages can be more easily traced or kept in order. These features allow detailed records to be straightforwardly maintained. Equally important is that any e-mails you receive can be kept (e.g. in your folders).

The address of an e-mail follows a standard convention. It is a combination of the user's name with a domain name (often the e-mail's computer host or Internet Service Provider) joined by the @ symbol. Some examples of e-mail addresses are:

- ajones@acme.co.uk
- alison.jones@acme.net
- jones@harry.org.uk
- a.jones@acme.com.

Many organizations standardize e-mail addresses so that if you know one e-mail address you can work out other ones. For example, you know one member of staff's e-mail address is d.harrison@acme.co.uk. If you know another person is called James King then his e-mail address may be j.king@acme.co.uk.

Exercise 61

Send an e-mail

1 Load Microsoft Outlook® using either the All Programs menu or by clicking on the Outlook icon on the desktop.

2 Open a new message by selecting the New button on the toolbar to reveal the e-mail window (Figure 8.13).

3 If you are studying OCR CLAiT 2006 as part of a class, ask your learning colleagues if you can send them an e-mail or ask a work colleague for her address.

Enter the following text:

To: e-mail address of your colleague

Subject: Practice e-mail

This is my first e-mail and I would be grateful if you would reply to it so that I can see what happens.

Name

4 Before you send your e-mail check that you have entered the address accurately. It must be 100% correct or it will not be delivered. If you send a message to an unknown address you will receive an error message saying that there is no such address. Often this is the result of a tiny error.

5 Click on the Send button as soon as you have completed the message. If you are not connected to the Internet you will see the message added to the Outbox (number in brackets will increase by one). If you are connected then the message will be sent immediately and a copy placed in the Sent Items folder. Check this folder and see if your message has been added.

6 If you are not connected to the Internet you should then connect and you will see your message sent. It should only take a moment or two.

7 Explore Outlook® by clicking on menus and buttons and investigating the different options. Observe the changes to the display.

8 When you are confident that you understand the layout of the application, close Outlook® by selecting the File menu and the Exit option or click on the Close button in the top right-hand corner of the application window.

Receiving e-mails

E-mails that have been sent to you will appear in the Inbox which you access by clicking on the Inbox function in the Folders List or in the main working area (i.e. right-hand side of the opening display). Figure 8.10 shows the Inbox. A list of e-mails is shown in the Inbox which presents you with details of who the message is from, its subject and the date and time it was received. This information can be preceded by a symbol (e.g. a paperclip indicates an attachment and an exclamation mark, an important message). If you

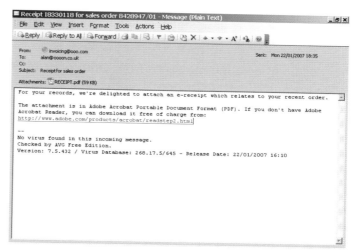

Figure 8.14 Open e-mail

single-click on a message it will be highlighted and its contents revealed in the box to the right of the list. If you double-click on the message then it will open fully (Figure 8.14). Figure 8.14 shows that it has an attachment and that it has been checked for viruses.

When you receive an e-mail you have a variety of options. You can:

- read then delete the message (with the e-mail highlighted or the message window open, select the Edit menu and the Delete option or press the Delete key)
- read and save the message (with the e-mail highlighted or the message window open select the File menu and the Save As option)
- read and reply to the original e-mail sender (with the e-mail highlighted or the message window open, click on the Reply button on the toolbar)
- read and reply to everyone who received the original e-mail (i.e. copies) (with the e-mail highlighted or the message window open click on the Reply to All button on the toolbar)
- read and forward the message to someone else (with the e-mail highlighted or the message window open, click on the Forward button on the toolbar and enter the e-mail address of the person you want the message copied to)
- read and copy the message to a folder (with the e-mail highlighted or the message window open, select the Edit menu and the Copy to Folder option. This allows you to place a copy of the message into one of the existing local folders or to a new local folder. This is useful within Microsoft Outlook®, you begin to create a filing system for your communications. Alternatively you could use the Save As option we discussed earlier)
- read and copy the message to another person (with the e-mail highlighted or the message window open, click on the Reply button on the toolbar. Enter the address of the person you want to copy your reply to in addition to the sender in the To ... box or delete the sender's address and enter the address of the person you are copying the message to)
- print the message (with the e-mail highlighted or the message window open, select the File menu and the Print option).

E-mails are often printed and it is important always to print the e-mail header. This shows the details of the sender, receiver, date sent and subject of the message. This allows you to trace the background to the message and to link it to other related items. It is quite common to print a series of messages to read and answer while travelling and then to send the answers when you return to the office. In order to avoid mistakes it is clearly vital to have the details on the printout. During the assessment for this chapter you will be required to print e-mails with the headers.

The process of deleting messages from your Inbox once you have acted on them is important since very quickly after starting to use e-mail you are likely to have a vast number of old messages. It is vital that these are organized (e.g. saved into folders) or deleted. Otherwise you will rapidly become confused by the mountain of correspondence.

Some of the e-mails you receive will be accompanied by attachments. If you look at the top line of the Inbox you will see a variety of headings – one is a paperclip. If you now look down the list of messages, if any have a paperclip it indicates a message with an attachment. These are files of information (e.g. word-processor files). To open an attachment double-click on it; it will open providing you have the appropriate application available on your computer. A Word file requires Microsoft® Word, an Excel® file requires Microsoft Excel® and so on. Figure 8.14 has an Adobe Acrobat file, a type of file often used, and the message explains where you can locate a copy of the application in order to read the file. If the appropriate application is not present then you will see an error message stating that it cannot identify the application. Once an attachment is open you can save or print it using its application. The appropriate application will be opened automatically by the attachment.

Viruses are frequently transmitted by e-mail attachments. It is therefore important not to open an attachment unless you know who has sent you the message. Equally important is to have up-to-date virus protection software on your computer. Many virus protection systems allow you to check attachments automatically before opening them. It is good practice to check e-mail attachments even if you know the sender. Some viruses automatically send e-mail messages to spread their effects. Figure 8.14 shows that this message has been checked.

Netiquette

Many organizations have established codes of conduct for using e-mail. E-mail messages are often informal and short making them easy to misunderstand. This has given e-mails a reputation for causing offence or causing an argument without intending to do so. Many people do not realize that the same laws apply to e-mail as to letters (e.g. libel). These codes of conduct are called netiquette. Netiquette rules vary but some widely used ones are:

- never send or reply to a message in anger
- always introduce your message (e.g. Dear ... or Hi ...)
- always end your messages (e.g. Best Wishes)
- do not include items in an e-mail that you would not send in a letter
- do not send any form of material that could cause offence.

There are potentially other rules and it is important to find out what your employer's netiquette code is and to follow it.

Formatting e-mail

E-mails are often informal and can easily be misunderstood so it is important to consider how to format messages to make them clear. When creating a new message you can select from a range of formatting options by selecting the ▸Format◂ menu and a series of options including:

- ▸Font◂
- ▸Paragraph◂
- ▸Background◂ .

The ▸Font◂ option allows you to select the font, style (e.g. underlined, italics or bold), colour of text and character size. The ▸Paragraph◂ offers options to align (justify) your message left, right and centre as well as a bullet list, while the ▸Background◂ option offers the possibility of using a picture of your choice as a background for the message or changing the colour of the background.

This range of different options provides powerful ways of presenting your messages to give them impact. However, the main purpose of any message is to ensure that the receiver understands it. It is therefore important not to overuse the different features since they can sometimes distract the reader from the message.

Exercise 62

Receiving e-mails

1 Load Microsoft Outlook® using either the ▸All Programs◂ menu or by clicking on the ▸Outlook◂ icon on the desktop.

2 Single-click on the ▸Inbox◂ which will be highlighted and a list of e-mails received will be listed. E-mail messages that you have not opened are shown in bold. You will possibly find a reply to your previous e-mail but, even if no one has sent you

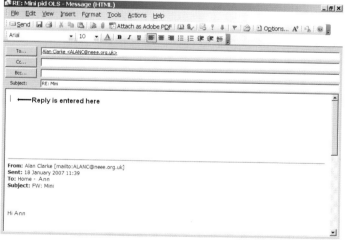

Figure 8.15 **Reply**

a message, Outlook® usually shows a welcome e-mail from the Outlook® team when you initially install it.

3 Single-click on a message. You will see the content displayed. This is very useful if you are seeking to check your e-mail rapidly.

4 Double-click on a message and you will see the Message window open.

5 Click on the ▸Reply◂ button and a new window will appear (Figure 8.15) showing the

original message but it reverses the sender and receiver. In the space above the original message you enter your reply. This enables both the original message and reply to be sent. If this e-mail provokes a response, the e-mail will have the original, the reply and the second reply. E-mails can contain the whole communication.

6   Enter a reply that is appropriate to the message you have opened. In my example:

Hi Alan

Could you please give me some more details about the mini – e.g. how many miles, number of owners and colour etc

Best Wishes,

Ann

7   Click on the `Send` button as soon as you have finished. If you are connected to the Internet your message will be sent. If you are working off-line then the message will be stored in the Outbox and you will see the number in the box increase.

8   Open the e-mail again and this time, click on `Reply to All` and you will see the same window (Figure 8.15) open. This is because the original e-mail was sent only to you. If the original message had been copied to other people then your reply would go to everyone. To close the window select the `File` menu and the `Exit` option or click on the `Close` button in the top right-hand corner of the window.

9   Open the e-mail again and click on the `Forward` button. You will see the same window (Figure 8.15) open again but with a blank To ... line. This lets you send your message to another person. You can also add an extra message. To close the window select the `File` menu and the `Exit` option or click on `Close` button in the top right-hand corner of the window.

10 Open the e-mail again and click on the `Reply` button. You will see the same window (Figure 8.15) open again with the sender and receiver reversed. Delete the address in the To ... box and enter another address (perhaps another student if you are taking a course) and copy the e-mail to the new person.

11 Repeat step 10 but instead of substituting the address in the To ... box insert the address of the person you are copying to in the Cc box.

12 Compare the `Reply` , `Reply to All` and `Forward` functions.

13 When you are confident that you understand the three functions, close Outlook® by selecting the `File` menu and the `Exit` option or click on the `Close` button in the top right-hand corner of the application window.

Attaching files

Attaching files to an e-mail can be very useful. You initially need to start a new e-mail (click on the New button) which opens the E-mail window (Figure 8.13). To add an attachment, click on the Insert File button (i.e. paperclip) on the toolbar. This will open the Insert File window (Figure 8.16).

This window gives you access to all your saved files. To move around the different drives, use the drop down arrow next to the Look in: box and then click on the selected folder or drive. When you have identified the file, double-click on it or single-click the file and then click on the Insert button. The attached file will appear on your message.

Electronic address book

An important function that Microsoft Outlook® provides is the storage of e-mail addresses. You can copy addresses from e-mails that are sent to you or enter new ones manually. Once you have created an entry in the electronic address book, you can send an e-mail directly from it.

The address book can be opened by selecting the Address Book icon (i.e. an open book) on the toolbar when you have an open e-mail. This opens the Select Names window (Figure 8.17). You can enter new addresses by selecting the Advanced button, which will open a short menu with the option New. When you click on New , the New Entry window will appear. This offers you

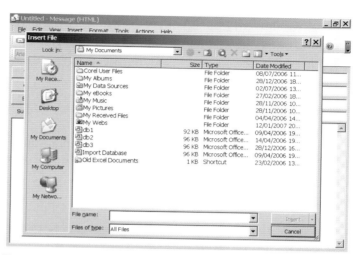

Figure 8.16 Attachment

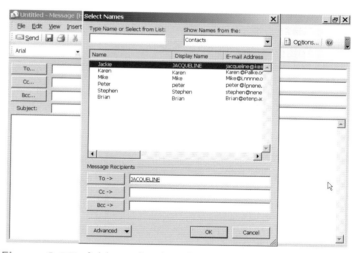

Figure 8.17 Address Book – Select Names window

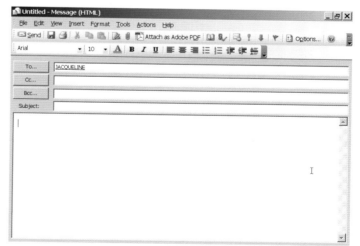

Figure 8.18 Send e-mail from Select Names Window

two choices: to enter a new contact or a new distribution list. A distribution list contains a group of contacts under a common name so that when you send an e-mail to the common name everyone on the list is sent the same message. If you select New Contact then the Contact window will open (Figure 8.19). This allows you to enter the details about the person or organization such as name, address, e-mail addresses, telephone numbers etc. Once you have entered a new contact click on the Save and Close button and their name will appear in the Select Names window.

A useful function provided in the Select Names window is the ability to send an e-mail from it. If you highlight the contact you wish to send an e-mail to and click on the To button or double-click on the name you will see the name appear in the To: box (Figure 8.17). Click on the OK button to see an e-mail message window appear addressed to the contact (Figure 8.18).

Exercise 63

Using an address book

1 Load Microsoft Outlook® using the All Programs menu or by clicking on the Outlook icon on the desktop.

2 Select the New button to open the e-mail window. Click on the Address Book icon (i.e. an open book) to open the Select Names window (Figure 8.17), click on the Advanced button and click on the New option to open the New Entry window. Select the New Contact option to open the Contact window (Figure 8.19).

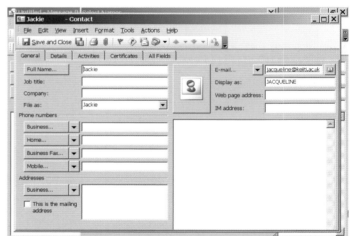

Figure 8.19 Contact Window

3 Add the following information to create a new record

Jackie
Keiiti College
11 New Way
Newtown

020 345 7896

jacqueline@keiiti.ac.uk

When you have completed the entry, click on the Save and Close button and you will see the new entry in the Select Names window.

4 Try entering the contact details and e-mail addresses of some people you know. If you are using this book as part of a course, ask the other learners for their details. Practise until you are confident of adding new addresses. You can delete entries by highlighting them and right-clicking the mouse button when they are highlighted to reveal a list of options which includes delete.

5 If you double-click on a name in the Select Names window it will appear in the To box. Click on the OK button to open an e-mail window with the name inserted as the address.

6 Select a name and send a new e-mail. Experiment with the different formatting options (e.g. fonts, character size, alignment and background colours) for presenting your e-mail.

7 Explore the other Select Names functions by clicking on the Advanced button until you are confident you understand what it can offer you. The Properties option allows you to open the contact details of any name you have highlighted.

8 Close Microsoft Outlook® by selecting the File menu and the Exit option or click on the Close button in the top right-hand corner of the application window.

Web-based e-mail

Another way of providing yourself with an e-mail account, if you have access to the Internet, is through web-based e-mail suppliers. To send or receive messages you must gain access to the World Wide Web. This has the advantage that you can access your messages from any computer in the world connected to the Internet, although it does have the disadvantage that you must be online to read or send messages.

Almost all the web-based services have a free option but you will find advertising related to both the sites you have to visit and in some cases the e-mails you send. In order to establish an account you normally only have to visit the site, complete some online forms, and choose a user name and password. Once this is done you are ready to send and receive e-mail.

Some Internet Service Providers will offer you both a web-based account and one linked to your home computer. This gives you the opportunity of reading and replying to your mail when you are away from home.

Company policy and legislation

Although the World Wide Web provides a huge amount of useful information, it also contains offensive material, pornography and information which is incorrect. Many employers have established policies about the use of the World Wide Web. It is critical that you are aware of your organization's policy.

Companies frequently forbid the use of the World Wide Web to access offensive material and in many cases it is a serious disciplinary offence to breach the policy. The legal position should also be considered. There have been several prominent court cases about using the World Wide Web to access pornography. It is important to be aware of both the law and access policy. In a similar way learning centres, colleges and libraries which provide public access to the Internet also place restrictions on the use of the system.

Many organizations have also developed policies regarding the use of e-mail which you should be fully aware of. In simple terms, it is always best to include in an e-mail only material you would write in a letter. You are just as liable for what you write in an e-mail as in a letter.

More Practice

Activity 1

Locate a website

1 Access the website at www.movinghere. org.uk, which is a website developed by the National Archive to allow people to learn more about migration to Great Britain. It contains a wealth of material. Figure 8.20 shows the home page today but, since websites are dynamic, it is likely that it will have changed to some extent when you view it.

2 Use the site search facility to locate information about stories from Ireland.

3 Save the page as a favorite so that you can locate it again.

4 Print the web page.

Figure 8.20 Moving Here. We would like to acknowledge The National Archive for their permission to use the screen capture of Moving Here.

5 On the printout of your web page write your name and the date you accessed it.

6 Use the links on the website to locate the gallery and return to the home page.

7 Save the home page as a favorite so that you can locate it again.

8 Print the home page and write your name and the date you accessed it.

9 Close your browser when you have completed the task.

Activity 2

Searching the World Wide Web

1 Using a search engine of your choice, locate a picture of The Fighting Temeraire which is a famous painting by the artist J.M.W. Turner.

2 Use the links to find a page with a copy of the painting.

3 Save the page as a favorite so that you can locate it again.

4 Print the web page.

5 Write your name on the printout and indicate the Painting of The Fighting Temerarire.

6   Close your browser when you have completed the task.

Activity 3

Sending an e-mail message

The website linked to this book (www.hodderclait.co.uk) has an e-mail bin into which you can send e-mails but you will not get a reply.

1   Using Microsoft Outlook® or another e-mail editor, send an e-mail message to a friend or colleague. Use the formatting options to present your message in an attractive and effective way.

Title: Practising E-mail

Text: I am learning how to send e-mails. I would be grateful if you would e-mail me and attach a picture file to the message. I have attached a file with an image.

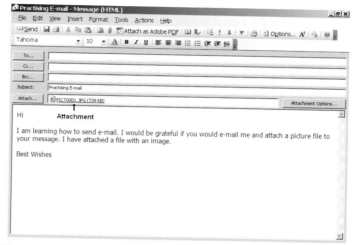

Figure 8.21   E-mail with attachment

2   Attach an image file to the message (the images used in this book are available from the associated website if you do not have access to one). Figure 8.21 illustrates a sample message.
3   Check your message for mistakes.
4   Close Microsoft Outlook® or your chosen e-mail editor.

Activity 4

Replying to an e-mail

1   Open your e-mail system and access your Inbox to check if you have received any messages.
2   Open the message from your friend and read it.
3   Ensure that the attachment is checked for viruses.
4   Save the e-mail attachment to a folder you have created.
5   Reply to the message:
Many thanks for your help.
6   Make sure your e-mail system will save your reply.
7   Send your reply.
8   Close your e-mail system.

Activity 5

Managing e-mail

1 Open Microsoft Outlook® or another e-mail system and access your Inbox.
2 Create a series of folders to store your e-mail within the Inbox folder.
3 Create four folders for e-mails relating to work. They are:
   1 Proposals
   2 Confidential Matters
   3 Staff
   4 General.
   Figure 8.22 indicates the structure of the Inbox folders.
4 Close Microsoft Outlook®.

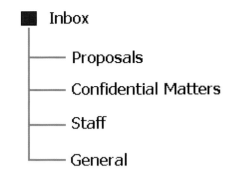

Figure 8.22 E-mail folders

Activity 6

Address Book

1 Open Microsoft Outlook® or another e-mail system and access your Inbox.
2 Open the Address Book (i.e. Select Names window in Outlook®) and add the following new addresses.
Sheila Davidson
Unicorn Enterprises
234 High Road
Hatson

s.davidson@unicornenterprises.com

Janice Lord
Gold Ltd
Gordon House
Rose Street
Firstville

Janicelord@ltdgold.co.uk

Frank Stevenson
Philips plc
675 Lion Court
Kilston
FS@philplc.co.uk

3 Select a name and send a new e-mail to them.
4 Close Microsoft Outlook® or your chosen e-mail editor.

SUMMARY

1 **Load Internet Explorer** Use either the `Start` button and the `All Programs` menu or double-click on the `Internet Explorer` icon on the Windows® desktop.

2 **Close Internet Explorer** Click on the `File` menu item and the `Exit` option or click on the `Close` button in the top right-hand corner of the application window.

3 **Load Microsoft Outlook®** Use either the `Start` button and the `All Programs` menu or double-click on the `Outlook` icon on Windows® desktop.

4 **Close Microsoft Outlook®** Click on the `File` menu and the `Exit` option or click on the `Close` button in the top right-hand corner of the application window.

5 **URL (Uniform Resource Locator)** Website addresses are unique and consist of http (Hypertext Transfer Protocol), www (World Wide Web), the website host, a code to explain the type of organization and a country code (e.g. http://www.bbc.co.uk). Perfect accuracy is essential.

6 **Links** Links connect different web pages both within a particular website and to other websites. Links are indicated by underlined words, coloured text, the mouse pointer changing shape (e.g. from an arrow to a hand) or areas being highlighted by the mouse moving across them.

7 **Retracing your route** Internet Explorer provides you with `Back` and `Forward` buttons. These allow you either to retrace your steps or to return along your route.

8 **Searching** Complex websites often provide a means of searching for distinct pages. In a similar way there are search engines that will locate websites which relate to a user's interest. The search engines tend to operate by matching words which the users enter describing their interest. They match the words in different ways such as:

- Whole Words – any of the words you have entered match any whole word in the content
- Exact Phrase – the search phrase is matched exactly in the content
- Wild Cards – this matches the structure of the search terms used, such as *ard that will match with yard, card and any other four-letter word ending with ard. The wild card can be any letter.
- Case – the search must match the case (i.e. lower- or upper-case) of the search words.

9 **Saving web addresses** Internet Explorer lets you save URLs (website addresses) so that you can return to the website later. From the chosen website select the `Favorites` menu and the `Add to Favorites` option to save the URL. Alternatively select the `Add to Favorites` icon on the toolbar and click on the `Add to Favorites` option.

10 **Saving a web page** Select the `File` menu and the `Save` or `Save As` options.

11 **Save an Image displayed on a web page** Right-click on the image to open a menu of options. Select `Save Picture As` to open the Save Picture window.

12 **Printing a web page** Select the `File` menu and the `Print` option.

13 **Create a new e-mail** Select the `New` button on the toolbar of Microsoft Outlook® and the E-mail window will be revealed. Enter your message and address, then click on the `Send` button. If you are connected to the Internet, the e-mail will be sent immediately. If you are working off-line (i.e. you are not connected to the Internet) then the e-mail is stored in the Outbox and the number of messages stored will be shown in brackets next to the title Outbox.

14 **Read a message** E-mails are stored in the Inbox. Clicking on the `Inbox` will reveal a list of messages. If you single-click on a message it will be highlighted and its contents revealed in the box to the right of the list. If you double-click on the message then a new window will open showing the message.

15 **Reply, Forward, Copy and Reply to All messages** With the message window open, you can reply to the person who sent the e-mail, forward its contents to another person, reply to everyone sent the original message or copy the message to a folder.

Reply With the e-mail highlighted or the message window open, click on the `Reply` or `Reply to All` buttons on the toolbar.

Forward the message With the e-mail highlighted or the message window open, click on the `Forward` button on the toolbar and enter the e-mail address of the person you want the message copied to.

Copy the message to a folder With the e-mail highlighted, select the `Edit` menu and the `Copy to Folder` option. This allows you to place a copy of the message in one of the existing local folders or a new local folder.

16 **Attached files** To open an attachment double-click on it and it will open providing you have the appropriate application available on your computer.

To attach a file start a new e-mail (click on the `New` button) and click on the `Insert File` button (i.e. paperclip) on the toolbar. This will open the Insert File window from where you can select a file.

17 **Save and recall e-mail addresses** Select the `Address Book` icon (i.e. an open book) to open the Select Names window. This offers a series of options that allow you to add (i.e. `Advanced` Button), delete (i.e. right-click on highlighted name) and send e-mails (i.e. double-click on the name and then the `OK` button).

18 **Send an e-mail using a saved address** With the Address Book open, highlight the chosen address (single-click), select the `New Message` button and a blank e-mail will appear with the To line completed.

19 **Print an e-mail** With the e-mail highlighted or the message window open, select the `File` menu and the `Print` option.

20 **Company policies and legislation** It is essential to be aware of both your organization's policy and the law relating to the use of the Internet.

Glossary

Alignment – a way of laying out text, e.g. left aligned means that text is aligned so that its left edge is parallel with the paper's edge when it is printed.

Application – a software program designed to perform a task such as desktop publishing, designing a database or designing a web page.

Bar chart – a chart which represents numerical information as bars of different lengths.

Bitmap – an image composed of many dots called pixels. The more pixels in a given amount of space (e.g. a square inch) the clearer the image or the higher the resolution of the picture.

Boot – the process that occurs when you switch on the computer. It involves the loading of the operating system (e.g. Microsoft® Windows® XP) and checking of the equipment to ensure that everything is ready for you to use.

Browser – an application which allows you to access a World Wide Web page. Each page has a unique address which is called a URL (Uniform or Universal Resource Locator) which, when entered into the browser, allows it to find the site and view its contents.

Byte – the basic measure of memory. A byte is sufficient memory to store one character (e.g. a letter or a number).

Column chart – a chart which represents numbers as columns of different lengths.

CPU – Central Processing Unit: a silicon chip which controls the operation of the computer.

Database – a way of storing information so that its contents can be extracted in many different combinations and ways.

Desktop – the main display of the operating system and normally the first display you see after the computer has loaded the operating system (e.g. Microsoft® Windows® XP).

Desktop Publishing – an application which allows text and images to be combined in many different ways so that many different forms of printed document can be designed (e.g. newsletters and posters).

Directory – a list of World Wide Web addresses related to a particular topic or subject.

DTP – see Desktop Publishing

E-mail – a message which is sent electronically through the Internet or over a local network.

Field – an individual piece of information stored on a database usually as part of a record.

File – a collection of digital (computer) information. There are many types of file such as word-processing, graphic and spreadsheet files.

Floppy disk – a small magnetic disk on which you can store a small amount of information in the form of files.

Folder – a location on the computer in which you can store files.

Font – characters can be printed and displayed in many different styles. These styles are known as fonts.

Format – a way of structuring the computer information stored in a file on a disk or drive. There are many different types of file format.

Formula – a method of calculating parts of a spreadsheet automatically.

Greyscale – a way of describing an image which is shown in a range of shades of grey rather than in different colours.

GUI – Graphical User Interface: a display in which icons, windows and a mouse pointer interact to produce an easy to use environment.

Hard disk – a magnetic disk located inside the computer, on which a large amount of information can be stored.

Hardware – the physical components which make up the computer.

HTML – Hypertext Markup Language: a presentation language which is used to design World Wide Web pages so that they can be read using a browser.

HTTP – Hypertext Transfer Protocol: specifies how to access documents on the World Wide Web (e.g. http://www.bbc.co.uk)

Hypertext – Pages of a web site are linked together through a number of hypertext connections. These are shown by underlined words, coloured words, icons and graphic pictures. The links allow the user to jump between different parts of the site or even between sites.

Icon – a small picture which represents a computer function or operation.

Internet – a super network of networks which links millions of computers throughout the world.

ISP – Internet Service Provider: a commercial company that provides connections to the Internet for individuals and companies.

KB – Kilobyte: a measure of memory (i.e. 1024 bytes).

Laptop – a portable computer with a screen built into its cover.

Line Graph – a graphical way of comparing two or more sets of numerical information.

MB – Megabyte: a measure of computer memory (approximately a million bytes).

Memory – a measure of the computer's capacity to perform tasks and to store information.

Menu – a method of displaying options.

Operating System – software that provides the instructions to make the hardware work.

Password – a series of alphanumeric characters that limits access to a computer system.

Personal computer – an individual computer which is normally used by one person at a time.

Pie chart – a graphical representation of information by showing it as slices of a circle so that the size of each slice is proportional to the data.

Pixel – graphic images are made up of many small rectangular areas which are called pixels.

Port – a way of connecting peripheral devices (e.g. printers) to a computer.

Query – a way of asking a database of information a particular question. Normally, this takes the form of identifying particular combinations of information (e.g. all customers who have ordered more than £100,000 of goods during the last three months).

QWERTY – this is the order of the top line of alphabetical keys on the keyboard.

RAM – Random Access Memory: the computer's working memory in which the computer carries out its functions once it is switched on. It only exists while the machine is on. If the power is switched off, so is the memory.

Record – a group of related fields of information which you find in a database.

Resolution – this is a way of describing the quality of an image, monitor or printer. The quality is described in terms of the dots which make up the image. That is, the more dots the higher the quality of the image, monitor display or printer output.

ROM – Read Only Memory: the computer's permanent memory, built into the structure of the silicon chips. It is not lost if the power is switched off.

Search engine – an application that allows you to search the World Wide Web for a web page containing information on a specific topic or to search within a website for a particular item of information.

Software – computer programs written to allow you or the computer to carry out certain tasks such as constructing databases.

Sort – a way of presenting information in a spreadsheet or database (e.g. alphabetically).

Surfing – the process of wandering around the World Wide Web in search of interesting information.

Table – the part of a database in which information is stored as a series of records and fields.

URL – Uniform Resource Locator: the unique address of a World Wide Web site that allows a browser to locate the site.

Vector – an image that is defined by mathematical formulae rather than pixels. This defines the start and finish of the line and allows it to be easily changed. A vector image can be resized and it will stay in perfect proportion.

Virus – a computer program designed to cause harm to a computer.

Web page – a document which forms part of a website.

Website – a collection of pages on the Internet.

Word processor – an application which allows you to create and manipulate documents.

WWW – World Wide Web: a collection of millions of websites and documents spread across the world as part of the Internet.

Window – rectangular area of the screen in which computer applications and information are displayed.

Wizard – Many Microsoft® Windows® applications include Wizards that are used to perform complex tasks more easily by allowing the user to choose between options.

Index

Salads

(c) 2003 Feierabend Verlag, OHG,
Mommsenstr. 43, D-10629 Berlin.

Idea: Peter Feierabend
Recipes, Styling, Production: Frauke Koops - www.frauke-koops.de
Recipe Assistant: Ute Ritter
Styling Assistant: Bodil Haslehner
Introduction and Captions: Susanna Birnmeier
Photography: Günter Beer - food.beerfoto.com
Assistant: Kathi Günter
Photos taken at BuenavistaStudio, Barcelona
Layout: Kathi Günter, Sarah David-Spickermann

Multilingual Management: LocTeam, Barcelona
www.locteam.com
Translated from German by Sheila Hardie

(c) 2003 Text, Design, Photography, Recipes:
Günter Beer, Frauke Koops, Feierabend Verlag

Printing and Binding: Eurolitho s.p.a., Mailand
Printed in Italy
ISBN: 3-936761-59-0
61-08022-1

Important: All ingredients – especially fish and seafood – should be fresh and in perfect
conditions. Lettuces must be washed very carefully. Those vulnerable to Salmonella en-
teritidis infections – in particular the elderly, pregnant women, young children and those
with weakened immune systems – should consult their doctor before consuming raw
eggs, raw fish or seafood.

Frauke Koops · Günter Beer

Salads

Feierabend

Contents

Level of difficulty

Preparation time

40

Salad days!

Does a three-star salad have to be something particularly luxurious or a one-star salad simple and unpretentious? The stars in this book do not perform the same function as hotel ratings, because good food is always a luxury. Here, one star means easy and three, difficult. And, just so everyone knows right away how long each salad is going to take to make, preparation times are printed nice and clearly alongside the stars. All the recipes contain cooking techniques, tips and tricks of the trade written in plain English.

The fact that the book is indexed in three ways – alphabetically, by preparation times and by the additional salads, which absorb taste and aroma overnight – should make choosing easier. And you are unlikely to ask questions such as "Where can I find that ingredient?". You should find all you need in any well-stocked supermarket or greengrocer's.

Oscar Wilde would definitely have liked this book, since he said: "I have the simplest tastes. I am always satisfied with the best". These salads, whether it be the fruity Mediterranean ones or the hearty Scandinavian dishes, call for extra virgin olive oil and the freshest fruit and vegetables you can find. Substitutes such as garlic powder, tinned food or dried herbs are only to be used if there really is no alternative. If you work with first-class fresh ingredients, you will create salads just as beautiful as the ones in the photos. The pictures were taken in a kitchen overlooking the Mediterranean – hence the soft, golden light, as pure and natural as the ingredients themselves, which created a wonderful aroma of fresh oregano, thyme, fennel and rosemary. It is no wonder that all the salads were quickly polished off by the camera team as soon as they had finished shooting.

One final word of advice: use your imagination with these recipes. Imagination is always a starting point, never an end. Try things out, improvise, substitute ingredients – that is what makes a real cook, not following recipes slavishly. No white pepper in the house? Black will do instead. No penne? Another type of pasta will do fine!

What can possibly go wrong?

Susanne Birnmeyer

Marinate and serve in a covered bowl

Like a miniature washing machine: a salad spinner for lettuce leaves

Just like in the ice-cream parlour, you can make pretty little balls with the melon ball scoop (pages 132/133)

The fruit and vegetable grater is good for grating kohlrabi, carrots and cheese
(pages 16/17)

Designed for cucumbers, useful with lots of other things: the cucumber slicer
(pages 32/33, 170/171)

The flat whisk above is good for stirring pots

The heavier it is, the more air the whisk beats into creams and sauces.

Delicate items can be cut into very fine slices with a truffle slicer (pages 12/13, 24/25)

Not just for peeling: use the potato peeler to cut fine slices of coconut and courgette (pages 44/45, 122/123)

The single-blade chopping knife nestles in the curved herb chopping board. If need be, you can also use a large knife on a wooden board.

No point trying it out with marbles: olive spoon

9

Blood oranges with coriander

4 blood oranges
80 g / 3 oz red onions
200 g / 7 oz white radish
1/2 - 1 bunch of coriander, torn leaves
3 chillis
Salt
30 minutes marinating time

Peel the oranges and cut the flesh into thick slices.
Peel the red onions and the radishes and slice finely.
Deseed the chillis and cut into fine strips.

Layer the orange slices, red onions and radishes.
Sprinkle coriander, chilli strips and some salt between layers.
Marinate in the fridge for around 30 minutes.

Tip: Instead of white radish, other kinds of radish can also be used.

*15

Oranges and olives with pasta

200 g / 7 oz capellini
Salt

3-4 oranges
60 g / 2 oz / 2/3 cup black olives, pitted
6-8 stems coriander, torn leaves
30-40 ml / 1-1 1/2 oz / 2-2 1/2 tbsp olive oil

Orange slices as a garnish

Break the capellini approximately in half
and cook until al dente in boiling salted water.
Drain.
Rinse with cold water to cool.

Peel the oranges and cut up into rough cubes.
Mix the capellini, olives, orange cubes, coriander
and olive oil. Marinate for 30 minutes.
Serve with orange slices.

Tip: Garlic chives, mint or flat-leaf parsley also taste
delicious instead of coriander. The main thing is to use
fine pasta.

*30

Carrots and kohlrabi with Roquefort vinaigrette

350 g / 12 oz carrots
250 g / 8 oz kohlrabi
Fleur de sel, alternatively fine sea salt

Dressing:
2 tbsp fruit vinegar
20 ml / 3/4 fl oz / 4 tsp nut oil
40-50 g / 1 1/2-1 3/4 oz Roquefort

Garnish:
Flower petals (from edible flowers)
Dill tips (or fennel greens)

Peel the carrots and the kohlrabi and grate with
a cheese grater. Season with a little salt and mix.
Divide into individual portions.

To make the dressing, break up the Roquefort into
small pieces with a fork and mix with the vinegar
and oil. Pour over the salad. Serve with flower
petals and dill tips.

Tip: You can find edible flowers in the greenhouse,
e.g. snapdragons, carnations, tagetes, marigolds,
pansies.

*15

16

A grater with rubber feet doesnt slip-
this makes grating easier and quicker

Carrots and kohlrabi with Roquefort vinaigrette

Finely grated, kohlrabi and carrots
stay crunchy and juicy

Lemon salad

2 unwaxed organic lemons
(alternatively bergamot oranges or citron)

1 tsp black pepper, ground
1/2 tsp salt
4 tbsp olive oil
1 tbsp rosemary, cut

Allow 1 hour for marinating

Some coriander or flat-leaf parsley as a garnish

Wash the lemon in hot water, dry and cut into
wafer-thin slices using a slicing machine
(if you have one).

Mix with pepper, salt, olive oil and rosemary
and marinate for 1 hour.

Tip: Serve in small portions with cold white fish,
fried and steamed fish or pies.
The intense flavour can be made milder by adding
some green salad.

*10

It takes several hours for the lemons
and the rosemary to blend their aromas

Flower and salad green tips salad

200 g / 7 oz / 8 cups of mixed salad greens tips
(escarole, frisée, oak leaf lettuce, lollo rosso, romaine)

8-12 organic pansy flowers
(alternatively nasturtium or marigold flowers)

6 tbsp olive oil
3 tbsp raspberry vinegar
Pepper
Salt

Wash the salad green tips and spin dry.
Pick the flowers off the stems and separate the large
ones into petals.
Arrange everything in a colourful display.

Whisk the olive oil and the raspberry vinegar until
blended and season with salt and pepper. Pour over the
salad before serving.

Tip: All edible, cultivated flowers can be used in this
recipe. An overview of different types of salad greens can
be found on pages 50-54.

Spinach & button mushroom salad with truffles

120 g / 4 1/5 oz / 4 1/2 cups leaf spinach
150 g / 5 1/4 oz button mushrooms

100 g /3 1/2 oz peppered goats cheese
2 tbsp lemon juice
30 ml / 1 fl oz / 2 tbsp herb olive oil
10-20 g / 1/3-3/4 oz fresh truffle

Pick through the spinach and discard any
unwanted leaves, wash and spin dry. Gently brush
off any dirt or debris from the mushrooms and
slice finely. Mix with the spinach leaves.

Break the cheese up into small pieces using a
fork. Place evenly on top of the salad.
Sprinkle the lemon juice and olive oil.
Slice the truffle finely with a truffle slicer and
sprinkle onto the salad. Mix everything together
before serving.

Tip: The amount of truffle you use depends on
the size of your wallet. Tinned truffles do not have
such an intense aroma, but are an acceptable
substitute.

Keep the noble truffle in a closed
jar in the fridge.
Kitchen paper helps keep it fresh

Use a soft brush to carefully
remove any earth from the truffle

The ingredients could also be used for a dessert.

The delicate blue mould gives the Gorgonzola cheese its sharp, spicy flavour

If you use firm varieties of pear, the cooked slices will keep their shape. Laid out individually, the pear slices cool down more quickly.

Pears with Gorgonzola

300 ml / 10 fl oz / 1 1/4 cups wine vinegar
1/4 litre / 1 3/4 pints / 4 1/4cups dry white wine
40 g / 1 1/2 oz fresh ginger, peeled
200 g / 7 oz / 3/4 cup sugar
6-8 cinnamon sticks
1 vanilla pod, halved lengthways
3 medium-sized pears (ca. 360 g / 13 oz)

120 g / 4 1 / 5 oz Gorgonzola
1 small frisée lettuce
20 g / 3/4 oz / 1/8 cup pine nuts, roasted

Dressing:
6 tbsp pear stock
2 tbsp walnut oil
1 pinch of salt

Bring the wine vinegar, wine, sliced ginger, sugar,
cinnamon sticks and vanilla pod to a boil.
Meantime, peel the pears. Halve the fruits and, starting
with the cut surface, cut into thin slices on a slicing
machine.
Blanch for 2 minutes in the boiling stock.

Remove the pear slices. Leave the stock to simmer for
around 5 minutes in an uncovered pot and let it cool.

With two forks, break the Gorgonzola cheese (which has
been kept at room temperature) into small pieces. Cut up
the frisée lettuce, wash the leaves and spin them dry.
Mix the Gorgonzola flakes, pear slices, frisée and pine nuts
together and serve on a plate.

Whisk the pear stock and the oil together until blended,
add a little salt and pour over the salad.

Cinnamon, vanilla and ginger season the pear stock

Tip: The pear stock tastes excellent with
cold meat, fried fish, pies or in dessert sauces.
It keeps in the fridge for 5-7 days.

*15

Chicory with mascarpone

1 unwaxed organic lemon

Dressing:
125 g / 4 1/2 oz / 1/2 cup mascarpone
125 ml / 4 fl oz / 1/2 cup LC1 yoghurt
3-4 tbsp white elderberry syrup
3-4 tbsp lemon juice
2 dashes of Tabasco
Sugar

280 g / 9 3/4 oz / 11 cups chicory

Wash the lemon with hot water. Grate the peel.

Stir the mascarpone, yoghurt, and elderberry syrup together with ¾ of the grated lemon peel until the mixture reaches a smooth consistency. Season with lemon juice, Tabasco sauce and sugar.

Wash the chicory and cut away the bitter cores. Serve the chicory leaves with the mascarpone dressing and sprinkle with the remaining lemon peel.

Tip: This is delicious with red and white chicory and alternatively with celery, apple slices, crisp salad or melon.

*20

Beetroot and strawberries

300 g / 10 oz strawberries
180-200 g / 6-7 oz beetroot,
cooked and peeled
50-60 g / 1 3/4-2 oz / 2-2 1/4 cups
watercress

Mayonnaise:
1 egg yolk
1 tbsp white balsamic vinegar
1 tsp mustard
Salt
Freshly ground black pepper
80 ml / 3 fl oz / 1/3 cup olive oil

1 tsp rosemary, chopped
1 tbsp pickled green pepper

Tip: A few nasturtium flowers would be
a nice finishing touch to this dish.

An unusual trio:
beetroot, strawberries and rosemary

Not all vinaigrettes
require a mixer

Remove the stalks from
the strawberries and halve the fruit.
Cut the beetroot into wafer-thin slices
with a slicing machine or a vegetable slicer.
Tear the watercress leaves off the stalks.
Arrange all the ingredients.

Beat the egg yolk, balsamic vinegar, mustard, salt,
pepper and oil into a thin mayonnaise.
Spread on top of the salad.
Sprinkle with rosemary and green pepper.

20

Warm olive salad with cherry tomatoes

1 unwaxed organic lemon
50 ml / 1 3/4 fl oz / 3 1/2 tbsp olive oil
3 garlic cloves, chopped
Freshly ground black pepper
200 g / 7 oz green olives, with stones
300 g / 10 oz cherry tomatoes
1 bunch flat-leaf parsley, torn leaves

Salt

Squeeze the juice from the lemon

Heat the lemon juice, olive oil, garlic and pepper.
Add the olives, tomatoes and parsley leaves, mix
well together and heat. If you like, season with salt
and pepper and then serve immediately.

You can also sprinkle chopped nuts over the salad.

Tip: The salad is also delicious cold and can be
served with grated Pecorino or Parmesan.

In garlic chives we can see the relationship between onions and leeks.
The cloves dont appear until later on.

There's nothing finer: garlic press

Something for your eyes, to stop you crying:
a covered pot for garlic and onions

…and purple skinned heads of garlic

And this is how you find them in
the supermarket: white skinned…

Varieties of garlic

Wild strawberries with sprouts

250 g / 8 oz wild strawberries

1 tbsp white balsamic vinegar
1 tbsp olive oil
1 tbsp mint, cut up
1 tsp icing sugar

8 small to medium-sized leaves of romaine lettuce
130-150 g / 4 1/2-5 1/4 oz / 1/2-3/4 cup cottage cheese
6 tbsp alfalfa sprouts
Pepper to taste, ground

Sort through the strawberries and discard any you do not like. Wash in cold water. Place on kitchen paper and leave to drain thoroughly.

Mix the balsamic vinegar, olive oil, mint and icing sugar together and add to the strawberries.

Arrange the strawberry salad on top of the green leaves. Cover with cottage cheese and sprouts and sprinkle with pepper.

Tip: This also tastes really delicious with fresh goat's cheese or mozzarella instead of cottage cheese.

*20

Tiny berries with a big taste: wild strawberries

Figs and dry-cured serrano ham

8 small figs (around 300 g / 10 oz)
1tbsp sugar
2 tbsp balsamic vinegar
2 tbsp olive oil
Black pepper, pounded

8 slices of serrano dry-cured ham

Halve the figs lengthways. Place on silver foil with the wider curved end facing down. Sprinkle with sugar. Place under the grill for 4-5 minutes until brown. Arrange on a dish. Add the balsamic vinegar and olive oil and sprinkle with pepper.
Allow to cool.

Cover with plenty of serrano dry-cured ham and serve.

Tip: Instead of serrano ham you could also use Parma or Black Forest ham.

Dry-cured serrano ham from Iberian pigs has a spicy, nutty taste - this is thanks to the pigs rich diet of acorns

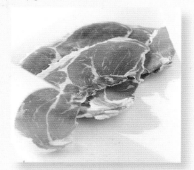

*15

Bean salad with sheep's cheese and tomato sauce

500 g / 1 1/4 lb shelled haricot beans (soak overnight)
Salt
1/2 bunch of savoury (alternatively marjoram)

60 g / 2 oz / 1/2 cup sun-dried tomatoes in oil
Olive oil
1 bunch oregano, chopped
300 g / 10 oz tomatoes

120-150 g / 4 1/5-5 1/2 oz sheeps cheese
Freshly ground black pepper
2-3 garlic cloves, peeled

Soak the beans in cold water overnight. Add salt and the
savoury and boil for 30 minutes. Let the contents of the
pot cool. Drain the beans.

Drain the oil from the tomatoes, remove and replace with
100 ml / 3 1/2 fl oz / just under 1/2 cup olive oil.
Slice 40 g / 1 1/2 oz of the drained tomatoes into fine
strips. Add to the oil along with the oregano.
Chop 150 g / 5 1/4 oz of the tomatoes into rough cubes
and mix with the beans.

Cover the salad with sheep's cheese and season with
pepper.

Purée the remaining sun-dried tomatoes with
the rest of the fresh tomatoes and garlic.
Season to taste.
Serve separate from the bean salad.

Tip: The tomato sauce can be mixed with the lettuce;
this makes the flavour more intense.
Tuna can be used in this recipe instead of sheeps
cheese.

Courgettes and mozzarella

600 g / 1 lb 5 oz courgettes

Salad dressing:
2 tbsp lemon juice
5 tbsp olive oil
1/2 bunch flat-leaf parsley, torn leaves
Salt
Freshly ground white pepper

2 buffalo milk mozzarella cheeses, each weighing 125 g / 4 1/2 oz
1/2 bunch basil, cut into strips

Wash the courgettes and cut lengthways into very thin strips
with a potato peeler.

Whisk together the lemon juice, oil, parsley, salt and pepper
into a salad dressing, or purée with a hand blender.
Toss the courgettes in the dressing.

Cut the mozzarella into fork-sized pieces. Add to the courgette salad
and sprinkle with basil.

*15

45

Celery with salmon tartar

200 g / 7 oz fresh salmon
2 tbsp lime juice
1 tbsp olive oil
1 tbsp tarragon, chopped
1 tbsp chives, cut into rings
1 tbsp chervil, torn leaves
1 tbsp flat-leaf parsley, leaves torn and chopped
1 tsp sea salt
Allow one night for marinating

400 g / 14 oz celery
Salt

Tarragon leaves as garnish
Freshly ground white pepper

Remove any skin and bones from the salmon and cut the fish into small cubes. Mix with lime juice, olive oil, herbs and sea salt. Marinate overnight in the fridge.

Cut the celery into strips and blanch for 1 minute in boiling salted water. Plunge into iced water immediately in order to cool.

Drain the celery well and arrange on a plate with the salmon tartar and tarragon. Sprinkle with pepper.

Bring to the boil for a short time and then plunge in cold water to cool: blanching helps conserve the celerys colour and vitamins

*30

Varieties
of lettuce

Oak leaf lettuce

Lollo rosso

Red chicory

Lettuce hearts

Lambs lettuce

Radicchio

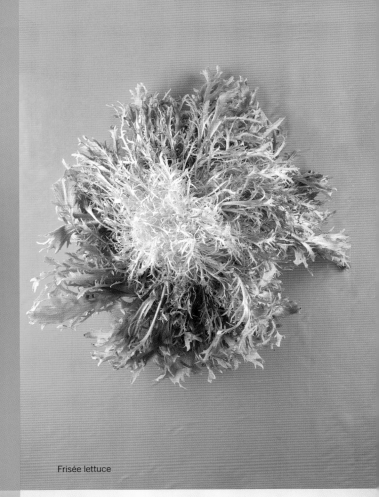

Frisée lettuce

Head lettuce

Radicchio di Treviso

Iceberg lettuce

Green spinach

Wild rocket

Yellow cultivated dandelion greens

Rocket

Escarol

Chicory

Lollo Bianco

Romaine lettuce

Mustard greens

53

Veal and tuna on
green vegetable salad

Veal and tuna on green vegetable salad

250 g / 8 oz lean veal
1 tbsp olive oil
Salt
Pepper

Dressing:
3 tbsp olive oil
3 tbsp tarragon vinegar (alternatively orange vinegar)
2 tbsp orange juice
2 tbsp tarragon, chopped

200 g / 7 oz / 1 cup sugar peas
80 g / 3 oz / 1/2 cup green peas
25 g / 1 oz shallots / 1/8 cup, chopped
150 g / 5 1/4 oz tuna in oil

Sear the veal quickly over a high heat
to make sure the meat is pale pink and juicy inside

Fry the meat for 2 minutes on each side in the frying pan in 1 tbsp of oil. The meat should stay pink in the centre. Season with salt and pepper and leave to cool in the frying pan. Cut into narrow strips.

Whisk all the ingredients for the dressing until blended. Add the meat juices from the frying pan.

Bring the sugar peas, green peas and shallots to the boil in salted water. Then drain and cool with cold water. Drain the tuna and break up into fork-sized pieces. Arrange the vegetables on a dish.
Place the veal strips and the tuna on top of the vegetables and cover with generous amounts of salad dressing.

Tip: Dill or lemon balm can be used instead of tarragon.
Bonito (white tuna from Spain) or freshly fried tuna fish can be used instead of the conventional tinned tuna. Instead of raw veal, you can use roast veal and that will save time.

40

Young artichokes
and Parmesan

Young artichokes
and Parmesan

Vinaigrette:
80 ml / 3 fl oz / 1/3 cup olive oil
80 ml / 3 fl oz / 1/3 cup lemon juice
Salt

6 tender artichokes weighing 60-80 g / 2-3 oz each
100 g / 3 1/2 oz medium mature Parmesan

Whisk the oil and lemon juice with salt in a large bowl
until blended.

Remove the hard outer leaves and stems from the
artichokes. Cut off the hard leaf tips. Halve lengthways
and remove the hairy choke.
Cut the artichoke halves lengthways into very fine slices.

Put the artichokes in vinegar immediately, to avoid them
oxidising and turning brown.

Break up or finely slice the Parmesan, mix with the salad
and serve immediately.

It is worth the effort:
the finely cut artichoke slices are also delicious raw.

**20

Kitchen scissors can be used
to cut off the hard leaf tips

The innermost, unripe leaf tips are called the choke:
it does not have much of a taste

Unless you place them in vinaigrette immediately,
the artichokes will oxidise and turn brown

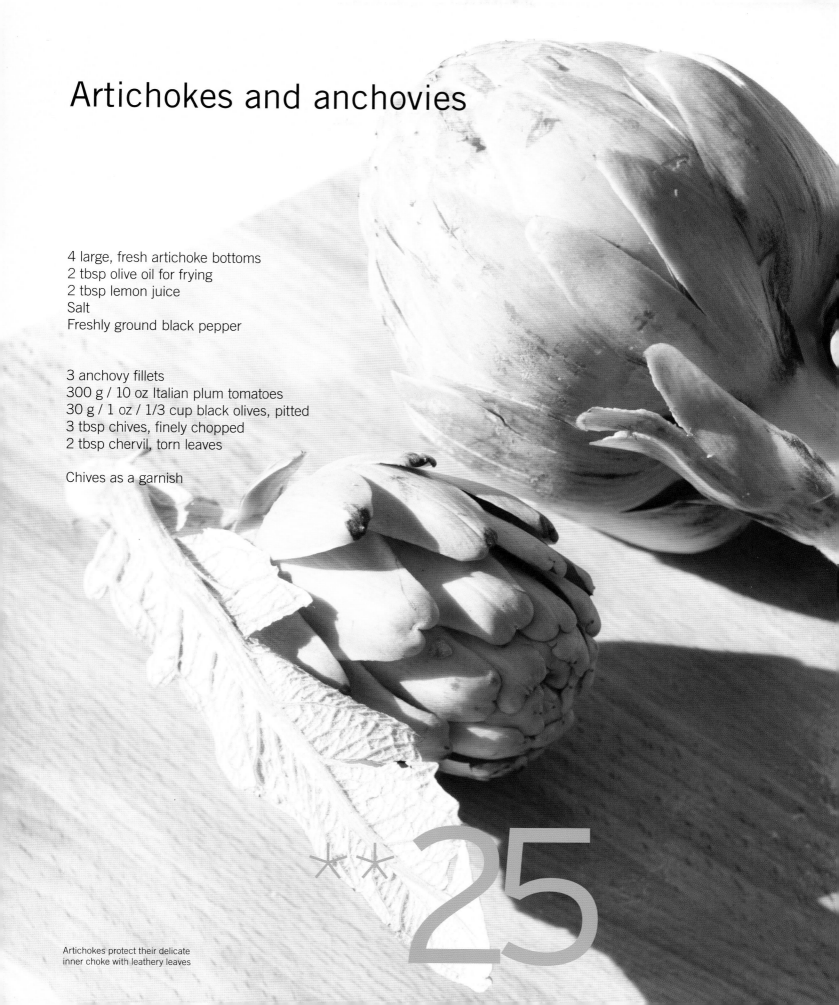

Artichokes and anchovies

4 large, fresh artichoke bottoms
2 tbsp olive oil for frying
2 tbsp lemon juice
Salt
Freshly ground black pepper

3 anchovy fillets
300 g / 10 oz Italian plum tomatoes
30 g / 1 oz / 1/3 cup black olives, pitted
3 tbsp chives, finely chopped
2 tbsp chervil, torn leaves

Chives as a garnish

**25

Artichokes protect their delicate
inner choke with leathery leaves

Artichokes and anchovies

First step: tear off the hard outer leaves one by one

Next, snip off the tips of the leaves and cut the bottom to make it smooth

Cut the artichoke bottoms into slices.
Fry in oil until golden brown.
Season with lemon juice, salt and pepper
and leave to cool in the frying juices.

Cut the anchovy fillets into strips. Halve the tomatoes,
deseed them and cut into slices. Mix the anchovies,
tomatoes and olives with the cooled artichoke bottoms.
Toss with herbs and drizzle with the frying juices. Serve
on a bed of chives.

Tip: Artichoke hearts can be used instead of the
bottoms.

First step towards the artichoke bottom:
cut off the stem base

When the tip is removed,
the tender inner choke is revealed.

Bottom or leaves?
Both parts of the artichoke are delicious.

The fine strips fry quickly.

Rum eggs on iceberg salad

4 eggs
60 ml / 2 fl oz / 4 tbsp rum
1/4 l / 1/2 fl oz / 1 cup red wine vinegar
1-2 garlic cloves, chopped roughly
1/2 tbsp salt
1 tsp sugar
1/2 tbsp peppercorns
1/4 bunch thyme
1 fresh red chilli
40 ml / 1 1/2 fl oz / 2 1/2 tbsp olive oil
Allow 6 hours for marinating

300 g / 10 oz / 12 cups iceberg lettuce

1/4 bunch of chives, chopped finely

Cook eggs for 6-7 minutes until medium-boiled,
place in cold water to cool and peel carefully.

Bring the rum, red wine vinegar, garlic, salt, sugar,
peppercorns, thyme and chilli to a boil. Pour the hot
mixture over the peeled eggs. Add oil and mix well.
Marinate for at least 6 hours, turning over the eggs in
the marinade now and again. Remove the eggs from
the marinade.

Wash the iceberg lettuce and cut into fine strips.
Add 6 tbsp of rum marinade, place the eggs on top
and sprinkle with chives. Serve garnished with the
thyme from the marinade.

Tip: The eggs can be kept in the fridge for 4-6 days.

Aubergines with two dressings

600 g / 1 lb 5 oz medium-sized aubergines
Salt
Drain for 20 minutes

Olive oil for frying
Pepper

Salad dressing 1:
40 ml / 1 1/2 fl oz / 2 1/2 tbsp olive oil
3 garlic cloves, pressed
1/2 tsp cumin
1 tsp rose paprika
1/2 tsp cayenne pepper

Salad dressing 2:
100 g / 3 1/2 oz / 1/3 cup Greek yoghurt
2 garlic cloves, pressed
1 tsp salt
Freshly ground black pepper
1 tbsp lemon juice
30-40 ml / 1-1 1/2 fl oz / 2-2 1/2 tbsp white wine
1 bunch flat-leaf parsley, chopped

1 unwaxed organic lemon

½ bunch parsley, torn leaves

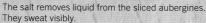

The salt removes liquid from the sliced aubergines. They sweat visibly.

Split the aubergines in half lengthways or crossways into 1 cm/ 1/2 inch slices. Sprinkle with salt and drain for 20 minutes. Rinse with cold water and dab dry with kitchen paper.

Fry the aubergines in portions with a little oil in a frying pan until both sides are golden brown. Place on kitchen paper to remove excess fat. Season with salt and pepper.

Stir together the ingredients for both salad dressings.

Peel the lemon and cut the flesh into slices. Divide the aubergine slices into two portions. Arrange lemon slices and pour the second salad dressing onto one half and serve the second half of the aubergines with dressing number one. Sprinkle both with parsley.

Freshly cut aubergine slices, just fried. They only turn this beautiful brown colour if they have been drained sufficiently.

Peppers in a glass

300 g / 10 oz red pepper
300 g / 10 oz yellow pepper
30 minutes roasting time
1/2 bunch of flat-leaf parsley

3 garlic cloves, chopped
2 tbsp lime juice
4 tbsp olive oil

Halve the peppers, remove the seeds and place the cut side onto silver foil and roast for around 30 minutes at 200 °C / 400 °F / Gas Mark 6 until the skins blister. Remove from the oven and cover with a cold, wet kitchen cloth and leave to cool. Remove the skin. Tear the parsley leaves off the stems, wash them and chop up roughly.

Dice the red and yellow peppers.
Put equal amounts in each glass. Sprinkle with garlic and parsley. Drizzle with lime juice and olive oil.

Serve with toasted pitta bread.

Tip: Green peppers are not so suitable because they have a slightly bitter taste.

** 20

Finely dice the roasted, peeled peppers

After 30 minutes in the oven, the skin comes off quite easily

Peppers in a glass

Long and narrow, yellow, storage, or cooking onions: the classic all-rounders

Shallots:
the Queen of the tearjerkers, with a delicate and intense taste (pages 56/57, 92,93, 170/171)

Italian red onion:
sweet enough to eat raw and very decorative (pages 12/13)

Pearl onions:
the smallest ones taste delicious braised or pickled in a mild, sweetish vinegar (pages 148/149)

Spanish onion:
the Great Dane of the onion family:
large, tranquil and real
(pages 78/79, 174/175)

Round yellow, storage,
or cooking onions: easy to find
and very versatile
(pages 100/101)

Spring onions: stronger than chives,
milder than leeks, and beautiful too
(pages 104/105, 122/123)

Varieties of onion

Fried onions and elderberry syrup

400 g / 14 oz white onions (or mild yellow onions)

3 tbsp walnut oil
Salt
Pepper to taste, pounded
60 ml / 2 fl oz / 4 tbsp dark elderberry syrup
4-5 tbsp balsamic vinegar

200 g / 7 oz iceberg lettuce
4-6 Amaretti biscuits, crumbled

Peel the onions, halve them and cut into thick slices.

Fry the onion slices lightly in hot oil on the cut side until brown.
Season with salt and pepper. Add elderberry syrup and balsamic
vinegar and toss.

Wash the iceberg lettuce and cut into fine strips. Serve the onions
lukewarm or cold with the salad strips.
Sprinkle with Amaretti and serve immediately.

Quicker to prepare than slices,
so you cry less: onion wedges

Balsamic vinegar and elderberry syrup
add a spot of colour to the frying pan

35

Warm mustard beans and marinated meat kebabs

200 g / 7 oz fresh broad beans
Salt
200 g / 7 oz French beans
150 g / 5 1/4 oz climbing beans
1 tbsp fresh horseradish, grated
1/2 cinnamon stick
200 ml / 7 fl oz / 3/4 cup white wine vinegar
70 g / 2 1/3 oz / 1/3 cup sugar
1 tsp mustard powder
1/2 bunch savoury

Marinade:
2 tbsp oil
1 tbsp lime juice
1 tsp mustard powder
Salt
Pepper

160 g / 5 1/2 oz beef fried until pink and cut into fine slices
4 wooden skewers

3 tbsp rocket

Olive oil to serve

Blanch the beans for 3 minutes in boiling water. Plunge into cold water to cool and shell the beans.
Cut the French beans diagonally into strips, leave the climbing beans whole. Cook for 3 minutes
in boiling salted water and drain.

Bring the horseradish, cinnamon stick, vinegar, sugar, mustard powder and savoury to a boil.
Place the beans in the vinegar stock and leave to cool down until it is lukewarm. Stir the beans from time to time.

Mix the lime juice, mustard powder, salt and pepper together.
Add the slices of meat to this mixture and marinate for 10 minutes. Thread onto the skewers in cloud shapes.

Wash the rocket, sort through and discard any unwanted leaves, drain and cut into strips. Remove all the beans
from the marinade and mix together. Arrange on a plate and sprinkle with rocket strips. Make the kebabs, drizzle
with the remaining meat marinade and some of the bean stock. Then drizzle with olive oil.

Tip: Instead of mustard powder pounded mustard seeds can also be used

Beetroot salad with leaves

350-400 g / 12-14 oz young beetroots with leaves
2 tbsp neutral oil
Salt
40-50 minutes roasting time

5 garlic cloves, peeled
1 small unwaxed organic lemon
60 g / 2 oz / 1/3 cup black olives
30 minutes marinating time

Salad dressing:
50 ml 1 3/4 fl oz / 3 1/2 tbsp wine vinegar
50 ml 1 3/4 fl oz / 3 1/2 tbsp herb olive oil
Salt
Freshly ground black pepper

Cut the leaves off the beetroots and put them aside.
Scrub the beetroots and then toss them in oil and salt.
Place on a baking tray perhaps on baking paper and roast for
around 40-50 minutes at 200 °C / 400 °F / Gas Mark 6.
Allow to cool down for a short time, until the beetroots are cool
enough to handle. Remove the skins and chop roughly.
Leave to cool.

Wash the beetroot leaves and separate them from the stalks.
Cut the leaves into strips. Cut the garlic into thin slices and slice
the lemon into wafer-thin slices with a slicing machine.
Pit the olives.

For the salad dressing whisk the vinegar and herb olive oil
together.
Season with salt and pepper. Add beetroot, garlic, lemon slices
and black olives and marinate for 30 minutes.

Mix the salad with the beetroot leaf strips and serve.

Tip: Beetroots bleed and can stain your hands.
It is advisable to wear rubber gloves when preparing them.

Gnocchi and ground cherries

160 g / 5 1/2 oz / 5 cups radicchio rosso di Treviso
150 g / 5 1/4 oz fresh, ready-made gnocchi
2 tbsp olive oil
80 g / 3 oz / 1/2 cup ground cherries

100 g / 3 1/2 oz / 1/3 cup mayonnaise
100 g / 3 1/2 oz / 1/3 cup yoghurt, full-fat
2 tbsp flat-leaf parsley, chopped
Salt
Pepper
1 heaped tsp Madras curry powder

Wash the radicchio, separate the leaves and leave to drain.

Cook the gnocchi in boiling salted water until they come up to the surface. Drain, cool with cold water and cover in oil. Remove the ground cherries husks and cut the fruit in half.

Mix the mayonnaise and the yoghurt. Stir in the salt, pepper and curry powder into this mixture and season well. Add the ground cherries and the gnocchi and arrange on top of the radicchio.

Tip: Alternatively, you can use chicory or crisp iceberg lettuce. If the leaves are small, this salad can be eaten with one's hands.

**30

Oils

Oil infused with dried herbs

For salads, raw fruit and vegetables, pasta, pizza, marinades for grilled or fried meat and fish.

2 thyme twigs
2 rosemary twigs
2 lavender twigs
500 ml / 16 fl oz / 2 cups olive oil

Place the herbs in a wide-necked bottle. Cover with olive oil.
Keeps for 2-3 weeks. Sieve before using.

Tip:
You can also add summer or winter savoury to this oil.

Chilli and habanero pepper oil

For salads, to drizzle over spicy soups and pizzas, spicy fruit salads, stews and vegetable purées.

2 chilli peppers
1 habanero pepper
500 ml / 16 fl oz / 2 cups olive oil

Pound the chilli peppers roughly using a pestle and mortar. Halve the habanero pepper. Place in a wide-necked container and cover with oil.

Keeps for around 3 weeks, stored in a cool, dry place.

Tip:
Dried peppers can be used instead of fresh ones.
If habanero peppers are not available, you can use 4 chilli peppers instead.
Use this oil sparingly, as it is very hot.

Oil infused with herbs and spices

For nice big salads, exotic dishes, grilled or fried meat, fried salt-water fish, vegetable dishes, and hors doeuvres.

1 tbsp coriander seeds
1 tsp peppercorns
3-4 cardamom pods
2-3 bay leaves
1 cinnamon stick
500 ml / 16 fl oz / 2 cups olive oil

Gently toast the coriander seeds, peppercorns, cardamom, bay leaves and cinnamon in a frying pan. This makes the taste more pungent. Place these ingredients into a container and cover with olive oil.
Store in a cool, dry place.
Sieve the oil before using.

Tip:
The herbs and spices can also be used untoasted. This oil also tastes delicious if you add cumin and mustard seeds.

Truffle oil with garlic

For delicate salads, pasta, meat and fish carpaccios, delicate-tasting soups and potato dishes.

6 g / 1/5 oz truffle peel or bits, cleaned
1 young garlic clove, peeled
250 ml / 8 fl oz / 1 cup olive oil
Chop the truffle peel or bits and the garlic.
Cover in olive oil.
Keeps for around 3 weeks.

Tip:
Adding onion, leek and celery will make the truffle oil even tastier.

Wether you use virgin olive oil, sunflower or seed oil: in a few hours it can be converted into fine infused herb oil.

For example (from front to back):

with dried herb, chilli and habanero peppers, with all kinds of herbs and spices, truffle and garlic and garlic with fresh herbs.

Garlic oil

For cold and hot spicy soups, vegetable and green leaf salads as well as with meat, fish and pasta, stews, cream cheese and quark dips.

1-2 garlic chives, cleaned
3 garlic cloves, peeled
500 ml / 16 fl oz / 2 cups olive oil
Cut up the garlic chives. Halve the garlic cloves.
Place in a container and cover with olive oil.
Keeps in a cool, dark place for around 3 weeks.

Tip:
The garlic cloves can be chopped or pressed and used again.
If garlic chives are not available, you can also use wild garlic, Asian garlic chive flowers or chives.
If you only have garlic cloves, then you should use a total of 5-6.

Ready-made flavoured oils and vinegars are not to be scoffed at.

The advantages:
they save you time and are relatively long lasting, just as long as they are kept in a cool, dry place out of direct sunlight.
The use-by date is of particular importance with oils: they go rancid very easily.

Oil infused with fresh garden herbs

For salads with light meat, fish, pasta and cooked vegetables. For green salad or raw fruit and vegetables. For cream cheese and quark dips.

1stalk basil
1 stalk peppermint
1 stalk oregano
500 ml / 16 fl oz / 2 cups olive oil
Wash the herbs and dry well using kitchen paper.
Place in a container and cover with oil.
Keeps for around 3 weeks.

Tip:
You can add garlic chives and peppercorns to the herbs. Other delicious additions include tarragon, hyssop, sage, marjoram, lavender and rocket.

Corn oil

Sunflower oil

Cardamom oil

Nut oil

Extra virgin olive oil

Herb infused olive oil

Smoked salmon
on asparagus

1 bunch of green asparagus
Salt
50-60 g / 1 3/4 -2 oz / 2-2 1/4 cups purslane
120 g / 4 1/5 oz smoked salmon

Melon dressing:
100 g / 3 1/2 oz ogen melon flesh,
alternatively cantaloupe or galia melon
100 g / 3 1/2 oz / 1/3 cup creamy yoghurt
1 pinch salt
Pounded pepper

Peel only the lower parts of
the asparagus and cut off the woody
ends. Halve lengthways.
Cook in well salted boiling water
for 2 minutes. Remove the asparagus
and plunge into iced water
to cool. Wash the
purslane, pick through
and discard any unwanted
leaves and allow to drain.
Dice the salmon finely.

Arrange the drained
asparagus on a plate and cover with
the diced salmon and purslane.

For the dressing, dice and purée
the melon. Mix with the creamy yoghurt
and season with salt.
Sprinkle with the pounded pepper,
pour over the salad and then serve.

Tip: White asparagus can also be used here instead of
green.

**25

Shallots in oil with oak leaf lettuce

300 g / 10 oz shallots

1/2 litre / 16 fl oz / 2 cups wine vinegar
1/2 tsp salt
1/2 tbsp peppercorns
5 cloves
1 garlic clove, chopped
1/2 cinnamon stick
2 bay leaves

100 ml / 3 1/2 fl oz / just under 1/2 cup olive oil
12 hours marinating time

100-150 g / 3 1/2-5 1/4 oz / 4-6 cups oak leaf lettuce

Place the shallots into a pan of boiling water.
Drain immediately, plunge into cold water and then peel.

Bring the vinegar to the boil with 1/4 litre of water and
the spices.
Add the shallots and boil for around 5 minutes.
Remove the shallots, place in a dish,
cover with olive oil and marinate overnight.
Collect the vinegar stock.

Wash the oak leaf lettuce and spin dry.
Remove the shallots from the oil. Let them drain and
divide into portions.
Moisten the salad leaves with a little of the marinating
oil and vinegar stock and serve with the shallots.

Tip: Use the leftover vinegar stock to prepare aspics,
brawn, salad dressings and marinades.

Courgette flowers with penne

220 g penne / 7 oz / 5 cups
Salt

4-6 courgette flowers
2-3 tbsp olive oil

Salad dressing:
For each tbsp:
Thyme, chopped
Oregano, chopped
Basil, chopped
Dill, chopped
50 ml / 1 3/4 fl oz / 3 1/2 tbsp oil
3 tbsp white wine vinegar

3 tbsp pumpkin seeds, toasted
Allow 30 minutes for marinating

Whether you use penne, farfalle or fusili: the main thing is to drain them when they are al dente.

Cook penne in salted boiling water until al dente.
Rinse with cold water.

Separate the courgettes from the flowers and slice finely.
Halve the courgette flowers lengthways and fry in hot
olive oil with the courgette slices for a short time. Then
toss the penne with the ingredients in the pan.

Stir together all the ingredients for the salad dressing,
marinate with the penne and courgette mixture for 30
minutes. Serve with the courgette flowers and sprinkle
with pumpkin seeds.

**40

Fried cep salad

Leek is more robust.
Sautéed, it tastes absolutely delicious with ceps.

Fried cep salad

8 medium-sized firm ceps
4 tbsp olive oil for frying
Salt
Pepper

1 garlic clove, peeled

40 g / 1 1/2 oz young leeks
2-3 tbsp white wine

4 oregano twigs
1 thyme twig
Olive oil for deep-frying

2 tbsp garlic oil for drizzling

Clean the ceps and rub them dry and cut into slices.
Fry on both sides in the frying pan until golden brown.
Season with salt and pepper. Leave to cool.

Rub a plate with half a garlic clove. Arrange the ceps on
this dish.

Rinse the leeks and cut into fine rings.
Sauté the leek in the frying pan and deglace with white
wine. Place the leeks on top of the ceps.

Deep-fry the herbs in a little olive oil over a medium heat
and distribute over the salad.
Drizzle the salad with garlic oil.

Tip: Instead of ceps, large portobello mushrooms, oyster
mushrooms or other large seasonal mushrooms may be
used. If the leeks are large, use the white part only.

98

Rice salad with calamaretti

2 tbsp oil
200 g / 7 oz / 1 cup risotto rice
1 onion, finely diced
1 garlic clove, chopped
225 ml / 7 1/2 fl oz / 1 cup vegetable
stock
175 ml / 6 fl oz / 3/4 cup white wine

300 g / 10 oz
ready-to-cook calamaretti
Salt
40 ml / 1 1/2 fl oz / 2 1/2 tbsp
Olive oil
Pepper
2 tbsp lemon juice

20 g / 3/4 oz / 3/4 cup celery leaves
Lemon wedges as a garnish

Heat the oil. Sauté the rice, onion and garlic
until they become transparent.
Gradually add vegetable stock and wine.
Stir the rice constantly while it absorbs the liquid.
After 15 minutes take the pot off the heat.
The rice should be al dente and have a creamy
consistence.
If it is a little dry, add some more stock.
Place a lid on the pot and leave to cool.

Sprinkle the calamaretti with salt and cook for
about 2 minutes in a covered frying pan.
Remove the lid and sauté until all the liquid has
gone. Turn the heat up high. Add some olive oil
and brown the calamaretti briefly. Season with
salt, pepper and lemon juice. Leave to cool.
Mix the creamy rice with the fried calamaretti.
Serve in portions, garnished with celery leaves
and lemon wedges.

Tip: When you buy them, the calamaretti are
normally already cooked and ready to eat.
Sensitive souls can clean them following the
instructions given under the photos.

Carefully remove the calamaretii
heads from the bodies. Press
the bodies lightly so that the ink
drains out. Rinse the calamaretti
clean and continue.

Warm cauliflower with lentil salad

The yellow spice, turmeric, give dishes like curry their intense colour.

80 g / 3 oz brown lentils
Salt

Salad dressing:
2 tsp turmeric
3 tbsp lime juice
2 garlic cloves, chopped
50 ml / 1 3/4 fl oz / 3 1/2 tbsp olive oil
30 g / 1 oz / 1/8 cup garlic chives, finely chopped
80 g / 3 oz tomatoes

350 g / 12 oz cauliflower
1 lemon
2 tbsp red wine vinegar
1 tbsp oil

Cooked lentils are very delicate: drain carefully!

Cook the lentils in boiling salted water for 10-15 minutes. Drain and pour cold water over the lentils to cool them. Drain well. Stir the turmeric, lime juice, garlic, olive oil and garlic chives together. Cut the tomatoes diagonally up to the stem. Remove the seeds, dice finely and add to the salad dressing with the lentils. Season with salt.

Boil the cauliflower for 8-10 minutes with sliced lemon and salt until it is al dente. Remove and allow to drain. Break into rosettes and cut into rough slices. Toss in oil and vinegar.

Arrange the cauliflower and the lentil salad on a plate and serve immediately.

By adding turmeric vinaigrette, you can transform everyday vegetables such as cauliflower into exotic specialities.

**45

Fried green tomatoes

600 g / 1 lb 5 oz green tomatoes
Salt
Pepper

100 g / 3 1/2 oz firm tomatoes
120 g / 4 1/5 oz beef tomatoes
30 g / 1 oz garlic chives / 1/8 cup
(alternatively 2 garlic cloves)
1 small habanero pepper
1/2 tsp rose paprika
2 tbsp olive oil
Salt
1/4 tsp cumin

Thin strips of spring onion to serve.

Cut the stems off the green tomatoes. Cut the tomatoes into generous 1 cm / ½ inch thick slices. Fry them on both sides in a non-stick frying pan over a medium-high heat until they become golden brown in places.
Arrange on a dish, season with salt and pepper and leave to cool.

Dice the firm tomatoes. Scald the beef tomatoes in boiling water, cool down with cold water and remove the skins. Crush the tomatoes or chop them up very finely. Cut the garlic chives into very fine rings. Deseed the habanero pepper and chop into small pieces.
Mix everything together. Season with paprika, olive oil, salt and cumin.

Place the fried tomato slices on strips of spring onion and cover with tomato sauce.

Fried green tomatoes

Two ways of preparing tomatoes: crushed (in the glass) and diced. In the front, chopped habanero pepper

Habanero peppers are easy to recognise

Not too hot and fat-free:
it is best to use a non-stick pan to fry the tomato slices

Sage

Dill

Chives

Flat-leaf parsley

Thyme

Lavender, dried

Rosemary

Sorrel

Hyssop

Tarragon

Peppermint

Basil

Herbs

voury, dried

Oregano

y leaves

ennel, dried

Chervil

Green salad with ricotta salata and potato dressing

Potato dressing:
80 g / 3 oz floury potatoes,
cooked in their skins
150-200 g / 5 1/4-7 oz /
1/2 - 3/4 cup full-fat yoghurt
3 stems of chervil
1 garlic clove, peeled
Salt
1 large pinch of cayenne pepper

180-200 g / 6-7 oz / 7-8 cups green
salad leaves (escarol, lollo rosso)
1 tbsp lemon juice
1 tbsp olive oil

125-150 g /4 1/2 - 5 1/4 oz / 1/2 - 3/4 cup ricotta
1 tsp green pepper, pounded

Ricotta salata is a firm-textured cheese

The hand blender quickly turns everything
into a purée: or rather, a potato dressing

Peel the potatoes. Purée with yoghurt, chervil and garlic.
Season well with salt and cayenne pepper.

Wash the green salad, tear and leaves off roughly
and spin dry. Add the lemon juice and olive oil.

Arrange the salad leaves on a plate,
cover with ricotta and sprinkle with pepper.
Serve the potato dressing separately.

Tip: The salad is also delicious with the potato dressing
alone or just with the ricotta (add more seasoning in this
case).

** 30

Vinaigrettes & dips

Anchovy dressing

2 egg yolks, hard boiled
1-2 garlic cloves, peeled
6 tbsp olive oil
2-3 anchovies, drained
3 tbsp red wine vinegar
Salt
Freshly ground black pepper

Purée the egg yolks, garlic, olive oil and
anchovies.

Season with vinegar, salt and pepper.

Use with:
Salads with cold meat, potatoes, tomatoes, cold
vegetable hors d'oeuvres.

Tip:
Instead of olive oil, sunflower or seed oil can be
used - this will give the dressing a more neutral
taste.

Red tomato cream

150 g / 5 1/4 oz tomatoes
20 g / 3/4 oz sun-dried tomatoes
2-3 garlic cloves, peeled
Salt
Freshly ground black pepper

Cut the tomatoes diagonally up to the stem, cut
out the seeds. Chop the tomatoes roughly.

Purée the cut up tomatoes, sun-dried tomatoes
and garlic. Season with salt and pepper.

Use with:
Bean salads, Mediterranean salads and pasta
salads.

Tip:
Add olive oil to the purée and stir until a soft
consistency has been reached.
Rose paprika or cayenne pepper can be used
instead of black pepper.
In order to improve the vinaigrette and for
variety, all kinds of Mediterranean herbs, sheep's
cheese, fresh cheese, crème fraîche, olives,
shallots and celery can be added.
Moreover, you can add dried chopped ceps;
in this case there is no need to remove the
tomato seeds, the dried ceps will absorb the
liquid.

Vinaigrette with egg

2 eggs, hard boiled
2 tbsp olive oil
3 tbsp white wine vinegar
(alternatively red wine or herb vinegar)
Salt
Freshly ground black pepper
2 tbsp chives, finely chopped

Peel the eggs, chop up with a knife or an egg
slicer.

Whisk the oil, vinegar and pepper until
blended and season well. Add the chopped
egg and chives and stir.

Use with:
Hearty green salad, potato salad.

Tip:
The vinaigrette can be varied with the addition
of capers, shallots, spring onions, gherkins,
cooked beetroot, tart apples, mustard powder
or mustard, all kinds of garden herbs and crisp
grilled bacon.

Herb dressing

3 tbsp mayonnaise
2-3 tbsp full-fat yoghurt
3-4 large stalks of each of the following herbs: flat-parsley, tarragon, chervil and sorrel
Salt
Freshly ground black pepper

Stir the mayonnaise and yoghurt together.

Tear the fresh herb leaves off the stalks, add to the mayonnaise and yoghurt and then purée.
Season with salt and pepper.

Use with:
Salads with fish, shellfish and crustaceans, cooked vegetables, light meat and pasta.

Tip:
This dressing tastes milder if the herbs are blanched briefly before making the purée. To do this, dip them rapidly into boiling water and then plunge into cold water to cool.The more herbs you use the more intense the colour and the flavour will be.
Cress and blanched, squeezed spinach leaves can also be used.You could use crème fraîche instead of yoghurt.

Mustard vinaigrette

2 tbsp herb vinegar
1/2 tsp salt
1-1 1/2 tsp coarse grained mustard
1 garlic clove, pressed
7-8 tbsp olive oil
Freshly ground black pepper

Mix the vinegar and salt together until the salt has dissolved.

Add the mustard and garlic and gradually stir in the olive oil until you have a mayonnaise-like cream.
Season with pepper.

Use with:
Salads with raw and cooked vegetables and meat.

Tip:
If possible, prepare the vinaigrette just before serving as it separates very quickly.

Truffle vinaigrette

1 ½ tbsp white wine vinegar
1 tbsp salt
Freshly ground black pepper
70-80 ml / 2 1/3-3 fl oz / 1/3 cup olive oil
10-20 g / 1/3-3/4 oz fresh truffle peelings or bits, cleaned

Mix together the white wine vinegar with salt and pepper until the salt has dissolved. Stir in the olive oil.

Chop up the truffle peelings or bits and add to the vinaigrette.

Use with:
Fine green salad, potato, pasta and egg salads.

Tip:
Only use preserved truffle in an emergency, the aroma of fresh truffle cannot be beaten.

Balsamic vinegar and olive oil dressing

1 tbsp balsamic vinegar
3-4 tbsp olive oil
Salt
Freshly ground black pepper

Pour all the ingredients over the prepared salad and toss well.

Serve immediately.

Use with:
This dressing is particularly suitable for salads containing fruit and for all vegetable and green salads.

Tip:
Instead of red balsamic vinegar, you could also try white vinegar. Other ingredients that taste delicious with this dressing are Parmesan, Pecorino, grilled goats cheese, Alpine cheese or quark, garlic or deep-fried herbs.

Vinaigrette with Roquefort

100 g / 3 1/2 oz Roquefort
1-2 tbsp white wine vinegar
4 tbsp olive oil
1/2 tsp medium strength mustard
3 garlic cloves, pressed
Freshly ground black pepper
Salt

Break the Roquefort up into the small flakes using a fork.

Whisk the white wine vinegar and olive oil with mustard, garlic and pepper until blended.
Add the Roquefort and season with salt.

Use with:
All kinds of strong-tasting green salad leaves, salads with dark meat, potatoes or pasta.

Tip: Orange vinegar can also be used instead of white wine vinegar.
Gorgonzola can be used instead of Roquefort, the taste will then be milder.

Green pesto

35-40 g / 1-1 1/2 oz basil, torn leaves
4 garlic cloves, peeled
40 g / 1 1/2 oz / 1/4 cup pine nuts, toasted
80-100 g / 3-3 1/2 oz Parmesan, grated
Around 175 ml / 6 fl oz / 3/4 cup olive oil

Mix all the ingredients together and purée.
This is easiest with a food processor, but you can also use a hand blender or pestle and mortar.

Season with salt and pepper.

Use with:
Pasta salads, salads with cooked vegetables with light meat and salt-water fish.

Tip:
Instead of basil you can use rocket, flat-leaf parsley, mixed wild and garden herbs.
Instead of pine nuts you can use walnuts, almonds, pumpkin and sunflower seeds or pistachios.
Instead of olive oil you can use nut, pumpkin seed, pistachio, peanut, thistle or grape seed oil.

Grilled goat's cheese
on a bed of lettuce

150 g / 5 1/4 oz / 5 cups mixed escarole leaves
120 g / 4 1/5 oz cherry tomatoes

Vinaigrette:
4 tbsp olive oil
2 tbsp red wine vinegar
1 tsp coarse grain Dijon mustard

4 goat's cheeses, weighing 40 g / 1 1/2 oz each
4 small thyme twigs
1 tbsp olive oil
Freshly ground black pepper

Grilled croutons as a garnish

Wash the escarole leaves, tear leaves up and spin dry.
Halve the tomatoes. Arrange both on individual plates.

Whisk all the ingredients for the vinaigrette together
 until blended.

Cover the goat's cheese with thyme, drizzle with olive oil and
place on silver foil under the grill until golden brown.
When still hot, place on top of the salad. Drizzle the salad with
vinaigrette and season with pepper. Serve immediately with
the grilled croutons.

**30

Two cheese pomegranate

50 g / 1 3/4 oz / scant 1/2 cup flat-leaf parsley
200 g / 7 oz / 8 cups spinach and red chard
1 pomegranate

Salad dressing:
6 tbsp olive oil
1 tbsp balsamic vinegar
2-3 tbsp white wine
1 scant tbsp Dijon mustard
Salt
Freshly ground black pepper

80-100 g /3-3 1/2 oz French soft cheese
80-100 g / 3-3 1/2 oz fresh Parmesan

Tear the leaves off the parsley stalks, sort through the spinach and discard any unwanted leaves. Then wash all the leaves and spin them dry. Cut the pomegranate into quarters and remove the seeds and separate them from the fibrous white membranes.

Whisk the olive oil, balsamic vinegar, white wine, Dijon mustard, salt and pepper until blended into a salad dressing. Then toss with parsley, spinach and red chard. Arrange on individual plates. Sprinkle with pomegranate seeds.

Cut the soft cheese into fine slices. Slice the Parmesan into long strips. Arrange both on top of the salad. Season with plenty of pepper.

Tip: All kinds of bitter green salad leaves can be used in this recipe. Alternative cheese: Alpine cheese.

The seeds almost tumble out of the open pomegranate.
The fruit's membranes do no harm, but they don't have much flavour

**15

Two cheese pomegranate

Parmesan and, in the foreground, Camembert from
Isigny Sainte-Mère matured in Calvados- a soft cheese
from Normandy- taste wonderful with spinach

120

122

Marinated chicken breast with fresh coconut

250 g / 8 oz chicken breast fillet

Marinade:
1 lime, cut into slices
1 tsp salt
Freshly ground black pepper
1 tbsp ginger, freshly grated
1 pepperoni, crushed in a mortar
Allow 30 minutes for marinating

1 tbsp neutral oil for browning

Dressing:
125 ml / 4 fl oz / 1/2 cup cream
1-2 tbsp rum
3-4 tbsp lemon juice

40 g / 1 1/2 oz fresh coconut flesh, shelled
300 g / 10 oz full-flavoured melon
1 small romaine lettuce

2 tbsp spring onion, finely chopped

Clean the chicken breast of any skin and sinews.
Marinate with the lime, salt, pepper, ginger and pepperoni.
Allow to drain and then sear the chicken in hot oil.
Cover the pan with a lid and cook for 4-5 minutes
over a low heat. Allow to cool.

Mix together all the ingredients for the dressing.
Season well. Slice the coconut flesh with a potato
peeler. Peel the melon, remove the seeds and
then dice the flesh.

Wash the romaine lettuce, drain and cut lengthways
into fine strips. Arrange on a plate. Serve with
chopped chicken breast, melon cubes and
coconut. Cover with plenty of dressing
and sprinkle with spring onions.

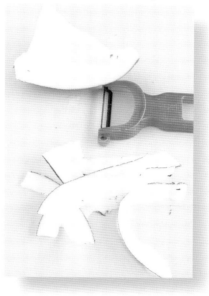

A little trick that is very effective: use a potato peeler to create fine coconut shavings

Remove any skin and sinews from the chicken breasts

Not all marinades are liquid: in this case, the chicken breast is infused with intense flavours in 30 minutes

**25

Nuts, seeds and croutons

Croutons:
fine toasted cubes of bread for adding to soups and salads

Walnuts:
delicious on their own or with honey

Pistachios:
often salted, occasionally sweet, easy to crack open

Pumpkin seeds:
contain valuable amino acids

Unshelled sunflower seeds:
a popular snack in southern Europe

Shelled sunflower seeds:
delicious in muesli and lots of other dishes

Pine nuts:
toasted to bring out the flavour

Peeled whole almonds:
their delicate oil is superb for moisturising dry skin and for cooking

Cucumbers with caramelised amonds

450-500 g / 1-1 1/4 lb cucumbers
Salt

150 g / 5 1/4 oz / 1/2 cup Greek yoghurt
30-40 ml / 1-1 1/2 fl oz / 2-2 1/2 tbsp dark port
1 garlic clove, pressed
1-2 dashes of Tabasco sauce
Salt

30 g / 1 oz / 1/8 cup butter
30 g / 1 oz / 1/8 cup sugar
50 g / 1 3/4 oz / scant 1/2 cup whole almonds, peeled
4 tbsp Port

Purslane or sprouts as a garnish
Freshly ground black pepper

Peel the cucumbers and cut into 2 cm / 3/4 inch thick slices. Scoop out the middle of the cucumbers with an apple corer. You are left with thick cucumber rings. Heat some water. Sprinkle the cucumber rings with salt and steam for 8-10 minutes in a steamer or a sieve over boiling water in a covered pan. Leave to cool.

Mix the yoghurt, port and garlic and stir until a smooth consistency is reached. Season with Tabasco sauce and salt.

Melt butter and sugar in a frying pan. Add the almonds and let them caramelise until they are of a light brown colour. Toss the contents of the pan constantly whilst doing this. Remove the almonds and leave to cool on baking paper. Try as far as possible to make sure that the almonds are laid out individually and are not in contact one with another. Add some port to the pan to deglace the caramel juice.

Pour the yoghurt dressing over the cucumber rings. Scatter with almonds and purslane. Drizzle with caramel juice and season with freshly ground black pepper.

** 35

Potato carpaccio with tapenade

600 g / 1 lb 5 oz firm-cooking potatoes
Salt

Tapenade:
2 tbsp capers
80 g / 3 oz / 1 cup black olives, pitted
6 anchovies
2 bay leaves
6 tbsp olive oil
2 tbsp lemon juice
1 tsp black pepper

1 thyme twig

Peel the potatoes. Cut into wafer-thin slices with
a slicing machine. Cook for 2-3 minutes in boiling
salted water. Cool with cold water, and drain well.
Serve on a plate.

For the tapenade, pound the capers, olives,
anchovies and bay leaves in a mortar.
Then stir in the oil and lemon juice and season with
pepper. Spread out on top of the potato slices.
Serve with broken up bay leaves and the thyme twig.

With the pestle and mortar
capers, olives, anchovies and
bay leaves are transformed
into tapenade

In ancient Rome and
Greece, the bay leaf
was a symbol of glory,
honour and victory

Use a melon scoop to create uniform-sized little potato balls. This is easiest with raw potatoes or other vegetables. No scoop handy? Diced potatoes will do the trick!

Princess potatoes, quail eggs and fresh herb mayonnaise

1 kg / 2 1/5 lb large, firm-cooking potatoes
1/2 litre/1 3/4 pints / 4 cups vegetable stock
12-16 quail eggs

2 sprigs of parsley
2 sprigs of tarragon
2 sprigs of chervil
2 sprigs of basil
2 heaped tbsp mayonnaise
2-3 tbsp olive oil
1 scant tbsp coarse mustard
Salt
Freshly ground black pepper

50 g / 1 3/4 oz / 2 cups rocket leaves
2 tbsp drained capers

Peel the potatoes and scoop out the
princess potatoes with a melon baller.
Cook for 7-8 minutes in vegetable stock, then
drain. Cook the quail eggs for 4 minutes, place
them into cold water and then peel off the shells.

Wash the parsley, tarragon, chervil and basil
and then pick the leaves off the stems.
Purée the herbs, mayonnaise and olive oil.
Add the mustard and season with salt and pepper.

Wash the rocket, sort through to discard any unwanted
leaves and then let them drain. Mix the potatoes with the
herb mayonnaise and arrange on the rocket leaves,
surround with quail eggs and finally sprinkle with capers.

A quick whiz with the blender,
and olive oil, mayonnaise and mustard
are transformed into herb mayonnaise

Quails camouflage their eggs to
look like large pebbles

The pieces of potato left over after scooping out
the princess potatoe balls can be used in soups,
stews or purées

★★ 45

132

Types of vinegar

Raspberry vinegar

For salads and dips.

250 g / 8 oz freshly picked raspberries
500 ml / 16 fl oz / 2 cups white wine vinegar
180-200 g / 6-7 oz / 3/4-1 cup sugar

Remove the raspberry stalks. Place the fruit in
a wide-necked container and fill up with vinegar.
Leave for 3-4 days. Sieve the vinegar and remove
the raspberries. Bring the strained vinegar to the boil
with sugar. Pour into bottles and cork them.

Keep in a cool, dry place.

Tip:
Brambles can be used instead of raspberries.
Water or soda water with a small dash of
raspberry vinegar makes a really refreshing and
thirst-quenching drink in summer.

Orange vinegar

For vegetable salads, hors d'oeuvres and preserving fruit.

2-3 unwaxed organic oranges
500 ml / 16 fl oz / 2 cups white wine vinegar

Wash the oranges with hot water, then dry them.
Remove the orange peel in fine strips using a potato peeler.
Squeeze out the juice until you have around 100 ml /
3 1/2 fl oz / just under 1/2 cup. Thread the peel onto a long
wooden skewer (to make it easier to handle). Put the peel
and the juice into a container and fill up with vinegar.

Keeps for 2-3 weeks.

Tip:
Blood oranges are particularly suitable for this vinegar.
The peel can be chopped or cut into strips and used
in other recipes.Lemon vinegar prepared in the same
way is also delicious.

Ginger and garlic chive vinegar

For fruit and vegetable salads, Asian dishes and
marinades. Can also be combined with soy sauce.

30 g / 1 oz fresh ginger
10 g / 1/3 oz / 1 dsp garlic chives, cleaned
500 ml / 16 fl oz / 2 cups apple cider vinegar

Brush the ginger clean under cold running water and
cut into fine slices keeping the skin on. Pound the
garlic chives roughly using a pestle and mortar.
Put the gingerand the garlic chives into a container
and pour the apple cider vinegar over them.

Keeps for 2-3 weeks.

Tip:
Instead of ginger you can also use galangal or turmeric.
The preserved ingredients can be chopped finely and
used again in another recipe.

In a flash, a simple, relatively good wine vinegar can be transformed into a real delicacy: by simply "infusing" it with aromatic ingredients for a few days. For example (from front to back): peeled shallots, fresh herbs and cloves of garlic. Behind, from left to right: raspberries, orange peel twists, ginger and garlic.

135

Garlic vinegar

For vegetable and green leaf salads or hors d'oeuvres with cooked aubergines, mushrooms and courgettes.

1 young head of garlic
1 large pinch of salt
500 ml / 16 fl oz / 2 cups white wine vinegar

Break the head of garlic up into individual cloves. Place them in a container and sprinkle with salt. Lay the container on a wet cloth. Bring the white wine vinegar to a boil and, whilst still hot, pour over the garlic.

Sieve after one week. Close the container.

Keep in a cool, dry place.

Tip:
The sieved ingredients can be chopped finely and used in other recipes.

Herb vinegar

For vegetable, fish, meat and green leaf salads.
For pickling, marinating, spicy brawn and aspics.

2 stalks flat-leaf parsley
2 stalks peppermint
2 stalks dill
2 stalks lemon balm
500 ml / 16 fl oz / 2 cups white wine vinegar

Wash the herbs and spin completely dry.
Place in a wide-necked container and cover with vinegar.

Keeps for around 2 weeks.

Tip:
Mixed or individual wild herbs also make very good additions to this vinegar.

Shallot vinegar

For green salads, pasta, potato salads.
For a fish marinade.

5-6 shallots, peeled
1 large pinch of sea salt
500 ml / 16 fl oz / 2 cups red wine vinegar
1 tsp peppercorns
Cut up the shallots or halve them and season with a little salt. Place them in a wide-necked container. Fill up with red wine vinegar and peppercorns.

Keeps for around 3 weeks,
stored in a cool, dry place.

Tip:
This also tastes lovely with white wine or apple cider vinegar. It is also delicious with fresh tarragon.

General advice on preparing flavoured oils and vinegars

You will need some wide-necked containers.
All containers must be spotlessly clean (sterile) and made of flawless, acid-resistant material: glass is the best choice.
A gauze cloth, fine sieve, filter bag (e.g. coffee filter) or kitchen paper placed in a sieve can be used for straining.

The oil and vinegar must be kept in a cool, dry place, away from direct sunlight.
The oil becomes rancid very quickly.
The vinegar goes cloudy. Close the lids tightly!
For small households, it is best to use half of the ingredients in the recipe.
Use the oil and vinegar quickly.

All salads can be improved with the addition of flavoured oils and vinegars – all that is required is a touch of creativity.

Champagne vinegar

Lemon vinegar

White wine vinegar

Red wine vinegar

White balsamic vinegar

Tarragon vinegar

Red balsamic vinegar

Sherry vinegar

Raspberry vinegar

Apple cider vinegar

Lettuce hearts
with two dressings

200 g / 7 oz lettuce hearts

Red wine vinaigrette with egg:
2 eggs, hard boiled
2 tbsp olive oil
2 tbsp red wine vinegar
Salt
Coarse black pepper
2 tbsp chives, finely chopped

Wash the lettuce hearts, tear up the leaves
and toss dry.

Peel the eggs and slice finely with the egg cutter.
Whisk together the remaining ingredients
and add the egg and chives.

Mix the lettuce hearts with the red wine and egg
vinaigrette and serve.

Tip: All kinds of light coloured leaf lettuce can
be used in this recipe. Each salad dressing will
serve 4 people. If you wish to use both salad
dressings at the same time, they will serve 2 people.

Lettuce hearts
with two dressings

200 g / 7 oz lettuce hearts

Warm lemon butter:
1 unwaxed organic lemon
1 garlic clove, chopped
50 g / 1 3/4 oz / 1/4 cup butter
Salt
Black pepper, pounded
Dill, chopped

Wash the lettuce hearts, tear up the leaves
and toss dry.

Wash the lemon with hot water and cut in half.
Cut one half into wafer-thin slices and extract the juice
from the other half. Sauté the lemon slices and garlic
in butter. Season with salt and pepper.
Add the dill and lemon juice to the butter.

Toss the lettuce hearts in the lemon butter and serve
straight away.

Head lettuce with crunchy bacon and deep-fried herbs

1 head lettuce

150 g / 5 1/4 oz lardo di Arnad
(smoked bacon fat with herbs from the Aosta valley)
1 shallot, finely diced

6 tbsp sunflower oil for deep-frying
6 small sage leaves
1 small rosemary twig

Sea salt
Freshly ground coarse black pepper

Cut up the head lettuce leaves. Wash the lettuce and spin dry. Cut the bacon fat into very thin slices with a slicing machine.

Deep-fry the sage leaves and broken up rosemary twig briefly in oil that is not too hot. Allow to drain on kitchen paper. Fry the slices of bacon in 1 tbsp of the oil until crunchy. Allow to drain on kitchen paper. Sauté the diced shallots in the remaining oil.

Season the lettuce and bacon strips with salt and pepper. Pour the bacon dressing and shallots over the salad and mix. Cover with the deep-fried herbs. Serve immediately.

Tip: You can use other types of bacon instead of the bacon fat with herbs.

Fennel and cooked ham

A slicing machine,
put to a rather different use here, creates fine fennel slices...

...and then finely sliced
cooked ham.

Whether you choose ciabatta
or chapata, Italian or Spanish,
crusty white bread tastes best
with this dish

Fennel and cooked ham

600 g / 1 lb 5 oz fennel

200 ml / 7 fl oz / 3/4 cup white wine
1 1/2 tsp salt
2 bay leaves
5 peppercorns
1/2 tsp coriander seeds
3 thyme twigs
3 tbsp lemon juice

2 tbsp olive oil

200 g / 7 oz cooked ham, sliced quite thinly
1 tbsp oregano, chopped

Clean and rinse the fennel and set aside the fennel
greens. Halve the fennel and cut into wafer-thin slices
on a slicing machine. Bring the white wine, salt,
bay leaves, pepper, coriander and thyme to a boil and
remove from the heat. Add the fennel and leave to cool.
Take the fennel out of the stock and season with lemon
juice and a little salt.

To make the vinaigrette, reduce the stock until you
are left with 5-6 tbsp of liquid. Mix with olive oil.

Tear the ham into small pieces, serve with the fennel,
sprinkle with oregano and drizzle with vinaigrette.

Serve with fresh crusty white bread.

Pearl onions in Marsala wine

Braised in Marsala wine and sugar, the onions take on a praliné-like appearance

400 g / 14 oz pearl onions (alternatively shallots)

30 ml / 1 fl oz / 2 tbsp nut oil
2 tbsp sugar
50 ml / 1 3/4 fl oz / 3 1/2 tbsp Marsala wine
1 tsp salt
1 large pinch of cayenne pepper

300 g / 10 oz beef tomatoes
100 g / 3 1/2 oz / 4 cups lamb's lettuce
1 tbsp red wine vinegar
1 tbsp cardamom oil

Place the pearl onions into a pan of boiling water.
Drain immediately, plunge into cold water and then peel.

Heat the oil in a saucepan then add the sugar.
Stir until it softens and becomes golden brown.
Add the onions and then the Marsala wine and salt.
Cover with a lid and cook for 5 minutes over a medium
heat and then simmer for a further 5 minutes without
the lid until the stock has thickened. Stir from time to
time. Season with cayenne pepper.
Leave to cool until the onion mixture is just warm.

Cut the beef tomatoes into thin slices. Arrange on a
plate. Season with salt. Pick through the lamb's lettuce
and discard any unwanted leaves. Wash the lamb's
lettuce and spin dry, then add the red wine vinegar and
cardamom oil. Place the onions and lamb's lettuce on
top of the tomato slices. Drizzle with the onion stock and
serve immediately.

Tip: To avoid your eyes watering when peeling the
onions, blanch them in boiling water beforehand.
The onions are delicious with cold meat, pies and
steamed fish. If you are unable to find cardamom
oil, use olive oil and season to taste with cardamom.
Sprouts can be used instead of the lamb's lettuce.

Brought up to the boil quickly and cooled in iced water, the pearl onions can be peeled without tears

**

45

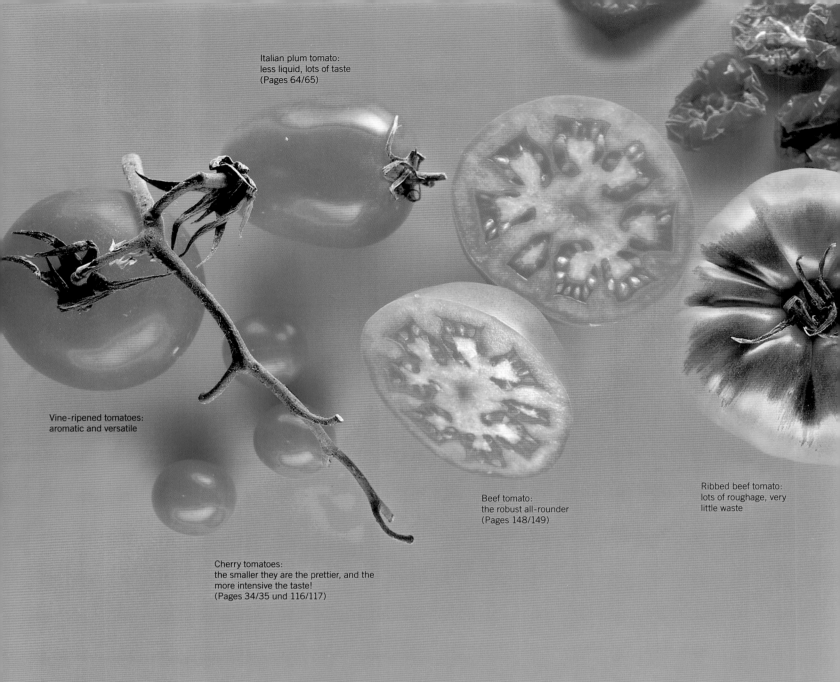

Italian plum tomato:
less liquid, lots of taste
(Pages 64/65)

Vine-ripened tomatoes:
aromatic and versatile

Beef tomato:
the robust all-rounder
(Pages 148/149)

Ribbed beef tomato:
lots of roughage, very
little waste

Cherry tomatoes:
the smaller they are the prettier, and the
more intensive the taste!
(Pages 34/35 und 116/117)

Sun-dried tomatoes:
concentrated sunshine, often presented in olive oil
(Pages 42/43)

Summer tomatoes, globe tomatoes, Dutch
tomatoes: available everywhere all year round

Green tomatoes:
preserved or fried, they are a real delicacy
(Pages 104/105)

Montserrat tomato:
easy to recognise by its colour

Varieties of tomato

Grapefruit and avocado salad with smoked fish

With a sharp knife and a deft hand, cut fine fillets out of the grapefruit segments.

3 pink grapefruit
1 large avocado
60 g / 2 oz / 2 1/4 cups rocket

Salad dressing:
2 tsp grated lemon peel
40 ml / 1 1/2 fl oz / 2 1/2 tbsp lemon juice
50 ml / 2 fl oz / 3 1/2 tbsp oil
Salt
Freshly ground black pepper
3 tbsp cognac
2 tsp sweet mustard

200 g / 7 oz smoked cod in strips (alternatively halibut, salmon or smoked salmon)

Peel the grapefruit, remove the flesh and cut each segment into thin fillets. Peel the avocado and dice the flesh. Wash the rocket, sort through and discard any unwanted leaves, drain and cut into strips.

Whisk all the ingredients for the salad dressing until blended.

Cut the cod into strips and thread them onto the wooden skewers so that they resemble rosettes. Mix together the salad ingredients and salad dressing and serve in cocktail glasses. Cover with the fish kebabs.

25

Citrus sardines

Citrus sardines

Patience! The tail fin stays but the head and bones must be removed

400 g / 14 oz fresh sardines (alternatively anchovies)

Marinade:
Juice of 3-4 limes
40 ml / 1 1/2 fl oz / 2 1/2 tbsp olive oil
1 1/2 tsp sea salt
Ground pepper
1 tbsp rosemary, chopped
Marinade over night

2 oranges
100-120 g / 3 1/2 oz-4 1/5 oz / 4-4 1/4 cups radicchio

Remove the sardines' heads and bones. Wash the fish and drain on kitchen paper. Place in an acid-proof, wide dish.

Mix the lime juice, olive oil, sea salt, pepper and rosemary. Pour over the sardines and marinate over night in the fridge.

Peel the oranges, remove the flesh and cut each segment into thin fillets. Wash the radicchio, drain and cut into fine strips. Divide the radicchio and orange mixture into portions. Cover with marinated sardines and drizzle with the marinade.

***30

Without their backbone, and cut open, the sardines soak up more marinade. Beforehand, they should be laid out to dry on kitchen paper.

Pointed cabbage with caramelised cranberries

Cranberries are related to blueberries

Pointed cabbage cooks quicker than normal white cabbage – and is easier to digest

161

Pointed cabbage with caramelised cranberries

Once the sugar is in the frying pan, it all happens very quickly:

On the edges the sugar is already beginning to dissolve

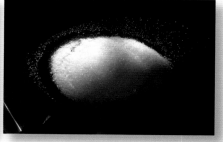

Stir, stir and stir again! The little lumps of hot sugar granules

Almost there: the sugar has just a dissolved

300 g / 10 oz tender pointed cabbage leaves, leaf ribs cut away
Salt
20 g / 3/4 oz / 3/4cup garlic chives (alternatively 2 garlic cloves)

30 g / 1 oz / 1/8 cup sugar
80 g / 3 oz cranberries
100 g / 3 1/2 oz / 1/3 cup mayonnaise
100 g / 3 1/2 oz/ 1/3 cup full-fat yoghurt
Salt
Freshly ground white pepper
Nutmeg, grated

2 tbsp white balsamic vinegar
1 tbsp olive oil

Finally, add the cranberries and caramelise them quickly

Blanch the pointed cabbage leaves in well-salted water for two minutes. Plunge into iced water to cool, drain well and toss dry. Slice the garlic chives.

Caramelise the sugar in the frying pan. Add the cranberries and toss quickly. Place a third of the caramelised cranberries insmall portions on baking paper using two forks. Reduce the heatfor the remaining berries. Cover the pan with a lid and cook thecranberries making sure they do not disintegrate. Leave to cool.Mix with mayonnaise and yoghurt. Season with salt, pepper and nutmeg.

Toss the pointed cabbage leaves and garlic chives with balsamic vinegar and olive oil. Serve with cooled caramelised cranberries and cover with generous amounts of salad dressing.

Tip: Instead of pointed cabbage, crisp lettuce, fennel or endives can be used.

Lightly browned, the caramel is ready

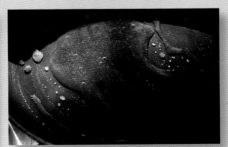

***40

Crab, papaya and mango

With a deft twist, break the pincers and legs off the cooked crab

Don't hit them too hard! Otherwise bits of shell might get into the meat.
It is better to break the shell open gently and then carefully remove the meat.

Press the crab's underside gently and remove the meat and the entrails

A pile of rubbish for some people - for others the start of a delicious crab stock: crab shells

Crab, papaya and mango

4 crabs (each weighing around 300 g / 10 oz)
Salt

2 garlic chives (alternatively, 2-3 garlic cloves)
1 ripe papaya
150 g /5 1/4 oz fresh mango

Mango vinaigrette:
3 tbsp olive oil
2 tsp mustard
4 tbsp mango juice
Freshly ground black pepper
Salt
2 tbsp chives, finely chopped

100 g / 3 1/2 oz / 4 cups green lettuce leaves, cut into strips

*** 40

Brush any dirt off the crabs and cook for around 5-7 minutes in boiling salted water. Remove and place in cold water to cool them down. Separate the legs and claws from the bodies. Crack or press the claws open and remove the meat. Break the undersides of the crabs open. Remove the meat and entrails. Break the meat up into small pieces.

Cut the garlic chives into fine rings. Peel the mango, cut the flesh into thick slices and dice. Peel the papaya, remove the seeds and dice up the flesh.

Mix the fruit and garlic chives with the crab meat.

Stir together the olive oil, mustard and mango juice and mix with pepper, salt and chives. Mix the crab salad, vinaigrette and lettuce leaves and serve.

Tip: Clean the crab shells thoroughly. Serve the salad in these shells.

Pepper

Dried black, white, green and red peppercorns and allspice.

It is a matter of taste which pepper you use.

Above, there is a photo of a pepper grinder alongside a colourful mixture of pickled green peppercorns and fresh red and green chilli peppers.

The green peppers tend to have a powerful effect on the mucus membranes and the respiratory tract.

Salt

Fleur de Sel:
the king of fine salts: the flower of
salt, handgathered like wild flowers
'growing' on the sea

Table salt:
that is what it is called in the
supermarket –iodised salt is
another variety

Fine sea salt:
it goes lumpy easily, and that is
why is has a wonderful taste

Sea salt flakes:
extremely soluble,
stick together easily

Grey sea salt:
with a particularly high mineral content

Coarse sea salt:
for cooking and for the salt grinder

Deep-fried silversides with parsley

400 g / 14 oz fresh silversides
500 ml / 16 fl oz / 2 cups beer
Marinate for 15 minutes

50 g / 1 3/4 oz/ scant 1/2 cup flat-leaf parsley, torn leaves
30 g / 1 oz / 1/8 cup shallots, diced
2 tbsp lemon juice
1 tbsp olive oil
1 tart apple, ca. 150 g / 5 1/4 oz
Freshly ground black pepper

250 g / 8 oz / 2 1/2 cups flour
500 ml / 16 fl oz / 1 pint olive oil for deep-frying

Coarse sea salt
Lemon wedges as a garnish

Wash the silversides under cold running water.
Drain well. Pour beer over the fish and marinate for
15 minutes. Allow to drain well.

Mix the parsley, diced shallots, lemon juice and olive oil.
Core the apple, slice finely and mix into the salad.
Serve in individual portions.

Dust each silverside in flour. Place the fish in a sieve
and shake off any surplus flour. The silversides should be
completely covered in flour. Deep-fry the fish in hot olive
oil until golden. Allow them drain briefly on kitchen
paper. Arrange the crisp silversides on top of the salad.
Sprinkle with sea salt and serve with lemon wedges.
Serve immediately.

✳✳✳ 40

Deep-fried silversides with parsley

Freshly washed silversides

A 15-minute beer bath
– good for the silversides

Not all at once! Deep fry in small
batches to make sure the fish cook
in a uniform manner.

Remove the fish from the beer,
drain them and sprinkle with flour

The golden-brown colour tells
you that the fish are cooked.
Now all you have to do is drain
them and they are ready to eat!

The flour should not mask the delicate
taste of these fish: place the silversides
in a sieve and shake off any surplus flour

Tartar salad

Marinate the soaked herring strips for 1 hour

1 Spanish salted herring (alternatively matjes herring)
40 minutes for salting (not applicable if using
matjes herring)
1 hour marinating time

Salad dressing:
3 tbsp wine vinegar
3 tbsp vegetable stock
2 tbsp olive oil
1 tsp coarse mustard
1 tsp salt
1/4 tsp pepper

300 g / 10 oz onions, cut into rings
1 tbsp olive oil
50 g / 1 3/4 oz / scant 1/2 cup pancetta
120 g / 4 1/5 oz / 4 1/4 cups head salad
80 g / 3 oz / 1/2 cup pickled gherkins, diced
300 g / 10 oz boiled potatoes, peeled and diced

Remove the herrings' skin and bones. Cut into strips.
Soak in water for 40 minutes, changing the water
frequently to remove the salt. Remove the roe.
Whisk all the ingredients for the salad dressing together
until blended. Leave the fish to marinate in this dressing
for 1 hour.

Fry the onion rings briefly in 1 tbsp oil. Leave to cool and
use them to form a bed of onions. Dice the pancetta and
fry until crisp. Wash the head salad and spin dry then
cut into strips. Add the pancetta, pickled gherkins,
potatoes and head salad strips to the fish vinaigrette.
Arrange the mixture on the bed of onions.

Pancetta tastes
delicious with
salted herring

✳✳✳ 40

174

Fresh herbs with tuna crêpe strips

Crêpes:
1 egg
1 egg yolk
125 ml / 4 fl oz / 1/2 cup buttermilk
45 g / 1 1/2 oz / 1/3 cup flour
25 g / 1 oz / 1/8 cup melted butter
1 1/2 tbsp lemon juice
Pepper
50 g / 1 3/4 oz / Scant 1/2 cup tinned tuna in brine, drained
30 minutes resting time

2 tbsp butter for frying

120 g / 4 1/5 oz / 4 1/4 cups mixed fresh herbs
(e.g. rocket, dandelion, chervil, mint)

Salad dressing:
4 tbsp olive oil
3 tbsp apple vinegar
Salt

The tender yellow cultivated dandelion greens are milder than their wild sisters

Blend all the ingredients for the crêpes in the food mixer. Allow to rest for 30 minutes. Add a little butter to a non-stick frying pan and prepare wafer-thin crêpes. Cut into fine strips.

Pick the leaves off the fresh herbs' stalks, wash and spin dry.

Mix together the ingredients for the salad dressing. Toss the herbs in the dressing and serve with the crêpe strips.

Tip: It is preferable to use three types of fresh herbs – but you can use other varieties than the ones suggested in this recipe.

*** 40

Mixed shellfish salad

In Galicia, they even decorate houses with
scallop shells (literally St. James' shells)
and hang them over their doors

179

Mixed shellfish salad

1 kg / 2 1/5 lb mixed shellfish (carpet shells, mussels, razor shells, winkles or scallops)

70 ml / 2 1/3 fl oz / 1/3 cup white wine
30 ml / 1 fl oz / 2 tbsp fish sauce
100 g / 3 1/2 oz leek, finely sliced
2 garlic cloves, chopped

1 shallot, finely diced
1/4 tsp saffron
250 g / 8 oz shelled scallops
Salt

120 g / 4 1/5 oz / 4 1/2 cups green salad
150 g / 5 1/4 oz tomatoes
2 tbsp lemon juice

Wash the mussels under running cold water and brush them. Remove the 'beards'. Discard any mussels with cracked, broken or open shells: they are unfit to eat.

Bring the wine, fish sauce, leek and garlic to the boil in a large pot. Add the mussels. Cover with a lid. Leave to boil until all the shells are open. Remove the flesh from the shells. Set aside the cooking liquid left in the pot.

Sieve the cooking liquid. Add the shallots and saffron. Reduce in an open pot until there is 60 ml / 2 fl oz / 4 tbsp left. Add the scallops and sauté for 2-3 minutes. Add the mussels and shake the pot. Season with salt and leave to cool.

Wash the lettuce and tear the leaves up. Remove the tomato cores and cut into slices. Arrange everything on a plate and drizzle with lemon juice. Add the mussel flesh to the salad with the white wine stock.

No pearls this time: cleaned mussel flesh

Off with their beards! Any uncooked mussels with cracked or open shells should be discarded immediately.

Mussel striptease: during cooking the mussels open up to reveal their true beauty. Any that remain closed should not be eaten.

Use one half of the mussel shell as a little spoon to scoop out the cooked flesh. Where's the sauce?

✳✳✳ 40

181

Watercress with carpaccio of salted cod

180 g / 6 oz salted cod, soaked and ready to cook
Freezing time

120 g / 4 1/5 oz / 4 1/2 cups watercress, sorted
1 tbsp olive oil
Salt

Truffle vinaigrette:
4 tbsp olive oil
1 tbsp white wine vinegar
1 tbsp truffle, chopped

Wrap the salted cod in cling film and freeze slightly.

Wash the watercress and spin dry.
Mix with oil and some salt.

Whisk the ingredients for the truffle vinaigrette together.

Create a mound with the watercress. Cut the salted cod into wafer-thin slices with a slicing machine and place directly onto the salad. Drizzle with truffle vinaigrette and serve immediately.

*** 25

Watercress wilts quicky, thereby losing vitamins and the nutty taste.

Preparation time index

35 ±

45 <